A Companion to Common Wo

D0809342

Volume 1

The Alcuin Club, founded in 1897, exists to promote the study of Christian liturgy in general, and in particular the worship of the Anglican Communion. The Club has published over 160 books, studies and pamphlets. The most recent annual collections have been a revised and enlarged edition of E. C. Whitaker's *Documents of the Baptismal Liturgy* by Maxwell E. Johnson, and *Eucharistic Origins* by Paul F. Bradshaw. Also in collaboration with SPCK, the Club is publishing a series of Liturgy Guides. Its recent titles include *Art and Worship* by Anne Dawtry and Christopher Irvine, and *Celebrating the Eucharist* by Benjamin Gordon-Taylor and Simon Jones. The Club works in partnership with GROW in the publication of the Joint Liturgical Study series, with two volumes being published each year.

Members of the Club receive publications of the current year free and others at a reduced price. The President of the Club is the Rt Revd Michael Perham and its Chairman is the Revd Canon Dr Donald Gray CBE. Information concerning the annual subscription, applications for membership and lists of publications is obtainable from the Secretary, Mr Jack Ryding, 'Ty Nant', 6 Parc Bach, Trefnant, Denbighshire LL16 4YE, or by email from alcuinclub@waitrose.com

Visit the Alcuin Club website at **www.alcuin.mcmail.com**

A Companion to
Common Worship

Edited by
Paul Bradshaw

Volume 1

Alcuin Club Collections 78

Published in Great Britain in 2001

Society for Promoting Christian Knowledge
36 Causton Street
London SW1P 4ST

Copyright © Alcuin Club 2001

British Library Cataloguing-in-Publication Data
A catalogue record for this book is available from the British Library

ISBN-13: 978-0-281-05266-0
ISBN-10: 0-281-05266-2

10 9 8 7 6 5 4

Designed and typeset by Kenneth Burnley, Wirral, Cheshire
Printed in Great Britain by Ashford Colour Press

Contents

Contributors

The Revd Dr Paul Bradshaw is Professor of Liturgy at the University of Notre Dame, and a Consultant to the Church of England Liturgical Commission.

The Revd Dr Anne Dawtry is Principal of Ordained Local Ministry and Integrated Education in the Diocese of Salisbury and a member of the Salisbury Diocesan Liturgical Team.

The Revd Gordon Giles is Succentor of St Paul's Cathedral, London.

The Revd Benjamin Gordon-Taylor served in parishes in Cornwall and Northampton, and is now Solway Fellow and Chaplain of University College, Durham.

The Revd Dr Donald Gray is Chairman of the Alcuin Club and formerly a Canon of Westminster Abbey.

The Revd Carolyn Headley is Tutor in Liturgy and Spirituality at Wycliffe Hall, Oxford.

The Revd Dr Simon Jones is Assistant Curate of Tewkesbury Abbey and Secretary of the Bishop of Gloucester's Advisory Group on Liturgy.

Simon Kershaw is Secretary of Christians on the Internet, and a member of the Ely Diocesan Liturgical Committee.

Dr Bridget Nichols is Lay Chaplain and Research Assistant to the Bishop of Ely.

The Very Revd Michael Perham is Dean of Derby and a member of the Church of England Liturgical Commission.

Dr Colin Podmore is the Secretary of the Church of England's Liturgical Publishing Group.

The Revd Canon Jane Sinclair is Precentor of Sheffield Cathedral and a member of the Church of England Liturgical Commission.

The Rt Revd David Stancliffe is Bishop of Salisbury and Chairman of the Church of England Liturgical Commission.

The Revd Phillip Tovey is Training Co-ordinator in the Diocese of Oxford.

Abbreviations

ACC	Alcuin Club Collections
ASB	*The Alternative Service Book 1980*
BAS	*The Book of Alternative Services of the Anglican Church of Canada*, 1985
BCP	*Book of Common Prayer*
CCP	Society of St Francis, *Celebrating Common Prayer*, Mowbray, London 1992
CLC	*The Christian Year: Calendar, Lectionary and Collects*, Church House Publishing, London, 1997
CPAS	Church Pastoral Aid Society
CSI	The Church of South India, *Book of Common Worship*
CW	*Common Worship*
ELLC	English Language Liturgical Consultation
GS	General Synod
IALC	International Anglican Liturgical Consultation
ICET	International Consultation on English Texts
JLG	Joint Liturgical Group of Great Britain
LHWE	*Lent, Holy Week, Easter*, Church House Publishing, London, 1986
MacDonnell	Charles L. MacDonnell, *After Communion*, Mowbray, London, 1985
MC	Church of the Province of Southern Africa, *Modern Collects*, 1972
PHG	*The Promise of His Glory*, Church House Publishing, London, 1991
PW	*Patterns for Worship*, Church House Publishing, London, 1995
RCL	Consultation on Common Texts, *The Revised Common Lectionary*, 1992
Silk	David Silk, ed., *Prayers for use at the Alternative Services*, Mowbray, London, 1980
SSF	Society of Saint Francis

Foreword

The text of *Common Worship* with its rubrics provides a template for the Church's worship. But this template needs an interpretative guidebook. All those who are responsible for designing and leading any part of the Church's worship need to understand the theological, historical and liturgical background to the texts that have been painstakingly crafted and carefully scrutinized on the way to formal authorization. They also need to be able to interpret the accompanying rubrics so that they can find their way and make principled choices among the variety of alternatives offered within the template of each clear structure. What the Church does and how it does it is often as significant as what is said.

This *Companion* fulfils this requirement of a guidebook admirably. It gives some background, and helps you to find your way. It helps you make choices among the variety of menus presented. It explains the genesis of the texts, and how the creative flow of each liturgy has developed. I hope that this scholarly but practical work will prove to be useful, informative and inspiring to all with responsibility for the worship of the Church.

† DAVID SARUM

Introduction

For just over 100 years the Alcuin Club has been involved in providing scholarly and educational material to serve the Church of England on each occasion it has found itself in the throes of liturgical revision. From the first, its publications had been preparing the ground for an informed examination of the Church's services. In the 1920s the Club produced a series of Prayer Book Revision Pamphlets; these critically surveyed the alternatives being put forward which resulted in the abortive 1927/28 proposals. After the 1939–45 War the Club's authors included many of the scholars who were to be intimately involved in the revision process which resulted in *The Alternative Service Book* in 1980 (R. C. D. Jasper, G. J. Cuming, E. C. Whitaker, Colin Buchanan, Michael Perham, P. F. Bradshaw, Colin Dunlop, Donald Gray) as well as others whose researches informed the nature of that book. Realizing that the *ASB* could never be the final word, the Alcuin Club produced two collections of essays in preparation for its revision: *Towards Liturgy 2000* (1989) and *Liturgy for a New Century* (1991). Many of the contributors to those collections have been involved in preparing *Common Worship*.

The present volume follows, then, in an established tradition, but with a difference. Instead of only involving the expertise of the current revisers, it also draws on the talents of the next generation of liturgical scholars. Geoffrey Cuming was the inspirer and motivator of many who have been involved in liturgical work in the past 25 years. At his death a memorial fund was set up, administered by the Alcuin Club, for which he had been both an author and editorial secretary. In recent years this fund has supported the Alcuin Club's younger scholars seminar. It is mostly the members of this group, imaginatively led by Professor Paul Bradshaw, who have worked collaboratively on this project, sharing their drafts and receiving helpful criticism from one another. They have also benefited from the unfailing willingness of David Hebblethwaite, Secretary of the Church of England Liturgical Commission and Alcuin Committee member, to answer queries and verify matters of detail, and also from the help given by Brother Tristam, SSF. To both of these the group would like to express their deep gratitude.

This two-volume work is intended as the successor to *A Companion to the Alternative Service Book* by Ronald Jasper and Paul Bradshaw (SPCK, London,

1985), and indeed Paul Bradshaw has very kindly permitted the historical material which he wrote for that commentary to be used by the contributors to this work and incorporated either more or less verbatim or in a condensed form into many of the chapters. However, it was not felt necessary for everything which was included in that earlier book to have its equivalent here, and parts of it can therefore still be consulted with profit. Yet while some things have been omitted, a number of new elements have also been introduced. This first volume deals chiefly, though not exclusively, with the contents of the main volume of *Common Worship*; and the second volume will cover the other liturgical material that forms part of the *Common Worship* 'family'. But, just as in the *Companion to the Alternative Service Book*, because of limitations of space many important aspects relating to worship – among them questions of architecture, the use of symbolism and music – will not be treated here. It is the Alcuin Club's hope that many of them will receive the attention they rightly deserve in new additions to our series of Manuals.

We trust that this latest offering of the Alcuin Club will serve to inform and enhance the common worship of the Church and consequently give glory to God.

DONALD GRAY

Chapter 1

Services and Service Books

The Jewish Background

Jewish worship in New Testament times was still officially centred around the sacrificial cult of the Temple at Jerusalem, as it had been for centuries. There offerings were made for the nation every day, morning and evening, and additional sacrifices were offered on Sabbaths and festivals. For the majority of people, however, such worship was rather distant, and did not really impinge on them, except at the annual festivals when they might go up in pilgrimage to Jerusalem, or at other important points in their lives. For most Jews, therefore, worship centred around the home and the synagogue. In the home, prayers would be said at regular times during the day and at meals, and special ceremonies were associated with the Sabbath and other festal occasions. The precise origins of the synagogue are uncertain, but it probably came into existence during or after the exile in Babylon in the sixth century BC, and it provided a place first for the study and proclamation of the Law (and eventually of the prophetic writings too), and later, but perhaps not until after the destruction of the Temple, also for regular acts of corporate worship.

In the New Testament period Jewish worship was still fluid in its nature: the broad outlines of its rituals and practices were established, but there were no written forms or service books, and different communities followed their own inherited traditions, often with quite significant liturgical variations from one another. Moreover, even within these conventions individuals were generally still free to vary the wording of prayers and the details of ceremonial observances. Only in later centuries did a measure of uniformity emerge. There was therefore nothing particularly heretical or remarkable in groups of early Jewish Christians forming themselves into a distinct liturgical assembly or synagogue of their own, with their own distinctive pattern of worship. Other Jewish groups had already done something similar, most notably the Essenes, who regarded the worship of the Temple as corrupt and had withdrawn from all association with it, evolving instead their own system of worship and waiting for the coming of the Messiah. A large number of them lived a communal life at Qumran, and were responsible for the composition of the writings known to us as the Dead Sea Scrolls.

The New Testament

Since both Jesus and the first Christian converts were themselves Jews, it is hardly surprising that one of the main influences on the shape of early Christian worship was the worship of Judaism, especially as the Christian faith was viewed by its adherents not as an alternative to the Jewish religion but as its proper fulfilment. We have no liturgical texts from this earliest period of Christian worship, not merely because none have survived, but because the Christians apparently adhered to the Jewish custom of not writing down their prayers but transmitting them orally. We have to rely for our information, therefore, on our knowledge of Jewish practice of the time, which is itself limited, and on the brief references and allusions to worship in the New Testament. The result is that, although by this means we can learn something of what early Christian worship was like, we cannot reconstruct it as fully as we would like to be able to do. What does emerge from the New Testament, however, is the strongly eschatological character of primitive Christianity: it was a movement which expected the imminent return of Christ and the fulfilment of the kingdom of God, and hence its worship and ritual practices were all powerfully shaped by this fact. This is shown, for example, by the nature of the Lord's Prayer itself ('your kingdom come, your will be done').

The Second and Third Centuries

In this period information about Christian liturgical practice is a little more plentiful. There are descriptions and allusions in a number of Christian writings, notably those of Justin Martyr at Rome around AD 165, and Tertullian and Cyprian in North Africa in the third century. Even so, there are many details about which we lack certainty. The general impression which emerges, however, is that Christian worship did not develop as a single organized whole, but, as in Judaism, with a number of variant traditions in different geographical areas, and with considerable liberty of improvization and adaptation being exercised. Earlier generations of scholars tended to search for an archetypal 'apostolic liturgy', believing that, behind the accretions of later centuries, there was a common nucleus which could be traced back to New Testament times. More recently scholars have recognized the existence of greater diversity in the practice of the early centuries, and have suggested that what was common was an archetypal shape or structure of the rites. Yet it is now emerging that even this cannot be accepted without some qualification: more variations in structure between different communities are beginning to be detected from the evidence, suggesting much more pluriformity in development from New Testament times.

The Apostolic Tradition of Hippolytus

Because of the relative paucity of other material, this document has come to be treated as a crucial source of information about the worship of the early Church. It consists of a collection of directions concerning the liturgical life of a community, including the text of many prayers, among them those for the Eucharist, for the initiation rites, and for ordination services. The original Greek version has not survived, and has to be reconstructed from an extant Latin translation, and from later Coptic, Arabic and Ethiopic versions, as well as from the use made of it by compilers of later liturgical documents. In the nineteenth century it was known as *The Egyptian Church Order*, but it was identified with the otherwise missing work of Hippolytus early in the twentieth century, and is now generally thought of as having originated in Rome around 215. A growing number of scholars have begun to doubt this attribution, however, and judge the document instead to be a composite work, containing material drawn from different historical periods, between the second to the fourth century, and from different geographical regions, and therefore not representing the practice of any single Christian community. Such uncertainties suggest that more caution is needed in using it as an historical source than has frequently been shown.

Worship in the Post-Constantinian Era

After the conversion of the Roman Emperor Constantine to the Christian faith in 313, the situation of the Church changed quite dramatically. No longer merely a tolerated sect, constantly exposed to the risk of sporadic persecution, it now became the established religion of the Empire, and large numbers rushed to join the Church now that it was not only respectable but also possibly advantageous to be a Christian. This inevitably had a profound effect upon the nature of the Church's worship, though one must be careful not to overstate this, as has often been done in the past. Many of the developments which can be seen at this period have roots reaching back well into the third century, when in many places the Church was already quite comfortably settled in society and undergoing a transformation from its earlier outlook and practices. Hence in these respects the so-called Constantinian revolution served more to intensify an already existing trend than to initiate one. Nevertheless, it is in general true that a marked contrast can be observed between the worship of the pre-Constantinian and post-Constantinian periods.

There were, first of all, the consequences of the movement from private to public worship. Whereas the first Christians saw themselves as set over against the world, and were careful to avoid any compromise with paganism and its ways, stressing rather what distinguished Christianity from other religions, the Church now emerged as a public institution within the world, its liturgy functioning as a *cultus publicus*, seeking the divine favour to secure the well-being of the state. Thus paganism was no longer viewed as a threat; the old division between the 'public' and 'private' elements in the liturgy disappeared; and the Church was quite willing to absorb and Christianize pagan religious ideas and ritual practices, seeing itself as the fulfilment to which the earlier religions had dimly pointed. Thus, for example, one finds the introduction into Christian liturgy of the common language, style and imagery of contemporary religious prayers; the use of such things as blessed salt and the burning of incense; and the taking over of sacred places as sites for Christian churches, and of pagan festivals as occasions for Christian feasts, with the inevitable dangers of syncretism which this brought.

Second, there were the effects of the growth in size of Christian communities, which meant that the relatively informal, intimate, quasi-domestic character of much pre-Nicene liturgy inevitably had to give way to much more formally structured services, taking place now in specially constructed church buildings instead of the private houses more generally used in earlier centuries. As a result of this, elements of the ceremonial of the imperial court were assimilated into Christian worship, as it provided the natural model for a style of liturgical practice more appropriate for these larger assemblies. Because of the corporate understanding of worship inherited from the past, there was at first a considerable reluctance to divide the congregation into smaller units as it grew in size, and even when this became inevitable, attempts continued to be made in some places to link together the different congregations in some way. However, one of the more significant consequences of the expansion in the number of separate congregations was that the liturgy was no longer under the regular presidency of the bishop in most places but of a presbyter.

Third, there was a growing clericalization of the liturgy and a decline in lay participation. The catechetical system was unable to cope with the great increase in numbers, and so very many of those entering the Church in the wake of the Constantinian peace were only half-converted barbarians with little understanding of the true meaning of the Christian mysteries, who brought with them attitudes and behaviour inherited from their pagan past. This led to a widening gulf between the liturgical roles of the clergy and laity, and although the theory of liturgy as a corporate action survived for several centuries, as time went on less and less of an active or vocal part was left to the laity, and they began to be little more than spectators of the professionals who performed the liturgy on their behalf.

The Emergence of Liturgical Texts

Not least as a consequence of the fear of the introduction of heretical teaching into liturgical formulations, the freedom of individual liturgical presidents and of local communities to extemporize prayer began to be curtailed to some extent by the regulations of provincial synods seeking to enforce conformity to alleged doctrinal and liturgical norms. Frequently it was insisted that any prayers used should be written down and subjected to the scrutiny of others. Although the composition of new prayers and formularies continued for several centuries under these conditions, it eventually declined virtually to the point of extinction, and ministers became expected to use traditional, agreed texts.

At first, the tendency seems to have been to write down single prayers – as for example the eucharistic prayer of the community – or collections of prayers for the presiding minister to use at various services and occasions, while allowing the remainder of the rite to continue to develop freely. The nearest thing at this time to the complete text of a service, including directions or 'rubrics' as they were later called, as well as prayers, were the 'Church Orders' which flourished for a while in the East. These were similar to the *Apostolic Tradition* of Hippolytus, and usually drew upon that as a major source, and they include the so-called *Canons of Hippolytus* from Egypt and the *Apostolic Constitutions* from Syria, both fourth-century documents.

The emergence of written liturgical texts in turn encouraged a growing standardization of liturgy, not only within a particular geographical area but also to a considerable extent between different areas. Travellers and pilgrims visiting the hallowed sites of primitive Christianity were able to observe the diverse traditions of other Christian groups, and tended to adopt them in their own countries, so that there was thus a mutual interchange of liturgical practices, and this promoted a greater measure of uniformity. For example, Syria adopted the Western practice of post-baptismal anointing, while the West took over the Syrian baptismal formula; and the East added the Western feast of the Nativity to its liturgical year, while the West absorbed the Eastern feast of the Epiphany. Some differences between geographical areas still remained, however, and distinct 'families' of rites, each stemming from a particular region, can be discerned; but the variations between them are concerned with relatively superficial features rather than with fundamentals, and the more extensive pluriformity which seems to have existed in the preceding centuries disappeared.

Eastern Rites

In the East at least three main groups or families of liturgical rites may be distinguished. There is, first of all, the West Syrian type, which originated from the great liturgical centres of Jerusalem and Antioch. From this source are ultimately descended such contemporary Eastern rites as the Jacobite, Maronite, Armenian, and even the Byzantine rite itself, which is practised by the Greek and Russian Orthodox Churches. Although this last rite stems from Constantinople, or Byzantium as it was once called, yet because that city had no special ecclesiastical importance until the Council of Constantinople in 381 recognized it as the New Rome, it had no indigenous liturgical tradition and was thus dependent upon Antioch and to a lesser extent Cappadocia for the principal features of its worship. Later the prestige which it enjoyed enabled it to influence and finally supplant all other local rites of Orthodox churches in the East, just as the Roman rite did in the West. Second, there is the East Syrian family, which because of geographical and political factors developed in relative isolation from the West Syrian rites. To this type belong the Nestorian and Chaldean rites. Third, there is the Egyptian or Alexandrian family, which includes the Coptic and Ethiopian rites.

Our knowledge of the historical development of Eastern liturgy is somewhat limited because of the fact that nearly all the liturgical texts which we possess are of a relatively late date when the various rites had already achieved what are substantially their present forms; and therefore attempts to reconstruct their earlier history and stages of evolution have to be rather tentative, and depend to a considerable extent on commentaries and other writings about liturgical practice from the earlier period. The oldest text of the Byzantine eucharistic rite, for example, dates from the end of the eighth century, and the texts of many other rites are much later than that.

In the course of their history, Eastern rites have accumulated much peripheral material, and frequently absorbed within a single service elements which were originally intended as alternative forms to one another, with the result that they are very long and repetitive, with a profusion of symbolic elaboration of what were formerly merely utilitarian actions. Because of the conservative nature of the tradition, however, they have often succeeded in preserving beneath the layers of later accretions many features of primitive Christian worship, even if only in a vestigial form, which have disappeared from Western rites. Moreover, unlike the West, the language of the liturgy has remained in the vernacular, even if in most places it has become archaic in the course of time and somewhat removed from the normal form of contemporary speech.

The Medieval West

Western rites may be divided into two main groups: the practice of Rome itself, which was followed throughout southern Italy, and the non-Roman family of rites. The latter may be further subdivided into the Ambrosian rite, stemming from Milan and practised throughout northern Italy; the Gallican rite, practised in France; the Mozarabic rite, practised in Spain; and the Celtic rite of the British Isles.

At first these various traditions evolved in relative independence. However, it was not long before they began to exercise a mutual influence upon one another. There was also a natural tendency for the churches of the West to turn to Rome as the ancient and apostolic centre of Christianity in that part of the world for authoritative guidance in matters of liturgical practice, and for missionaries from Rome to carry their own way of doing things into the countries to which they went. This was the way in which, for example, the Roman rite gradually supplanted the Celtic tradition in the British Isles. In the

Franco–German empire, rulers such as Pepin and his son Charlemagne in the eighth century tried to impose the Roman usage throughout their realm for both religious and political motives. In this process, however, a considerable element of intermingling took place between the imported Roman liturgical material and the indigenous Gallican tradition, so that what resulted was not the pure Roman rite but a form enriched and modified by Gallican elements. The ironical consequence of this was that at the end of the tenth century, when liturgical life at Rome had sunk to a very low ebb, it was revitalized by the importation of this Gallicanized version of its own rite. Thus, what eventually spread throughout the West in the later part of the Middle Ages was this mixed form of the Roman liturgy, which supplanted native traditions but gathered to itself local variations and customs wherever it went, so that there was substantial similarity everywhere but not total uniformity anywhere. In England, for example, in addition to the different customs followed in each of the various monastic traditions represented here, there were minor variations between different diocesan centres, though the use of Sarum (Salisbury) was particularly influential.

In the early Middle Ages the tendency was to provide separate liturgical books for the different ministers involved in the celebration of a rite, each containing the parts of the service needed by that person. Thus the bishop or priest presiding over a liturgical rite would have had a *Sacramentary* containing the prayers he was to say; those responsible for the readings at a service would have had a *Lectionary*, which would have indicated the beginnings and endings of the passages to be read; the singers would have had an *Antiphonary* containing musical parts of the service; and, at Rome at any rate, the ceremonial directions for the rite were contained in an *Ordo*. It was much later before it became general practice for the whole of a service, texts and rubrics, to be included in a single volume, and this came about largely as a result of the decline of the corporate celebration of liturgy and the growth of the practice of a single minister conducting the whole rite. Ordinary lay people did not usually have a copy of the service at all, partly because of the illiteracy of most people, partly because of the high cost of copying out texts by hand, and partly because liturgy had by now become something done by the clergy on behalf of the people, who were expected to occupy themselves meanwhile with their own private devotions. On the other hand, books of suitable devotions, or 'Primers' as they were called, were produced in the late Middle Ages for those lay people who were able to read and to afford their cost.

The Reformation

The rejection of many medieval doctrines by the sixteenth-century Reformers necessarily demanded a reformation in worship, for much of the teaching which they regarded as a corruption of pure Christianity was embodied and expressed in liturgical rites and practices. They sought to return to the model of the worship of the New Testament period, but because of the limitations of their scholarship and historical perspective, they were only able to do this to a limited extent, and in some ways were as much victims and heirs of medieval ways of thinking and acting as they were Reformers.

With regard to the ceremonial of worship, most Reformers tried to make a distinction between those things which they considered to be commanded by God in the New Testament, as, for example, the eating of bread and drinking of wine in the Eucharist or the pouring of water in the name of the Trinity in baptism, and those things which they regarded as merely human additions to the essential nucleus. They believed that the former had necessarily to be observed but the latter should be critically examined: if the practices were contrary to the gospel or encouraged superstition, then they should be abolished; but if they served a valuable purpose, then they might be kept (see for example 'Of ceremonies, why some be abolished and some retained' in the *Book of Common Prayer* (*BCP*)). Some extreme Reformers, however, regarded anything which they judged was not explicitly commanded in Scripture to be inadmissible in Christian worship.

Fundamental features of Reformation worship were the use of the vernacular and the restoration of the ministry of the Word to a prominent place, chiefly through the preaching and expounding of Scripture and through the inclusion within the services of the reading of long passages of doctrinal instruction and moral exhortation. With the exception of extreme Reformers, who believed that prayers which were read from a book were not really prayers at all, the majority were not opposed to set forms of liturgy. Indeed, fixed orders of service and prescribed texts were valuable instruments in ensuring that what was said and done in each congregation really was 'pure' and did not contain objectionable features. Although, therefore, they did tend to allow some freedom to individual ministers in shaping worship, the Reformers continued to produce orders of service as models to be followed, and thus the recent invention of printing was an important factor in enabling the Reformation ideas to be disseminated effectively and the orthodoxy of its worship to be controlled.

The Church of England

Reformation proceeded very slowly in England, for although Henry VIII had broken with Rome in 1532, he remained as solidly opposed to any major doctrinal or liturgical changes as he had been before. The first noticeable influence of the Protestant Reformation on worship, therefore, was in the use of the vernacular. Material for private devotions, including a number of Primers, appeared in English in the 1530s, and gradually elements of public worship also came to be translated. In 1537 Edward Lee, Archbishop of York, ordered the liturgical Gospels to be read in English in his diocese. In 1538 injunctions were issued which required an English Bible to be set up in every church in the land, so that it might be read outside services; incumbents were to recite the Creed, the Lord's Prayer, and the Ten Commandments in English to their people, so that they might learn them; and no one was to be admitted to Communion until he or she could recite them. In 1543 the English Bible began to be used liturgically, when it was ordered that every Sunday and holy day one chapter of it was to be read aloud, without exposition, after the *Te Deum* at Mattins and after the *Magnificat* at Vespers. Then in 1544 an English form of the litany appeared, from which the invocation of the saints was almost entirely purged and many other changes made. By a Royal Injunction of October 1545 it was to be used every Sunday and holy day.

When Edward VI, then only nine years old, came to the throne in January 1547 after Henry's death, Thomas Cranmer, Archbishop of Canterbury, could at last begin to put into effect the doctrinal and liturgical reforms which he desired. In July 1547 a book of homilies was issued by royal authority, and in August of that same year injunctions appeared which included the requirements that one of the homilies was to be read to the people every Sunday; the Epistle and Gospel at the Eucharist were to be in English; a chapter from the New Testament was to be read in English at Mattins, and one from the Old Testament at Vespers, the services being otherwise shortened to allow for this; Prime and the lesser hours of the day were to be omitted when there was a sermon, and when there was no sermon, the Creed, the Lord's Prayer, and the Ten Commandments were to be recited in English after the Gospel; images, pictures, and stained-glass windows before which votive candles had been burnt were to be removed; and only two candles could be left on the high altar. In January 1548 various traditional ceremonies associated with certain days of the liturgical year were also forbidden.

The First English Book of Common Prayer (BCP), 1549
Various experiments with whole services in English began to take place, and in December 1547 it was decreed that Holy Communion should be received in both kinds, bread and wine, an order for this being produced in March 1548. This was followed soon after by the first complete English *BCP*, on which a committee of bishops and other divines had begun work on 9 September 1548. Since the complete text was delivered to the king some three weeks later, it is obvious that a preliminary draft must have been prepared beforehand, doubtless by Thomas Cranmer himself. The book was finally approved by Parliament on 21 January 1549, and by an Act of Uniformity was to be used throughout the country from Whitsunday of that year, 9 June. The ordination services were issued later, in 1550, as was a musical setting of parts of the Prayer Book services by John Merbecke, under the title, *The Book of Common Prayer Noted*.

As will be seen from the accounts given of the individual services elsewhere in this book, this first English *BCP* was a quite conservative revision in comparison with much of the material being produced on the Continent, and it retained a considerable measure of the structure and some of the ceremonies of the medieval rites which had preceded it. It was essentially a compromise between the desires of the more extreme Reformers and the need to try to carry along the more conservative members of the Church, from bishops to ordinary lay people. Inevitably, therefore, it satisfied no one completely: it was criticized by some for not going far enough, and opposed by others for going too far. Further annoyance was caused to the more radical Reformers by the fact that some conservative bishops and divines claimed that its eucharistic rite could be considered compatible with traditional Catholic teaching, and by the fact that others were celebrating it in a manner not very different from the old rite. Obviously, both doctrine and practice needed to be made more explicitly Reformed.

The 1552 BCP

Further changes were not long in appearing. Indeed, some scholars believe that the first *BCP* was only ever intended as an interim step and that the text of the second book was already envisaged when the first was being produced. Certainly by January 1551 the bishops had agreed to many changes being made, and in April 1552 a new Act of Uniformity ordered the replacement of the first *BCP* by a second one from All Saints' Day onwards. As one would have expected, this was a thoroughgoing Protestant revision, with none of the ambiguity of doctrine or conservatism of practice of its immediate predecessor. This time the ordination services were bound up with the rest of the book. It was, however, short-lived, for in July 1553 Edward VI died, and the succession passed to the Catholic Princess Mary, who immediately repealed all the Edwardine legislation and restored the traditional liturgical practices of the medieval rites. Only in Scotland did the 1552 book continue in use. A number of leading English bishops and divines fled into exile on the Continent, where they came into direct contact with Calvinism. This served to encourage many of them to pursue doctrinal and liturgical change even further in a Reformed direction than the 1552 book, and tensions and quarrels developed over this issue among the exiles, some wishing to adhere to the English book, some demanding a Calvinist form, and others seeking a compromise between the two positions.

The 1559 BCP

In November 1558 Elizabeth I came to the throne and began by restoring the liturgical situation to what it had been immediately prior to the death of her father, Henry VIII. The English litany was reinstated, as were the English versions of the Epistles and Gospels, the Creed, the Lord's Prayer, and the Ten Commandments. However, the return of the exiles created pressure for further reform. They rejected as unacceptable a suggested return to the 1549 book, and insisted on going further. Faced with the possibility that some might demand the wholesale introduction of Calvinist forms of service, as in fact did happen in Scotland, there seemed no alternative but to agree to the compromise of the adoption of the 1552 book.

In April 1559, therefore, an Act of Uniformity was passed restoring the 1552 book with a few small alterations, the most important of which related to the service of Holy Communion and permitted a somewhat broader interpretation of the meaning of the rite. Thus once again, as in 1549, no one really wanted the book they were given: the Queen and others would have preferred something less Protestant, and the returned exiles something closer to the practice of the continental Reformed churches, such as had been adopted in Scotland. Many of the latter were extremely unhappy with the compromise book, and found even its few ceremonial directions (such as the wearing of the surplice by ministers and the use of a ring in marriage) objectionable because they were without scriptural warrant. Known as 'Puritans', this group continued to struggle for further change throughout the rest of Elizabeth's reign, but without success.

The 1604 BCP
When James I succeeded to the throne in 1603 on the death of Elizabeth, hopes rose among the Puritan party that, as a result of his experience as ruler of Scotland, he might be more kindly disposed towards them, and a petition expressing their desired reforms was presented to him. James referred the matter to a conference between the Prayer Book and Puritan factions, which met at Hampton Court in January 1604. After three days' discussion a number of very small concessions to the Puritan conscience were agreed upon for incorporation into the *BCP*. This was by no means sufficient to satisfy them, however, and their criticism of the book continued in the years which followed. They received an even less sympathetic hearing than in the previous century. There was no longer the same political necessity for appeasing the extreme Protestants in order to present a united front against the papists which had marked the early years of Elizabeth's reign, and there was a growing element among the adherents of the *BCP* who favoured a more Catholic theology and liturgical practice, usually known as 'Laudians', after William Laud, Archbishop of Canterbury from 1633 to 1645. Although they continued on the whole to retain the text of the *BCP* intact in their worship, they did make changes in the manner in which the services were celebrated, especially in the adornment of church buildings and in the vesture of ministers. The minister wore a cope for the celebration of the Eucharist, and the holy table was kept in its old 'altar' position against the east wall of the church, from which it had been removed in 1552, with a fine covering over it and surrounded with rails.

The Scottish BCP of 1637
After the accession of James I, bishops had been appointed in Scotland in place of the reformed Presbyterian system of church government which had

previously obtained, and, not surprisingly, there was pressure from the Laudian party for Scotland also to come into line with the liturgical practice of England. Strong resistance was encountered to this. However, during the reign of Charles I (1625–49) work began on the preparation of a prayer book for Scotland which was not dissimilar to the 1549 book and in many ways reflected what the Laudians would have liked to have introduced in England. Unfortunately, when it was published in 1637, it gave rise to such violent opposition in Scotland that it had to be abandoned.

Meanwhile, opposition to the Laudians had also been growing in England, and the Puritan party were in the ascendant, with the aim of total reform of the Church, including the abolition of both episcopacy and the *BCP*. No compromise was now possible, and in January 1645 Parliament declared the use of the *BCP* illegal, its place being taken by the Presbyterian *Directory for the Public Worship of God*. Both Laud and Charles I were executed, and the episcopal party lay low or fled into exile.

The 1662 BCP

In 1660 Charles II returned to England, episcopacy was restored once more, and the question immediately arose as to which form of the *BCP*, if any, was to be imposed. There was, naturally enough, strong support for a return to the book which had been in use prior to 1645, though the Presbyterians hoped that some concessions might be made to them, and some second-generation Laudians, among them Matthew Wren, Bishop of Ely, and John Cosin, Bishop of Durham, were engaged in preparing a possible revision of the *BCP* which would be more in accord with their theological position and include some of the features of the ill-fated Scottish book. Once again a conference was called to consider the different points of view. Known subsequently as the Savoy Conference, it met in 1661 and was composed of 12 bishops and an equal number of leading Presbyterian divines. The bishops were not disposed to accept any but the most insignificant of changes in the *BCP* proposed by the Presbyterians, and the conference broke up after three months without achieving any agreement.

Meanwhile an Act of Uniformity imposing the *BCP* of 1604 was already on its way through Parliament, a body which was equally unfavourable to changes in any direction and would have preferred to reprint the 1604 book without alteration. The Laudian party, therefore, arranged for Convocation to meet in November 1661 and to undertake the work of revising the *BCP*. A committee of eight bishops was entrusted with the preparatory work for this, and they presented their recommendations to full sessions of Convocation meeting briefly each day. The whole process was completed very rapidly, in a total of only 22 days. The final form was approved on 21 December 1661, and subsequently annexed to the Act of Uniformity in Parliament, which received the Royal Assent on 19 May 1662, and came into effect on St Bartholomew's Day, 24 August. Much of the less controversial material from Cosin's and Wren's work was incorporated, and other minor alterations made, including some small concessions to the Presbyterian objections, but both lack of time and, more significantly, the lack of sufficiently widespread support for a strongly Laudian version made the result something of a compromise. Neither the Laudians nor the Presbyterians achieved more than a small part of what they wanted, and the book that emerged in the end was very little changed from that of 1604.

The BCP after 1662

The imposition of the book was regarded as intolerable by many Presbyterian and Puritan ministers, and more than a thousand of them were deprived of their benefices in 1662 for refusing to submit to episcopal ordination, which was now written into the ordination services as a requirement for ministry in the Church of England. Nevertheless, even after this, efforts directed towards the 'comprehension' of dissenters within the Church of England still continued. An attempt was made in 1689 to produce a revision of the *BCP* which might be acceptable to all parties, but it had to be abandoned because of hostility to the idea in Convocation.

Enthusiasm for such schemes subsequently declined, but the desire to revise the *BCP* continued to surface among various groups of people from time to time in the following centuries. Generally, they were motivated by a wish to make the book conform more closely to their particular doctrinal position. Thus, for example, in the eighteenth century those with Unitarian leanings produced suggested versions which deleted overtly Trinitarian elements from the book. On the other hand, some scholars with knowledge of ancient liturgies, particularly among the Nonjurors, produced versions which tried to incorporate elements from these and so enrich the liturgical practice of the Church of England. All these attempts, however, eventually came to nothing, though the latter group did exert some influence on the Communion Service of the Episcopal Church in Scotland which appeared in 1764, and through that upon the revision of the *BCP* undertaken in the Episcopal Church in the United States of America in 1790.

A new problem emerged in the course of the nineteenth century. At first the pressure for revision came from extreme Evangelicals, who wished to remove from the *BCP* what they regarded as lingering traces of sacerdotalism and Romanism; but with the growth of the Anglo–Catholic movement in the Church of England there was a development in the opposite direction. The adherents of this party became increasingly dissatisfied with the provisions of the *BCP* and began to make additions to the worship of their churches, first by the introduction of furnishings which had not been seen for centuries (such as candles, crosses, credence tables, altar coverings, vestments and incense), and second by the incorporation of material from contemporary Roman Catholic sources into the text of their services. Feelings ran high against the 'ritualists', as they were called, and the bishops tried to settle the matter by appeal to law, to determine what might or might not legitimately be done in Anglican worship. Lawyers were divided as to the legality of a number of practices, and eventually a Royal Commission was appointed in 1867 to clarify, and if necessary amend, the directions of the *BCP* so as to secure uniformity of practice in what were deemed to be vital areas. Its final report, which appeared in 1870, failed to deal satisfactorily with the heart of the problem, much of it being taken up with controversy over the use of the Athanasian Creed, and the only real results of this protracted exercise were a revision of the lectionary in 1871 and the appearance of the Act of Uniformity Amendment Act (or 'Shortened Services Act' as it was generally called) in 1872. This mainly allowed Morning and Evening Prayer to be shortened on weekdays; additional services to be drawn up from material in the *BCP* or the Bible for Sundays or other special occasions; and Morning Prayer, the Litany and Holy Communion to take place separately.

Since the problem of ritualism still remained, a Public Worship Regulation Act was passed in 1874. This was aimed at enforcing the law with regard to conformity to the *BCP* and set up a special court with prescribed penalties. A series of prosecutions ensued, some resulting in the imprisonment of persistent offenders, which did nothing to lower the emotional temperature in the Church of England. Finally, in 1904 a Royal Commission on Ecclesiastical Discipline was appointed. This was to inquire into alleged breaches of the law with regard to worship and make recommendations for dealing with the situation. Its report appeared in 1906, and it concluded that the law was 'in our belief, nowhere exactly observed'; it was 'too narrow for the religious life of the present generation'; it should be reformed to admit of reasonable elasticity, and then enforced. The report recommended that Letters of Business should be issued to the Convocations to carry out the necessary work of amendment to the rubrics of the *BCP*. This was duly done, and official revision began once more.

The Proposed BCP of 1927/8
Many wanted to make only the minimum change necessary, but others saw an opportunity to make significant alterations and improvements to the *BCP*. Unfortunately, this common aspiration for revision did not tend in one uniform direction. Some were motivated by the desire to incorporate a broader doctrinal position, especially in a Catholic direction, others by a wish to provide more adequately for contemporary needs, and others by the hope of enriching current practice with the fruits of recent liturgical scholarship. This division of aims was to prove fatal for the project. For, though all these might have been agreed upon the need for revision, they were far from agreed upon the shape it should take.

The process dragged on tediously through the years until a final form was approved by the Church Assembly in July 1927, but, although it received overwhelming support in the Assembly (517 votes to 133, a majority of 79 per cent), it was not universally popular in the Church of England. Not only did Evangelicals remain resistant to any change at all in the *BCP*, seeing it as a weakening of the Protestant position of the Church of England, but Anglo–Catholics too were dissatisfied with the final form which the book had taken, since it did not represent what they themselves would have wished to have. The difficulties mainly centred around the structure of the eucharistic prayer in the Service of Holy Communion and the provisions for the reservation of the consecrated bread and wine after the service, provisions which went too far for Evangelicals and not far enough for Anglo–Catholics. Because of this opposition, when the book was submitted to Parliament in December, it was passed in the Lords by 214 votes to 88 but defeated in the Commons by 238 to 205.

The bishops then decided to reintroduce the book with a number of minor changes which they hoped might pacify the opposition, but their efforts were in vain: they merely resulted in further loss of support among Anglo–Catholics without winning over Evangelicals. Reservation remained the bone of contention, and though the book was again approved by the Church Assembly in April 1928 (by 396 votes to 153, a majority of 72 per cent), it was rejected by the House of Commons by 266 votes to 220. Fortunately such a relationship between Church and Parliament did not exist in other parts of the Anglican Communion, and many provinces were able to carry through similar revisions of the *BCP* at around this period, some very conservative, others going beyond what had been proposed in England.

The bishops now found themselves in something of a quandary, with a Prayer Book which commanded the support of a substantial majority in the Church Assembly having been defeated twice in the House of Commons. They dealt with what was clearly a difficult situation in three ways. First, they had the book published as it stood as a private venture, thus making it generally available to the Church. Since both in cost and appearance it was comparable with 1662, the ordinary lay person could be excused for regarding it simply as 'a new Prayer Book', even though the bishops were careful to state on the introductory page that 'the publication of this Book does not directly or indirectly imply that it can be regarded as authorized for use in churches'.

Second, they issued a statement in 1929 in which they declared that 'in the present emergency and until other order be taken' they would not 'regard as inconsistent with loyalty to the principles of the Church of England the use of such additions or deviations as fall within the limits of these proposals'. Taken in conjunction with the publication of the book, it was a clear invitation to ignore the decision of Parliament, and an implicit claim that they themselves possessed authority to determine matters of liturgy, a claim which had no legal basis whatsoever, but which was generally unquestioned by subsequent generations of Anglican clergy. Hence many of the provisions of the 1928 book came into widespread, if strictly illegal, use in the Church of England.

Third, they took the first steps in the search for some new method of dealing with liturgical revision which would prevent a repetition of the 1927 debacle. This involved an examination of the relationships between Church and State with a view to constitutional change. Little did they realize that the exercise on which they were embarking would last for more than 30 years. However, in 1930 the Archbishops appointed a Commission under the chairmanship of Viscount Cecil of Chelwood to examine the relations between Church and State. Despite a unanimous report in 1935, little or nothing resulted from its recommendations. Nevertheless, it did raise the important issue of what was meant by 'lawful authority' and suggested greater autonomy for the Church.

The Liturgical Movement

Meanwhile a movement had been growing in the Roman Catholic Church on the Continent since early in the nineteenth century which aimed at recovery and revitalization of the Church's liturgical heritage. The Benedictine order was the main force in this, which came to be known as the Liturgical Movement. It was at first too medieval and archaeological in character and insufficiently concerned with the pastoral aspects of the liturgy, but in the twentieth century it did begin to have some impact on the Church's worship, and led to more frequent reception of Holy Communion, a desire for more lay participation in worship, and, among scholars, to greater research into the early history of Christian liturgy and the building of a sound theology of worship.

Similar stirrings can be detected in the Church of England in the early years of the twentieth century, but the process really started to get under way and the influence of the Continental movement began to be felt with the publication in 1935 of *Liturgy and Society* by A. G. Hebert SSM, and two years later a collection of essays, *The Parish Communion*, also edited by Hebert. From this was born the 'Parish Communion movement', which aimed at restoring the Eucharist as the central act of worship in a parish on a Sunday morning. At first those involved simply tried to present the eucharistic and initiatory rites of the *BCP* in a way which would best bring out their full meaning, but eventually it became clear that liturgical revision was necessary if a real renewal of worship was to happen.

The Alternative Services Measure

The movement towards liturgical revision was taken a stage further in another Archbishops' Commission appointed in 1939 to consider the revision and modification of the canon law. Its report in 1947 not only contained a proposed revised code of canons but a valuable memorandum by Mr Justice Vaisey on the meaning of 'lawful authority'. His conclusion that in fact it had no precise meaning in law encouraged the Commission not only to give it meaning in its proposed Canon 13, but also to indicate how it should be used in liturgical revision: 'deviations (whether by way of addition, alternative use, or otherwise) from the said form [i.e. the *BCP*] as the Convocations of the respective Provinces of Canterbury and York may respectively order, allow, or sanction within the said respective Provinces' would be deemed to be ordered by lawful authority.

This whole process was set out in much greater detail in the report of a further Archbishops' Commission on Church and State which sat under Sir Walter Moberly from 1949 to 1952. It proposed the redrafting of Canon 13 to include experimental services which would require approval by the Convocations, with agreement by the House of Laity. Such services, alternative to those in the *BCP*, should be sanctioned for optional and experimental use for a period of seven or ten years, with the option of renewal for further periods; and every sanction would require a two-thirds majority in each House. By this means of trial and error, it was hoped that an acceptable revision of the services in the *BCP* might gradually be secured, after which they could be presented to Parliament by a Church Assembly Measure for statutory authorization. This was the basis of the proposals which were eventually embodied, after protracted negotiations, in the Prayer Book (Alternative and Other Services) Measure and passed by the Church Assembly in July 1965. On this occasion there was no objection from Parliament and the Measure received the Royal Assent in March 1965. It became operative on 1 May 1966. Under its terms, services alternative to those in the *BCP* could be used experimentally for a period of seven years, provided that they secured two-thirds majorities in all five Houses of the Convocations and the House of Laity. The Measure was, therefore, only operative until 1980.

Meanwhile, at the request of the Convocations, the Archbishops had already appointed a Liturgical Commission in 1955 to undertake the necessary preparatory work on new services. Its first major task was to prepare a report on the principles of Prayer Book revision, which was published in time for the consideration of the Lambeth Conference of 1958. In the following year it published its proposals for a revision of the Services of Baptism and Confirmation, even though the legislation for authorizing their experimental use was still in the distant future. Their preliminary airing in the Convocations was decidedly unfortunate: they came in for considerable criticism, and it was not surprising that the whole project was put into cold storage while the Commission turned its attention to the less contentious services of Morning and Evening Prayer.

Series 1, 2 and 3

The first task of the Liturgical Commission under the Alternative Services Measure was to secure the proper authorization of most of the services in the 1928 book, which had now been in unofficial use for over 30 years. Since the Commission had not been involved in the drafting of this material, it was agreed that the House of Bishops should be responsible for this operation, with the help and advice of one or two members of the Commission. With few exceptions, these services – known as Series 1 – were authorized for experimental use in 1966 for a period of seven years. Under this heading came Morning and Evening Prayer, Infant and Adult Baptism, Marriage, Burial, and Holy Communion. Confirmation failed to secure authorization by not receiving the necessary two-thirds majority in the House of Laity; Burial only narrowly secured authorization, owing to problems over prayer for the departed; and Holy Communion was an amended form of the 1928 rite. The 1928 Eucharistic Prayer had never been popular, and, unlike most of the book, was very rarely used. It was therefore replaced by a prayer which to all intents and purposes was that of the long-canvassed 'Interim Rite', and which could be used in a longer and a shorter form.

By this time the Liturgical Commission had already published the first set of its own proposals in *Alternative Services: Second Series* (1965), containing Morning and Evening Prayer, Intercessions and Thanksgivings, Thanksgiving after Childbirth, Burial, and an appendix. It was the appendix, containing an uncompleted draft of a new rite of Holy Communion, which created the greatest stir. Contrary to all expectations, it met with an enthusiastic reception from the Convocations and the House of Laity, all of which pleaded that it should be completed with all speed. This was done and, despite problems over prayer for the departed and the second half of the eucharistic prayer, it was authorized for use in 1967. Baptism and Confirmation, and Morning and Evening Prayer, quickly followed suit in 1968. The proposed services for Burial and Thanksgiving after Childbirth failed to secure authorization, and no proposals for Marriage or Ordination were made. The Series 2 range of services was, therefore, strictly limited.

It was also becoming clear by the mid-1960s that they were in a sense 'interim rites', for by that time ecumenical co-operation in liturgical matters was becoming a reality and there was a general movement towards the use of contemporary English. Significant in this respect were the publication of the New Testament of the *New English Bible* in 1961 (and of the whole Bible in 1970) and of the *Jerusalem Bible* in 1966. The use of such versions in public worship was facilitated by the passing of the Versions of the Bible Measure in 1965, which enabled the authorization for use in public worship of any versions approved by the Church Assembly (later the General Synod). Under this measure the *Revised Version*, the *Revised Standard Version*, the *New English Bible*, the *Jerusalem Bible*, and the *Revised Psalter* were all authorized in addition to the Authorized Version of 1611. Subsequently *The Bible in Today's English* was also authorized in 1978, and the *Liturgical Psalter* in 1979.

In 1967 the Liturgical Commission, with help from the Poet Laureate, C. Day Lewis, published its *Modern Liturgical Texts*, containing versions of the Lord's Prayer, the creeds, and the canticles in contemporary English, together with modern versions of the Series 2 Baptism, Confirmation and Holy Communion rites. This document was published in time for consideration by the Liturgical Consultation of the Lambeth Conference of 1968, and undoubtedly helped to stimulate discussion throughout the Anglican Communion. Shortly afterwards the International Consultation on English Texts (ICET), representing all the major English-speaking Churches throughout the world, came into being. Between 1968 and 1975 it produced three reports on *Prayers We Have in Common*; and its proposals on creeds and canticles ultimately secured general acceptance in English-speaking churches. Unfortunately it was less successful in its work on the Lord's Prayer; but even here only a single line ('lead us not into temptation') really stood in the way of success.

Significant moves were also taking place on the ecumenical front at home. Largely owing to Anglican initiative, the Joint Liturgical Group (JLG), composed of official representatives of all the main Churches in England and Scotland, came into being in 1963. In 1967–8 this group produced radical proposals for a revision of the Calendar, Lectionary and Daily Office, all of which were incorporated into the Church of England's programme of liturgical reform. They also had a profound influence on liturgical revision overseas, not least because of their timely publication before the Lambeth Conference of 1968.

Further constitutional change took place within the Church of England in 1970 with the advent of Synodical Government. This greatly simplified the procedure of liturgical revision, for instead of five Houses considering and voting on proposals, the three new Houses of Bishops, Clergy and Laity could now consider proposals together, although they still voted independently. A system was also devised whereby 'Provisional Approval' was first given to a service by a mere show of hands in the whole Synod; and this was followed by a revision stage, after which 'Final Approval' was required by two-thirds majorities in each House voting independently. One of the Synod's first major achievements was to secure freedom from parliamentary control in matters of worship and doctrine through the Church of England (Worship and Doctrine) Measure of 1974. Under its terms the General Synod was given power to produce and authorize forms of service as and when it was considered necessary, provided that the *BCP* remained available and unaltered. Thus it was only in matters concerning the 1662 Prayer Book that parliamentary approval was still required. Since it was now clear that 'lawful authority' lay with the General Synod, the Church was no longer faced with a possible repetition of the 1927–8 crisis. The Worship and Doctrine Measure also made the Alternative Services Measure of 1965 redundant, thereby releasing the Church of England from any obligation to work within a time limit of 14 years for its new services.

In this transformed atmosphere of the 1970s, the Liturgical Commission proceeded to produce its Series 3 forms of service, all in contemporary English. The first to appear was Holy Communion in September 1971, and this included both the ICET texts and the JLG eucharistic lectionary. Despite its radical approach it was approved by overwhelming majorities in the General Synod in November 1972, and came into use on 1 February 1973. Further proposals then appeared in rapid succession and were duly authorized – Funerals, and Morning and Evening Prayer in 1975; Collects in 1976; Marriage in 1977; the Ordinal, and Calendar, Lectionary, and Rules to order the Service in 1978; and Initiation and the Psalter in 1979.

The ASB

It was not enough, however, simply to authorize services and other relevant material for experimental use for limited periods of time: something with a greater degree of stability and permanence was required for the future. In 1973, therefore, a Working Party was appointed under Dr Habgood, Bishop of Durham, to consider future policy; and in February 1976 this group recommended that alternative services should be brought together into a single book. 1980 was fixed as the target date for publication, convenient not only as the original completion date of the old Alternative Services Measure but also because it was the latest possible date within the lifetime of the existing General Synod. It was agreed that all the contents were to be Series 3 services in contemporary English, with one exception – Holy Communion Series 1 and 2 Revised, modern in structure and content, but traditional in language.

Apart from this rite, all the services underwent a process of revision and then adaptation, whereby they all conformed to a uniform style and format. The synodical process was completed by November 1979, and *The Alternative Service Book 1980 (ASB)* was published in November 1980, being given authorization in the first instance for a period of ten years, which was later extended for a further ten years, until 31 December 2000. It was produced in a variety of editions – with Psalter, without Psalter, case-bound, soft-back, and so on – but in every case the pagination was identical, so that congregations could easily be directed to the right place by page reference.

References and Further Reading

For the general history of Christian worship:
Cheslyn Jones, Geoffrey Wainwright, Edward Yarnold and Paul Bradshaw (eds), *The Study of Liturgy*, 2nd edn, SPCK, London, 1992.

For Jewish worship:
Stefan C. Reif, *Judaism and Hebrew Prayer: New Perspectives on Jewish Liturgical History*, Cambridge University Press, Cambridge, 1993.

For early Christian worship:
Paul Bradshaw, *The Search for the Origins of Christian Worship*, SPCK, London, 1992.
Paul Bradshaw, *Early Christian Worship: A Basic Introduction to Ideas and Practice*, SPCK, London, 1996.

For the history of worship in the Church of England:

Colin Buchanan, *Recent Liturgical Revision in the Church of England*, Grove Books, Nottingham, 1973 (plus supplements for 1973–4, 1974–6 and 1976–8).

Colin Buchanan, *Latest Liturgical Revision in the Church of England 1978–84*, Grove Books, Nottingham, 1984.

G. J. Cuming, *A History of Anglican Liturgy*, 2nd edn, Macmillan, London, 1982.

Horton Davies, *Worship and Theology in England*, 5 vols, Princeton, 1961–76 provides rich background material.

D. E. W. Harrison and Michael C. Sansom, *Worship in the Church of England*, SPCK, London, 1982.

R. C. D. Jasper, *The Development of the Anglican Liturgy 1662–1980*, SPCK, London, 1989.

For the liturgical movement:

Donald Gray, *Earth and Altar*, ACC 68, Canterbury Press, Norwich, 1986.

John Fenwick and Bryan Spinks, *Worship in Transition: The Liturgical Movement in the Twentieth Century*, T & T Clark, Edinburgh, 1995.

Texts of various editions of the BCP can be found in:

F. E. Brightman, *The English Rite*, 2 vols, London, 1915; 2nd edn, 1921.

Colin Buchanan (ed.), *Background Documents to Liturgical Revision 1547–1549*, Grove Books, Nottingham, 1983.

D. E. W. Harrison (ed.), *The First and Second Prayer Books of Edward VI,* Everyman, London, 3rd edn, 1968.

Chapter 2

Liturgical Revision 1981–2000

The 1981–86 Commission

The Liturgical Commission of the Church of England that met for the first time in 1981 was a very different one from its predecessor that had seen through the liturgical reforms that led to the *ASB*. Only Colin Buchanan, then Principal of St John's College, Nottingham, Donald Gray, Rector of Liverpool, and David Silk, Archdeacon of Leicester, remained from the old Commission, with Dr Geoffrey Cuming continuing to bring his wisdom to bear as a consultant. Ronald Jasper had retired from the chairmanship, and indeed left behind the whole liturgical world, never once communicating with the new commission; and his replacement, Douglas Jones, the Lightfoot Professor of Divinity in the University of Durham, was a respected synodsman and a scholar, but made no claim to be a liturgist. Of the new team put together, only Trevor Lloyd, then Vicar of Holy Trinity, Wealdstone, remained on the Commission throughout the period between the *ASB* and *Common Worship* (*CW*), joined by Michael Perham, then Chaplain to the Bishop of Winchester, initially as a consultant, in 1982.

Many wondered what a new Commission would find to do. The new service book was in place and, as many saw it, the liturgical revision exercise complete. Indeed the appointment of a fairly conservative non-liturgist chairman perhaps indicated a desire on the part of the archbishops to see an end to the flow of new liturgies. It might have been expected that the new Commission's brief would be more in the form of an encouragement to liturgical formation, helping the Church to use the new book well, than to create yet more texts, but it was only later in the period under review that the new Commission began to move into this area.

The first authorized liturgical publication after the *ASB* was *Ministry to the Sick* (1983). It belonged to the *ASB* series of services and had been drafted by the 1976–81 Commission. It had simply missed the deadline for inclusion in the 1980 book, had been worked on by a synodical Revision Committee set up in July 1981 and was authorized for use from 1 June 1983. Thereafter its authority was in step with that of the *ASB*. It provided for Communion of the Sick, in hospital and at home, using both contemporary and traditional language forms, and allowing both for a celebration or for reception from the sacrament consecrated on a previous occasion. It also provided for the laying-on of hands with prayer and for anointing, both in public worship and more privately, and minimally for ministry to the dying, though this was later to be followed up by richer provision for those near to death (in *Ministry at the Time of Death*, 1991). It did not engage, in the way the *BCP*'s Visitation of the Sick had done, with issues of confession and absolution, the General Synod having failed to approve these in a dispute that was, at heart, about differing views of the *Absolvo te* ('I absolve you . . .') formula.

The Commission's first new work was a short paper (GS Misc 163, 1982) issued over the Chairman's signature, but drafted by two Commission members, Trevor Lloyd and Hugh Wybrew. In response to a question from Canon Peter Hawker, *Concelebration in the Eucharist* provided a succinct Church of England position on the question and, although the paper was never endorsed by either the General Synod or the House of Bishops, the line it took has, on the whole, been followed, except in those places where the Roman Catholic provisions have considerable influence. The paper makes a distinction between co-consecration, which it believes inappropriate, and what it calls 'ecclesial concelebration', seeing merit in the latter as an expression of collegiality, provided there is clear presidency and that the role of 'concelebrants' is more in terms of where they stand in relation to the president and the gestures they employ together than in terms of a vocal part in the eucharistic prayer. Subsequent authorized liturgy has never made provision for concelebration.

A more substantial piece of work by the 1981–86 Commission was 'Services of Prayer and Dedication after Civil Marriage', commended by the House of Bishops in 1985. Designed to meet the need for services in church after a registry office wedding, but carefully avoiding the more popular terminology of 'Blessing of a Civil Marriage', the service was a thorough reworking of a diocesan order (from Salisbury) with the incorporation of suitable parts of the 1980 Wedding Service. The introduction of Prayers of Penitence was a recognition of the realism that ought to be part of the service, the invitation to the congregation to uphold the marriage (with the response, 'We will') has found a place in the subsequent revision of the marriage rite, and some of the prayers engaged helpfully with issues in joining together two families, often with both partners bringing children to the new marriage. The nature of the authorization was also important, for a number of future provisions. The material was not subject to synodical scrutiny, but was 'commended', rather than 'authorized', by the House of Bishops.

Lent, Holy Week, Easter

The principal work of the 1981–86 Commission was *Lent, Holy Week, Easter: Services and Prayers* (*LHWE*). The House of Bishops invited the Commission to go to work in this area, but it was very much at the Commission's own request, and inevitably, after the period of preparation for the *ASB*, it had the sense of being the more leisurely occupation of an under-employed Commission. Published first in 1984 as a synodical document, subject then to a General Synod 'take note' debate, it was then commended by the House of Bishops and published for liturgical use in 1986. The lead publisher was SPCK, working with Church House Publishing and Cambridge University Press.

Even Commission members were surprised by the take-up of *LHWE*. Until this time the majority of parishes sat rather light to the liturgical possibilities of Ash Wednesday, Holy Week and Easter. There were parishes that already included special words and ceremonies, but they were a minority. Those that did use a special liturgy in some cases drew on the Roman Catholic provision, by then a generation old, and also on the JLG's *Holy Week Services,* first published in 1971, but reissued in a revised form in 1983. The expectation was to provide Church of England provision for churches already dipping into these forms and perhaps to reach some others where Holy Week provision was minimal. But the very widespread use of *LHWE* right across the Church gave a clear signal, both that the *ASB* had not ended the thirst for new liturgical material and also that there was a very high demand for good seasonal provision.

The heart of *LHWE* is a series of five full liturgies for principal holy days – Ash Wednesday, Palm Sunday, Maundy Thursday, Good Friday, and Easter. The material was very clearly *ASB*-based. Rite A Holy Communion is the norm from which the special liturgies are developed and there is no sense of leaving the *ASB* behind. In the end the new forms do not belong in the later world of infinite flexibility and a 'pick and mix' approach. They are set liturgies and, although there is freedom to use them or not, the orders of themselves, though they contain variants, are not simply outlines and resources. To that extent the material looked back to 1980 rather than forward to what might replace it.

Where *LHWE* did break new ground was in the provision of pastoral introductions to each rite, in a fresh approach to the use of Scripture, and in the much richer use of symbolic action than official Church of England texts had previously done. On Ash Wednesday ash was to be imposed on the forehead of the worshipper, on Palm Sunday branches carried (if possible in the open air), on Maundy Thursday feet washed, on Good Friday a large cross made the focus of the liturgy, and at the Easter Liturgy candles and much water. In all the rites there was more encouragement to movement and procession. A Watch was encouraged on Maundy Thursday night and a Vigil on Easter Eve.

In terms of lectionary, *LHWE* marked a first departure from the JLG's two-year thematic lectionary first published in 1967 and included, in a revised form, in the *ASB*. For *LHWE*, with more than a glance at the Roman Catholic Mass Lectionary for Holy Week and Easter, adopted a lectionary for a number of key days that sometimes broke into a three-year cycle and which abandoned the *ASB*'s relentless embrace of themes. It was the first move in a direction that the Church of England would adopt in a more thorough-going way in *CW*. *LHWE* also marks a recovery of earlier practice in its rich provision of lections for a Vigil at the Easter Liturgy.

Among the provisions in the five main liturgies, probably the most radical for most Anglicans was the advocacy of Holy Communion on Good Friday and the most creative the re-ordering of material in the Easter Liturgy from that in the Roman rite. On the former, the Pastoral Introduction states:

> The vexed question as to whether the Holy Communion should be celebrated on this day has been answered in the affirmative and provision so made. It would seem that on this, above all other days, it is wholly appropriate to eat the bread and drink the cup, thereby proclaiming the Lord's death until he comes. However, it is also recognized that there is a strong custom and tradition in many churches that the eucharist should not be celebrated, but that Holy Communion be given from the sacrament consecrated at the service of Maundy Thursday. Thus the eucharist which forms the commemoration of the Last Supper on Maundy Thursday night becomes the controlling celebration, as it were, both for the Communion on Maundy Thursday night itself and, by extension, for the Communion on Good Friday.

In relation to the Easter Liturgy, there was strong encouragement to celebrate the whole liturgy as a unity, whether in the evening, at midnight, at dawn or in the morning, rather than to celebrate separate parts on Saturday night and Sunday morning, and also the option (based on ancient precedent) of having the Vigil of Readings precede the lighting of the Paschal Candle and the singing of the *Exsultet,* rather than follow them in the way the Roman rite advocates.

Although the five set-piece liturgies for principal holy days are the heart of *LHWE*, there was other material: a rich resource of prayers for the seasons, two Services of Penitence, some guidance on giving distinctiveness to the seasons at Morning and Evening Prayer, the Passion narratives set out for dramatic reading, guidelines for a Holy Week *Agape,* and an order for Night Prayer (Compline), later published separately, a first attempt at an official form of a service long used in a variety of less-authorized versions, and, in reality, not particularly a Lent, Holy Week or Easter service in particular, but one for the whole year. It has been a mark of Liturgical Commission material in this 20-year period to 'smuggle' in material that needs to be given a chance, even when it is outside the strict subject matter of the provision in hand.

The 1986–91 Commission

LHWE was undertaken by the 1981–86 Commission, under Professor Jones' chairmanship, with a care for detail and oft-repeated reworking of material. The 'little red book', as it has been called, has been widely used since. In a sense it was that Commission that marked the end of the *ASB* era, for the Commission that replaced it in 1986 was very different and from the start worked with an expectation that the *ASB* would not last into the new millennium. This had been clearly signalled in the 'end-of-term' report of the 1981–86 Commission. Drafted by Colin Buchanan and entitled *The Worship of the Church* (GS 698), it emerged as a synodical document issued by the Standing Committee, with the additional weight and authority that implied. Its message was clear. It was too early to revise the *ASB* after ten years, but it would be necessary to do it after a further ten. A change in the year 2000 was on the agenda from that point onwards.

Of those who had served before 1980, only David Silk was left among the members of the new Commission. Trevor Lloyd, who had been a member since 1981, and Michael Perham, by now Rector of the Oakdale Team Ministry in Poole, a consultant since 1982 and now a member, were joined by others who were to see the Church right through to the *CW* provision of 2001. These were Jane Sinclair, then Liturgy Lecturer at St John's College, Nottingham, David Stancliffe, then Provost of Portsmouth, Kenneth Stevenson, then Rector of Holy Trinity, Guildford, and Michael Vasey, Liturgy Lecturer at Cranmer Hall, though his contribution, both as a thinker and a wordsmith, was tragically cut short by his death in 1998. It was a Commission where Evangelical membership seemed to be strong, though history reveals that churchmanship issues were rarely of importance in the Commission from this point onwards. In the Chair was Colin James, Bishop of Winchester, describing himself as a 'non-playing chairman', but with good liturgical instincts, and a willingness, probably not expected by those who appointed him, to let a new bright team of liturgists blaze a new trail. By now the Secretary of the Commission was David Hebblethwaite and it was he who provided the secretarial back-up through the next 15 years to 2000. Despite the sometimes desperate under-resourcing of the Commission, from his office at Church House the revision process was managed in a way that brought credit to the General Synod staff, in no more small measure because of David Hebblethwaite's own liturgical knowledge and instincts.

One of the first tasks of the new Commission was to address the question of gender-inclusive language in the liturgy. Although one member of the 1976–81 Commission, Jean Mayland, recalls raising the issue before the *ASB* was produced, that Commission had not responded to the new thinking in this area coming mainly from the United States and beginning to be an issue in England. The 1981–86 Commission had shown some understanding of it and *LHWE* is sensitive to it in a number of quite small ways. By 1986 a number of clergy and churches were modifying liturgical texts, not always in the most helpful or theologically precise way.

The new Commission was asked to engage with the issue. *Making Women Visible: The Use of Inclusive Language with the ASB* was the result, published in 1988. Although a small group of Commission members worked on the report, the introductory essay was principally the work of Michael Vasey, and it was also he who provided a version of Anselm's canticle, 'Jesus, as a mother you gather your people to you', that has since established itself in a number of books. The report's approach was threefold: to provide an alternative for each *ASB* exclusive word or phrase, to advocate that all new texts should be written with sensitivity to the gender issue, and to provide a number of additional texts that affirmed the feminine. The report was intended to help the Church through the remaining *ASB* years until new texts could be created in a replacement book, and indeed its recommendations were, on the whole, followed through the intervening years by all those who wanted to modify *ASB* texts. The later *Language and the Worship of the Church* (GS 1115, 1994), which set out the policy in relation to the forthcoming *CW* texts, followed the *Making Women Visible* principles, except in preferring to leave historic (*BCP*) texts unamended alongside new inclusive material.

Another small part of the 1986–91 Commission's early work was a *Funeral Service for a Child dying near the time of birth*. Although it drew on much of the material in the *ASB*, particularly the Funeral of a Child, there was new material, especially in the additional prayers. It was essentially a response to the growing recognition of the need for particular care for the parents and families of children dying near the time of birth, evidenced by the work of such bodies as the Stillbirth and Neonatal Death Society, with the consequent changes in hospital practice.

Yet another subject tackled early in the Commission's life was the liturgical ministry of the deacon. Although there was a desire by some to provide for the liturgical ministry of a number of permanent deacons not seeking priesthood, there was also the question of the ministry of many women admitted from 1987 to the diaconate, most of them believing themselves called to the priesthood, but at the time only able to serve as deacons. How could their ministry as deacons be liturgically enriching for them and for their congregations? *The Liturgical Ministry of Deacons* (GS Misc 281) was a discussion document, written mainly by David Stancliffe and published at the end of 1987. Although nothing came out of it directly, subsequent liturgical provision increasingly saw a place for a second minister, with a role complementary to that of the president, and this was finally enshrined in a significant Note on ministries in the *CW* eucharistic provision.

Other areas tackled by the Commission reflected the passions of Michael Vasey, who maintained a deep personal interest in large parts of the agenda. One was the theological reflection that led eventually to the new initiation services. A debate in the General Synod in 1991 led to joint work with the Board of Education and the Board of Mission leading to the House of Bishops' report *On the Way* (1995), and from that emerged the theological rationale in GS 1152 for linking Baptism and Confirmation with Wholeness and Healing and with the Reconciliation of a Penitent.

There was also Michael's Vasey's work on 'Rites on the Way', left unfinished at his death; and there was also, because of Michael Vasey's tenacity, strong

Liturgical Commission input into the *Code of Practice to the Ecumenical Canons* (B43–B44).

However, the main work of the 1986–91 Commission was in two major and very different publications, *The Promise of His Glory* (*PHG*) and *Patterns for Worship* (*PW*). Work on these two books went on in parallel for the first years of the Commission's life, though *PW* was the first to be published, in 1989. A commended, hard-back edition waited until 1995.

Patterns for Worship

Patterns for Worship emerged in response to two perceived needs. The first was the development of 'family services' and the labelling of some services as 'all-age worship'. Whereas in the past, those seeking a Sunday morning non-sacramental service had been content with Prayer Book Morning Prayer, which, with the addition of hymns and a sermon, had long been the staple Sunday morning diet of the majority of Anglicans, by the 1960s and 1970s this was ceasing to meet the need. Although Morning Prayer from the *ASB* had taken its place in some churches, it had not, in general, proved satisfactory; its emphasis on psalms and canticles, without any obvious alternative to Anglican chant, and its general inflexibility, made it a poor vehicle of worship for families in a mission-minded church. The result was that some churches had gone their own way and constructed Sunday morning worship that was often imaginative and creative, but that sometimes lacked shape and structure, balance or some of the marks that had characterized Anglican worship and made it distinctive. On the other hand, in some other parishes the lack of flexible provision was simply a source of frustration, with clergy and Parochial Church Councils loyally staying with the official services, but pleading for something different.

PW set out to address this situation, to encourage new forms and a more creative approach where people had held back, but also to suggest some guidelines and examples of good practice where enthusiasm had led people into some liturgical forms that were eccentric or poor. Although the majority of churches using or seeking family services were looking for a non-eucharistic service, either on a week-by-week model or for a service once a month to replace a eucharistic norm, there were parishes where the need was to loosen up the Eucharist itself to make it more obviously usable for all-age worship. Here the *ASB* was showing its inflexibility quite quickly. The result was that the Commission was at work on new provisions for the Eucharist within six years of its publication. For, although Holy Communion Rite A provided a number of alternatives in terms of text and structure, and although at many points the minister might use 'other suitable words', at a number of key points this possibility of choice and variety disappeared, notably in the use of the Nicene Creed every Sunday and in the length and similarity of style of the eucharistic prayers. The Eucharist needed loosening up.

The other pressure that led to *PW* was the report of the Archbishop of Canterbury's Commission on Urban Priority Areas, published in 1985 under the title *Faith in the City*. The report, which had said very little about worship (and that lack of engagement with the issue itself said something important), nevertheless included this paragraph:

> Many submissions included suggestions about books, services and groups. As we noted in Chapter 3 to give people a 1300 page *Alternative Service Book* is a symptom of the gulf between the Church and ordinary people in the UPAs. We have heard calls for short, functional service booklets or cards, prepared by people who will always ask 'if all the words are really necessary'. The work of re-forming the Liturgy has really only just begun for the UPA Church, and we recommend that the Liturgical Commission pay close attention to the needs of the Churches in the UPAs.

At first there was some thought that the Commission should be producing new material 'for use in Urban Priority Areas', but it did not take long for the Commission to be clear that this would be mistaken. If there was a need for greater flexibility, for some different kinds of text and for the presentation of material in a more user-friendly way, these should be available to everybody, not just to churches in a particular setting.

PW, responding to both the family service phenomenon and *Faith in the City*, was the first example of the 'directory approach', a compendium of suggested outlines, encouragement to good practice, and rich resources. There were four basic ingredients to the book.

First, there were Outlines and Instructions. These gave guidance about appropriate orders and structures for both eucharistic and non-eucharistic worship and loosened up the requirement to use particular texts, while holding the line in terms of there being a basic shape and order. Here was born 'A Service of the Word', a model for non-eucharistic worship that was more a contents list or a menu than the text of a service. Here also was Rite C, a form of Holy Communion a good deal more flexible than Rite A stretched to its limits.

Second was a series of sample services that were worked out examples of the new flexible services an authorized *PW* would allow. Some of them were published separately on cards, indicating new and simpler approaches to layout, with a variety of styles of illustration. Some of them included Holy Communion, but the majority assumed a non-sacramental service. They drew heavily on the next major part of the book.

In terms of pages, this third section was by far the largest. Entitled 'Resource Sections' it included a large number of introductions to worship, confessions, lectionary modules, affirmations of faith, intercessions, prayers of praise and thanksgiving, words introducing the peace or accompanying the breaking of bread, four alternative eucharistic prayers, blessings and endings and a wealth of canticles.

Finally there was the 'The Commentary', an extended essay to help people think through issues of good and bad practice and to find what was appropriate in terms of their own church with its particular building, community and tradition. The basic approach was to look at four imaginary churches – St Ann's, St Bartholomew's, St Christopher's and St David's – and to follow each through their approach to bringing their worship alive.

It is difficult to exaggerate the importance of *PW* in terms of the development of Anglican worship in England. Not all of it, of course, was commended or authorized, but it did represent a sea change in liturgical provision. If the *ASB* represented a move away from Prayer Book uniformity, *PW* marked a desire for a flexibility that seemed to some to threaten any sense of 'common prayer'. It was a subject to which the Commission itself returned in a series of essays a few years later (*The Renewal of Common Prayer,* 1993).

In terms of process, *PW* found its own level of acceptance over the next few years, although only available in a soft-cover synodical report edition. It was not until 1993 that certain parts of it had reached the end of a synodical authorization process and emerged as *A Service of the Word and Affirmations of Faith* and not until 1995 that most of the remainder of the original book was produced in a new edition, with some additional material, and commended by the House of Bishops. The only parts of the original book not to reach any kind of authorization or commendation were Rite C Holy Communion, though A Service of the Word opened up new possibilities for combining such a service with the Eucharist, and the eucharistic prayers, of which more will be said. As the Church entered the *CW* era in 2000, it took with it A Service of the Word, broadened to give a legal framework for a variety of forms of daily office as well as Sunday service, into its mainstream provision, and *PW* with a continuing life.

The Promise of His Glory

This was a very different book, though it shared with *PW* three important similarities. First, it did not look back to the *ASB* but forward to new provision. Second, it engaged afresh with the kind of liturgical language needed. Like *PW,* it looked for stronger images and metaphors, but perhaps more than *PW,* it looked for poetry, memorability and resonance. Third, it followed the directory approach, though in this case there were complete rites also.

The original brief, given to the Commission by the House of Bishops, but on the Commission's own initiative, was to provide for Advent, Christmas and Epiphany the equivalent of *LHWE*. It soon emerged within the Commission that a longer period, from All Saints' Day until the Presentation of Christ in the Temple, a three-month period of the year, needed integrated treatment, and indeed when it emerged in report form in 1990, it was entitled *The Promise of His Glory: Services and Prayers for the Season from All Saints to Candlemas.* Unlike *PW,* its progress from report form to final form commended by the House of Bishops was swift, with a joint publication by Church House

Publishing and Mowbray in 1991. The 'little green book' soon established itself alongside the 'little red book' of five years before.

In many ways *LHWE* and *PHG* are very alike. *PHG* includes a number of fully-worked-out rites for principal holy days and other festivals, including the Eucharist of All Saints' Day, All Souls' Day, Christmas Day and Candlemas, and a number of non-eucharistic occasions, from Christingles and Crib Services to an Epiphany liturgy celebrating not only the Magi, but the Lord's baptism and the first miracle at Cana. It also contains much free-standing resource material, seasonal provision and a further engagement with the three-year lectionary.

Yet *PHG* seems to belong to a slightly different world. It was partly the fact that the period of the year with which it engaged had a very different liturgical history. Holy Week had a strong tradition emerging from Jerusalem, Rome and the Mediterranean. Catholic Christianity had had a clear view of how one celebrated Holy Week and Easter. Christmas, however, had no such strong tradition, and the influences on its celebration came from Scandinavia and Germany as well as from Italy, and from the East as much as from the West. It was therefore a more creative task. There was also a need to take seriously a secular culture for which Christmas has retained a significance where Easter has lost it.

It was also at this stage in the year that the *ASB*, especially in its treatment of the month of November, with its 'Sundays before Christmas', but also, to some extent, in its lack of clarity on whether the Epiphany season extended the celebration of the Incarnation or returned to what is now more frequently called 'Ordinary Time', was at its least satisfying in terms of calendar and lectionary. Here the Commission went for radical solutions, proposing a new 'Season of the Kingdom' to encompass the period from All Saints to Advent, celebrating the reign of Christ and his saints, and an incarnation season of 40 days until Candlemas, with its bitter-sweet Gospel, making it a pivotal day between Christmas and Easter. From that basic calendrical decision flowed lections, prayers, rites and resources that celebrated the unity of the whole three-month period.

There were factors additional to the ones already mentioned that *PHG* had in common with *PW* – leaving the *ASB* mind-set behind, creating a new sort of poetic text, embracing a directory approach – that made this book seem different from *LHWE*. In the long term, many of its assumptions have found their way into *CW* and much of its text is in use. Its calendar and lectionary proposals (which were not formally commended) were modified in *Celebrating Common Prayer* (see below) and in general found their way into the *CW* provision, though, in the end, the General Synod rejected a novel 'Season of the Kingdom' and substituted 'Sundays before Advent' at the end of the liturgical cycle.

PRAXIS

One further initiative of the 1986–91 Commission needs to be recorded, though it had nothing to do with text. In 1990, very much on the initiative of Michael Vasey, PRAXIS came into being. With three sponsoring bodies, the Liturgical Commission, the Group for the Renewal of Worship (GROW) and the Alcuin Club, PRAXIS set out to be the 'provisional arm' of the Commission, engaged in liturgical formation, initially through London-based training days and seminars, but increasingly through regional meetings and the development of regional networks. The vision was that PRAXIS would determinedly transcend traditional churchmanship emphases and bring together people from right across the constituencies to engage with liturgical issues, especially practical and pastoral ones. Although throughout the 1990s the organization remained quite fragile because of lack of proper resourcing, it was able to do very significant work and establish itself as a key player in raising liturgical standards and awareness in the Church of England, finally attracting sufficient funding for a National PRAXIS Field Officer engaged in the work of liturgical formation.

This Commission ended its work with a report, *The Worship of the Church as it Approaches the Third Millennium* (GS Misc 364), drafted by Trevor Lloyd, that signalled the need to move quite quickly to decisions about key issues in replacing the *ASB*. Should there, for instance, be one book or a collection of books? What kind of issues needed to be addressed about questions of language? A clear liturgical agenda was emerging.

The 1991–96 Commission

There were only a few changes in the membership of the new Commission appointed to begin work in 1991. But there was a change of mood, for, with *PW* and *PHG* published and authority for the *ASB* extended only until 31 December 2000, the work of providing its successor began in earnest. Two years into its life the Commission acquired a new Chairman, when Colin James, who had guided the Commission with a light and encouraging touch, handed over to David Stancliffe, a member of the Commission since 1986, who became chairman in the same year as his appointment also as Bishop of Salisbury. It was he who was to lead the Commission through the years of preparation for *CW* and to shoulder much of the burden of seeing the Commission's proposals through the House of Bishops and the synodical processes.

From this point onwards for a number of years the Church heard less from the Commission as it moved into a new stage of its existence, returning to first principles in relation to all the rites that would go through a revision process. It is worth recording the Commission's working method on any project before it ever went to the House of Bishops, let alone the General Synod. What happened once it reached the Synod is a matter in the public domain; but not everyone is aware of the earlier stages.

Every new subject would begin with a broad discussion in the Commission, identifying the good and the less good in the material now to be revised, drawing new insights from scholars or from pastoral practice, noting developments in other provinces and Churches, leading more often than not to a discussion paper (not a draft) produced by a member of the Commission with a particular concern for the subject. This would then be the basis for a second discussion, in which matters would be clarified and some general sense of direction established. There would follow the establishment of a small group of Commission members (probably four or five with a range of skills and a variety of backgrounds) who would work on a first draft. The group would meet separately from the Commission, in some cases residentially. Sometimes other bodies would be consulted. Some of the material, for instance, notably the calendar, lectionary and collect provision, was also worked on in an Inter-Provincial Group with representatives of the Anglican provinces in England, Ireland, Scotland and Wales. A first draft would eventually come to the Commission, which would give a considerable amount of time to it, often suggest quite important changes and then send the text back to the group for further work. Only when the Commission was willing to own the material would it be sent to the House of Bishops and made public with their permission. Even at that stage the material was often in nothing like its final form because it awaited synodical revision, but from the moment it became public the Commission became less responsible for the changing form that it took.

Although these might be called the Commission's 'hidden years' (the first *CW* (as it was to become) report, *Calendar, Lectionary, Collects* (*CLC*), did not come before the General Synod until July 1995) and most of the work was behind the scenes, three developments need to be recorded.

The first was the publication of *The Renewal of Common Prayer: Unity and Diversity in Church of England Worship* (1993). This was a series of essays by members of the Commission, worked over by the whole Commission and edited by Michael Perham. The book attempts to define afresh what 'common prayer' might be for the Church of England in a new century. It rejects the uniformity that the Prayer Book years imposed, at least in terms of text, and explores the proper balance between commonality on the one hand, and diversity, variety and spontaneity on the other. The book is not without its tensions and inconsistencies. Michael Vasey's contribution speaks of 'promoting a common core', but his core is much more in terms of shape and structure and only minimally about text. Other contributions envisage a larger body of text that ought to be part of the 'liturgical knapsack' of Anglican Christians. The contributors who argue for a core that is textual as much as structural do so in terms of liturgical language carrying doctrine, of liturgy as an agent of unity in a divided Church and of the need for sufficient memorable text that the spirituality of worshippers is served by material they can commit to memory.

Coming a few years after *PW*, the effect of this book was to question gently the path to which the Church of England seemed to be committing itself.

To march resolutely down the path of diversity, where the local is thought more important than the national or universal, was fraught with dangers at the same time as bringing release and renewal. In revising the liturgy, the Church needed to engage again with getting the balance right. The services that then emerged from the Commission did indeed engage with that afresh. There were more freedoms, but they were less arbitrary. There was a greater sense of when diversity was appropriate and when a single common form alone should have authority. *CW* reflects that rethinking, though some of the tensions present in *The Renewal of Common Prayer* remain.

A second development was an attempt to heal the breach between the devoted followers of the *BCP* and the advocates of new liturgies. The introduction of the *ASB* had undoubtedly caused a lot of hurt and anger among those who felt that the Prayer Book was being marginalized. The spirit of the age seemed to see no possibility of new and old co-existing happily together, the one enriching the other, with individual Christians finding sustenance in both. Foremost among those defending the *BCP* was the Prayer Book Society, and there had been no love lost between this group and the Commission that had produced the *ASB*.

The 1991 Commission set about trying to create a new mood, helped by the fact that the Archbishops had appointed to the Commission a prominent vice-president of the Prayer Book Society, Baroness James of Holland Park. Through a series of meetings, and in particular through a symposium on 5 November 1992 attended by parliamentarians from Lords and Commons, representatives of the world of literature, theological college tutors, synod officers, academics, parish clergy and others, a new, more open and trusting atmosphere for debate was forged. Contributions to the symposium by David Stancliffe, Professor David Martin, Baroness James and Bishop Colin James were subsequently published in *Model and Inspiration* (SPCK, London 1993) and the fruit of this *rapprochement* has been seen in the way that *CW* more naturally holds together the old and the new, affirming the truth that liturgy must always be an evolving art, building on the past creatively and learning from it, not ensnared by it, but taking it seriously. There are those who continue to see no virtue at all in any new liturgical form and to believe that the Prayer Book alone will bring the nation back to Christ, but most in the General Synod and in the wider Church now seem to see merit in honouring the tradition as well as being bold in creating new approaches.

The third development was the publication in 1992 of *Celebrating Common Prayer* (*CCP*). At one level it is not relevant to this subject, for it was part of a prolific world of private liturgical enterprises which produced the writings of Janet Morley and Jim Cotter on the boundaries of orthodoxy, Susan Sayer with her apparently endless stream of books to resource the calendar and lectionary, and, nearer the Commission itself, such publications as *Enriching the Christian Year* by Michael Perham (SPCK/Alcuin Club, London 1993).

CCP was significant, however, because although an unofficial publication, it was in fact the work of a number of members of the Liturgical Commission, headed by David Stancliffe and Brother Tristam SSF, working with religious communities, in particular with the Society of St Francis, to produce a new daily office book that could be used across the Church in a whole variety of ways, from the solemn corporate celebration of the office in a religious community to the prayers of an individual Christian sitting on a train. *CCP* provided a richer form of office than any in the Church of England before, explored some new (for Anglicans) ways of using the Psalter and ordering the lectionary, took further some of the calendar proposals found in *PHG* and developed the celebration of the Christian mysteries through the days of the week in a fresh way. Sales exceeded all expectations and the book established itself as a popular quasi-official office book and also gave encouragement to others attempting similar, if less ambitious, experiments. The influence of *CCP* on *CW* can be seen both in *Calendar, Lectionary and Collects* and in its Sunday offices.

Many of these issues related to the need for a fresh approach to liturgical language, at the same time being more positive about historic texts and more creative and poetic in crafting new ones, while all the time having an eye to what was happening in the liturgical texts of other Churches and in ecumenical agreements. The Commission brought all these matters together in *Language and the Worship of the Church* (GS 1115), which was debated in the General Synod in 1994. From that point onwards the Commission and the Synod were committed to a particular approach, not least to a policy of holding old and new together in one volume, and also to a presumption in favour of using the English Language Liturgical Consultation (ELLC) texts whenever possible.

The 1996–2001 Commission

A rule that people should serve on Commissions for only ten years, introduced since 1980, would have meant the break-up of the team that was working on *CW* with the appointment of a new Liturgical Commission in 1996, had there not been a reprieve in order that the same team could see the venture through. There were few changes therefore in the Commission appointed in that year, at a stage where the most creative part of the exercise was over and the Commission members spent much of their time piloting material through synodical revision committees.

However, in one respect there was urgent new work to be done; for at the February 1996 meeting of the General Synod a set of eucharistic prayers, coming for final approval, was rejected because it failed to obtain a two-thirds majority in the House of Laity. These prayers were not an early piece of *CW* business; rather they were a late piece of *PW* business. *PW* had included four new eucharistic prayers and these were the starting point of the package for which final approval was sought in 1996. The four had been amended, become five with a request for a prayer more specifically for use with children present, and a sixth text had slipped in at the last minute.

The reasons for their rejection were complex. Probably chief among them was the fact that a new Synod at its second meeting did not feel it owned texts that had gone through all the other stages of their life in the previous Synod. Hearing some speeches against the prayers from those unhappy with them, sufficient of the House of Laity were persuaded to vote against them (135 for, 81 against), though the bishops voted in favour (25–10) as did the clergy, who had been pressing for these provisions for pastoral reasons (164–44). Those who made speeches against were in some cases against the theological emphases of the prayers, in some cases critical of their literary quality, in some cases still not convinced that they were suitable for children, and in some cases worried about the number of them or not persuaded of the need to have them. The defeat seemed an inauspicious start to a Synod that would need to engage with the whole of the liturgical revision programme until the year 2000.

But, perhaps in part because the Commission saw more clearly the need to take the Synod with it, in part because the Synod grew gradually in confidence when handling liturgical business and members became more willing to listen to people of differing views, perhaps because the later material (including the eucharistic prayers) was of better quality than the ones the Synod rejected, there was never again to be a rejection at final approval of a key liturgical proposal.

Perhaps the reason also was the use in the later stages of liturgical revision of 'experimental parishes'. A change in the liturgical canons in 1994 allowed the archbishops, under Canon B5A, after consultation, to allow an unlimited number of parishes to experiment for a set period of time with texts that had been introduced into the General Synod. These provisions were not employed for some of the earliest material to come to the Synod (including the *Initiation Services* that proved controversial after authorization), but some 800 parishes across the land were given authority to 'trial' the later proposals, notably the Wedding and Funeral rites and the second round of eucharistic prayers. As a result modifications were introduced and there was a better sense that there had been consultation and the material tested. Any future liturgical revision is likely to include this stage in the process.

During this final five years before *CW*, there were a number of problems relating to ecumenical texts. In 1994 the Church had recommitted itself to following ecumenical texts for common material, such as the *Gloria in Excelsis*, creeds, Lord's Prayer and Gospel canticles. These texts had in most cases changed since the versions incorporated in the *ASB*, partly through a desire to recover accuracy of text, but partly in response to the gender-inclusive language issues. As the General Synod found itself increasingly unhappy with some of the translations (notably in the Nicene Creed and the Lord's Prayer), questions began to be asked about where these texts came from and what authority they had. ELLC, which had revised its texts in 1990, turned out to have no Church of England member by the time the texts were being debated. English representation was through the Joint Liturgical Group. There was a sense that too much authority was being given to texts that were, in the end, no more than the work of a self-appointed group. Although this was not entirely fair, it has meant that the Church of England is likely to press for a greater accountability in the way international and ecumenical texts are determined in the future. In particular the texts of the Lord's Prayer and the Nicene Creed in *CW* are not the ELLC texts and the Church of England is committed to seeking new ecumenical work on them.

The final liturgical business of the 1995–2000 synodical quinquennium was a service that has no place in *CW*, but has a place alongside it. The service is *Public Worship with Communion by Extension* (GS 1230C), given final approval in July 2000. This service, which at some stages looked unlikely to secure final approval, meets a pastoral need, but has engendered much controversy. The debate was, however, not about the liturgical text (though this was much improved in a Revision Committee), but about the doctrinal principles at stake. Could it be right to take the consecrated elements from the Eucharist in one church to be shared by a congregation gathered in another? Liturgists were themselves divided, but the service did, in the end, secure the authority it needed, although the decision not to include it in the *CW* books is testimony to its provisionality.

In other ways the story of the final five years until the authorization of *CW* belongs to the other chapters of this book; for it was given over to synodical debates and the painstaking work of Revision Committees, as one by one the services came through the synodical process. Although the path towards *CW* was not always smooth, there was an aim shared by the Liturgical Commission, the House of Bishops and the General Synod to see the enterprise through successfully and to give the Church a flexible liturgy that drew on old and new and that could be a vehicle of worship and mission for a new century. Bit by bit this came about.

Chapter 3

The Calendar

A. HISTORY

The Christian Calendar consists of two overall cycles, customarily known as the *Temporale* and the *Sanctorale*. *Temporale*, as the Latin implies, refers to the course of times and seasons of the year, such as Advent, Easter, and what several traditions now call 'Ordinary Time', that is a period when no other season is being observed. The *Sanctorale*, as the word also implies, is the particular choice and sequence of saints' days through the year. In the Anglican tradition these have often been referred to as 'Red Letter' days (the principal celebrations), and 'Black Letter' days (the lesser observances), terms originating from the colours in which these categories of observance appeared in printed calendars in liturgical books, a custom which survives in some places.

The Week
The seven-day week was inherited by Christians from Judaism, where the Sabbath was the climax, marking the completion of the creation and the exodus (see Exodus 20.8–11; Deuteronomy 5.12–15) by abstinence from work and by acts of worship. Jesus observed the Sabbath by his attendance at the synagogue, although he also appears to have infringed its regulations (Luke 4.16ff; Mark 2.23ff). But while the post-resurrection Jewish Christian community continued to attend the synagogue (Acts 13.5, 14), Gentile Christians abandoned the Sabbath, and eventually all Christian communities came to celebrate the Eucharist on a Sunday, and for the first few centuries only on that day. It did not become a civil day of rest until 321 by order of Constantine.

Fasting emerged as a devotional practice among the early Christians, although on Wednesdays and Fridays instead of on Mondays and Thursdays like the Jews, and these days were observed with Services of the Word at 3 p.m. to mark the end of the period of fasting and to commemorate the death of Jesus.

Easter
This was originally the only annual festival of the Christian Church, and celebrated both the death and resurrection of Christ in a single feast. Some scholars believe it to have begun in apostolic times, while others would see it

emerging only in the second century. It was probably first observed on the date of the Jewish Passover itself, and only later on the Sunday following. From the end of the second century churches in North Africa and Rome showed a preference for Easter as the occasion for baptism, and this became universal in the fourth century. The Easter liturgy was preceded by fasting, for one, two, or even more days, and itself comprised a vigil of readings and prayer through Saturday night, with baptisms and the Eucharist at cockcrow on Sunday.

Ascension, Pentecost, Trinity

By the end of the second century the celebration of Easter had become extended to 50 days, terminating on the Jewish Feast of Pentecost, and was viewed as a continuous succession of Sundays. Influenced by the Luke–Acts chronology, the fiftieth day itself later became a celebration of the gift of the Holy Spirit as recounted in Acts 2. In time, this tended to lessen the emphasis on the 50 days as a single period of celebration, a trend which continued with a growing concentration on the first eight days, or 'octave', after Easter Day. Other feasts, including Pentecost, also came to have octaves. The English name 'Whitsunday' for Pentecost probably refers to the white robe of baptism, and reflects an increasing practice of baptism on that day as well as at Easter.

Ascension Day, on the fortieth day after Easter, also appeared alongside the separation of Pentecost in the fourth century, and it came to replace Pentecost as the end of the Easter season, with the resumption of normal fasting practices 'when the bridegroom is taken away' (Matthew 9.14–15 etc.).

Trinity Sunday emerged in the tenth century, and became a universal observance under the influence of Pope John XXII in 1334. The numbering of Sundays 'after Trinity' was begun in the medieval English Sarum calendar.

Holy Week

In fourth-century Jerusalem, a dramatic commemoration of the last week of the life of Jesus on earth was the origin of Holy Week. The community visited the sites of the events at the times they were thought to have taken place. For example, on Palm Sunday they went to the Mount of Olives and returned to the city in procession with palm branches, and on Friday there was worship before a relic of the cross, A Service of the Word in commemoration of the Passion, and a visit to the Holy Sepulchre with a reading of the account of the burial of Jesus.

The observance of Holy Week spread as a result of pilgrims sharing their experiences of Jerusalem in their own lands. Not all Christians could be present at the sites themselves, and so the dramatic commemoration came to be focused on the local parish church. The details varied considerably from place to place, and the ceremonies were subject to increasing elaboration into the Middle Ages.

'Maundy' Thursday, derived from the Latin *mandatum*, 'command', refers to Jesus' command in John 13 that the disciples love one another and wash each other's feet. Monarchs, bishops and kings came literally to wash the feet of those subject to them, as survives in symbolic form in England to this day. The washing of feet has been re-introduced in many Anglican parishes as part of their Holy Week observance. The oils for use in the initiation rites of Easter also came to be blessed on this day, the last occasion on which the Eucharist would be celebrated before the great feast.

Lent

This 40-day season of fasting in imitation of Christ's fasting and temptations in the wilderness seems to have originated among Egyptian Christians, where it was observed immediately after 6 January. In the fourth century it was adopted everywhere, but located immediately before Easter and combined with the preparation of candidates for baptism at that feast. It was also a time of public penance. Those who had committed serious sin were excluded from the Eucharist at the beginning of Lent, having the biblical penitential symbol of ash imposed on their foreheads. After fasting and doing works of charity, they were received back into communion just before Easter. Later the whole Christian community participated in what became known as Ash Wednesday and kept Lent as a penitential season.

Christmas and Epiphany

Originally these festivals seem to have been alternative versions of one another, 25 December in the West and 6 January in the East, but both celebrated the incarnation and included the birth, baptism and manifestation to the world of Christ. Scholars have commonly explained the choice of date as a reaction to the pagan observance of the winter solstice, but more recently an older theory has been revived that the dates were fixed through complex computation intended to determine the actual date of Christ's birth by reference to the supposed date of his death. The difference between East and West in these theories is accounted for respectively by different calendrical systems and calculations of the date of Easter. By the fifth century, both dates came to be observed in both East and West, with a separation of themes into the now customary Nativity (25 December) and Epiphany (6 January). While in the West the Epiphany came to centre on the visit of the Wise Men, in the East its focus was the baptism of Jesus and the wedding at Cana.

Advent

Like Christmas and Epiphany, the origins of Advent are not entirely clear. Some Christians appear to have intensified their regular fasting in December, perhaps in reaction to pagan feasting at the winter solstice, perhaps for other reasons. At the same time there was a tendency in some churches to read biblical texts that related to God's preparation for the coming of the Messiah on one or two Sundays before Christmas, such as the Annunciation or the mission of John the Baptist, while the preceding Sundays were treated as the end of the previous liturgical year and given over to readings that concerned Christ's second coming. Eventually, a distinct season emerged, at first of varying length and finally fixed as covering four Sundays immediately before Christmas, focusing on both the first and second comings. It never acquired the rigorous penitential character associated with Lent, and is not listed as a period of fasting in the 1662 *BCP*.

Saints' Days
As early as the second century local martyrs were celebrated on the dates of their deaths and at the places of their burial. Only gradually were other holy men and women added to local calendars, and saints celebrated in churches other than their own. Thus biblical saints were late additions to the calendar. By the late Middle Ages most days in the year had one or more saints associated with them.

The Calendar in the Church of England
The wholesale abolition of much of the Calendar, which characterized most churches of the Reformation, was not followed in England. Rather, the 1549 Prayer Book and its successors sought to simplify the liturgical year, with a drastic reduction in associated ceremonies and variable seasonal texts such as collects, readings and eucharistic prefaces. The commemoration of the saints, based on the Sarum calendar, was continued, but what came to be known as 'Black Letter' saints' days had no provision of proper texts, and may have been included only to assist in the calculation of secular dates.

The proposed 1927/8 revision retained the basic pattern of seasons and major festivals with some minor adjustments and improvements, such as the elevation of the Transfiguration (6 August) to the status of a Red Letter day with its own Proper texts, and the provision of more Proper Prefaces. There was by now a conscious intention to celebrate Black Letter days, and these were given common texts according to category. More controversially, an explicit 'Commemoration of All Souls' was restored on 2 November, indicating greater doctrinal breadth in the Church of England by this time, which in the matter of prayer for the departed was probably greatly influenced by the experience of the Great War.

The formation of the Liturgical Commission in the 1950s led to a further re-examination of the criteria for inclusion in the *Sanctorale*, and ultimately to the work which resulted in the Calendar of the *ASB*. Here for the first time officially, post-Reformation saints canonized by the Roman Catholic Church and many other Christian figures were added, and a more radical approach taken to the seasons, this time interlocking with the new two-year lectionary which began the Christian year on the Ninth Sunday before Christmas and entitled the Sundays after Trinity as Sundays 'after Pentecost'. The subsequent 'commended' material in *Lent, Holy Week and Easter* (*LHWE*) (1986) and *The Promise of His Glory* (*PHG*) (1991) indicated a desire to encourage a still richer observance of the seasons and feasts of the liturgical year, and the latter laid the foundations for some of the features now included in the latest revision.

B. COMMENTARY

To accompany the revised Calendar of the Church of England, the Liturgical Commission itself provided notes and a commentary in the first published edition in 1997, *Calendar, Lectionary and Collects* (*CLC*). It is significant that the Notes to the Calendar begin with a comment on Sundays, which declares: 'All Sundays celebrate the paschal mystery of the death and resurrection of the Lord' (*CLC*, p. 10). The Calendar is an aspect of the Church's call to celebration, not merely a lifeless structure. All Christian celebration is grounded in the paschal mystery, and this mystery historically and theologically finds its focus on Sunday. Thus the new Calendar is placed firmly in the contemporary understanding of liturgical time, whereby the historical, the christological and the eschatological aspects of Christian celebration may be seen as a coherent whole, with no exclusive emphasis, but still reflecting in the seasons and feasts different aspects of the one mystery of God in Christ.

Classification and Terminology

The definition of Principal Feasts, Principal Holy Days, Festivals, Lesser Festivals and Commemorations is clearly explained. It should be noticed that the number of categories has expanded since the *ASB*, and equivalent ranks have been given new names. Principal Holy Day in the *ASB* becomes Principal Feast, and Principal Holy Day is used in the new Calendar only to denote Ash Wednesday, Maundy Thursday and Good Friday. The Festivals and Greater Holy Days in the *ASB*, which included these three occasions, now no longer do so and are simply Festivals. A distinction is also made between Lesser Festivals and Commemorations, which was in the original proposals for the *ASB* but later abandoned. The *ASB* made the briefest of mentions of local celebrations, but the revision gives much more explicit encouragement to local *Sanctorales* and the celebration of Dedication and Patronal Festivals.

Principal Feasts

To the equivalent list in the *ASB* (Principal Holy Days) is added the Presentation of Christ, the Annunciation, Trinity Sunday and All Saints' Day. These additions partly reflect a more developed approach to seasons: the Presentation is being encouraged as a more appropriate end of the season of Christmas, Sundays in 'Ordinary Time' are now 'after Trinity' rather than 'after Pentecost', and the period following All Saints' Day is given more significance (see 'Seasons' below).

Principal Holy Days

Maundy Thursday and Good Friday, together with Ash Wednesday, become the only three Principal Holy Days, as they do not have a festal character, but have a status which precludes any other observances, just like the Principal Feasts.

Festivals

In the *ASB* these were also called Greater Holy Days. This confusion has now been removed, and some changes made to the list in order to resolve anomalies or respond to inter-Anglican, ecumenical and other interests. The Naming of Jesus *or* The Circumcision of Christ thus becomes The Naming and Circumcision of Jesus (1 January). The First Sunday after Epiphany is designated as the Baptism of Christ. St George's Day (23 April) is made a festival (to encourage the celebration of the Patron of England), as is the Visit of Mary to Elizabeth (31 May). St Peter's Day (29 June) becomes St Peter and St Paul, although the option remains to celebrate St Peter alone. The Day of Thanksgiving for the Holy Communion on the Thursday after Trinity Sunday may be kept as a festival and its common alternative title, Corpus Christi, is acknowledged, which is a recognition of the existing practice of some parishes. The main Festival of the Blessed Virgin Mary is moved to 15 August, thus bringing it into line with most other Anglican provinces and wider ecumenical practice, although the Commission is careful to point out that controversial doctrinal implications should not be inferred from this, and the option remains to keep it on 8 September, as in the *ASB*. Holy Cross Day (14 September) is now kept as a Festival. Following the Lectionary and ecumenical Western practice, Christ the King is celebrated on the Sunday before Advent.

Lesser Festivals and Commemorations

The former are intended to form the backbone of those feasts which occur on weekdays, but are nevertheless 'observed at the level appropriate to a particular church' (*CLC*, p. 13). The Commemorations are intended to be of less prominence liturgically, yet may still be celebrated as Lesser Festivals if local pastoral conditions suggest it. But in many cases all that is appropriate for a commemoration will be a mention of the saint or the causes with which he or she is associated in the intercessions and at other points in the rite rather than displacing the collect and readings of the day.

Several additions have been made to the *ASB* list, and as far as possible all the dates assigned for observance of particular saints have been adjusted to coincide with the Roman Catholic Calendar, although long-established celebrations on other dates have been retained as alternatives in a number of cases. There has also been an effort to reduce the number of saints' days in Advent, Lent, and the early days of the Christmas and Easter seasons so as not to detract from those important times of the year. Dates for new entries are not always those of the death of the individual, but may be of the birth, baptism, ordination, or other significant event. Overall, the revised *Sanctorale* does much to bring into the ambit of the liturgy figures whose contribution and witness has not necessarily been Anglican or indeed in England, thus reflecting ecumenical appreciation and the increasingly international character of Anglicanism. The list repays careful study. It would be difficult to draw attention to particular highlights, as these will be different for each individual and community, and rightly so.

The Seasons

Particular emphasis is now given in the Notes to the 50 days between Easter and Pentecost as a season of special importance. It is singled out there probably because it has not tended to be kept as a distinct season to the same degree as Advent and Lent, whereas its 'paschal character' ought to offer at least as much rich possibility in Scripture and liturgical celebration. To reflect this, Sundays in Eastertide are now 'of Easter' rather than 'after', and therefore the former 'First Sunday after Easter' (Low Sunday) is now the 'Second Sunday of Easter'.

The revision does not follow *PHG* in having a 'Kingdom' season as such between All Saints and Advent, although the Lectionary does reflect on the reign of Christ in earth and heaven during this period and the Sundays are counted as 'before Advent' rather than 'after Trinity'. Instead, there is an attempt to make the period after All Saints one of remembrance of the saints, and the option is therefore given of using red as the liturgical colour during this time, although this would seem to have no historical precedent. Nevertheless, the revision does away with the confusing *ASB* approach which began the liturgical year with the Ninth Sunday before Christmas. Advent Sunday has been restored to this status, and is also, of course, the day on which the Lectionary year changes. This is, overall, a much more coherent and indeed more ecumenical approach.

Outside the Seasons, the name Ordinary Time is used to refer to the period between the Presentation and Lent, and the period of Sundays after Trinity. This has been the subject of discussion focusing on the appropriateness of the word 'Ordinary' in the context of Christian worship. However, in actual fact each Sunday may be called by a number of different names, partly resulting from the differing terminologies employed by the Calendar and the Lectionary and the fact that the cycle of readings in Ordinary Time is calculated independently of the title of the Sunday. It will therefore be up to each community to decide how these names are to be used, but priority should be given to emphasizing the Seasons, and to the 'after Trinity' label, in order to avoid the sense that some Sundays of the year are somehow of less importance or interest.

Miscellaneous

Also given in the Notes are remarks on Days of Discipline and Self Denial, Ember Days, and Liturgical Colours, as in the *ASB*, and essentially these contain similar information and guidance. The section on colours has been expanded, and is now more appropriately linked with the Calendar, whereas in the *ASB* it was part of the notes to the Lectionary.

C. LITURGICAL COLOURS

One way in which the Calendar can be expressed visually is in the use of liturgical colours for fabric hangings and vestments. Only since the twelfth century have liturgical colours had more than incidental significance in the Western Church, save perhaps for a preference for white, referred to in Scripture (e.g. Revelation 3.4–5) and having associations with purity. The first real evidence of a connection between liturgical seasons and particular colours is the Augustinian Canons of the Latin Church in Jerusalem, a scheme which bears little relation to present-day practice: at the three Masses of Christmas, for example, the vestments were to be of black, red and white respectively, and the altar frontal was to be of unspecified colour but the best material. This appears to be typical of the local, informal uses which emerged. If these had anything in common, it was that the best hangings and vestments be used at the great festivals irrespective of colour, and sombre colours as an indication of penitential seasons.

The colour sequence familiar today developed only gradually, as even those drawn up by Popes, such as that of Innocent III (1198–1216), were not of universal obligation. Not until 1570 did Pius V define a formal sequence which is the basis of modern Roman Catholic and Anglican usage, but even this did not prevent local practices continuing, and indeed *CW* itself allows for such variations.

The effect of the Reformation was to associate liturgical colours largely with the practice of Rome, and so they tended to have little significance in the Reformed churches. They were preserved in a very limited way in some Lutheran churches and in the Church of England, as is suggested by the brief references to vestments in the 1549 *BCP* and the 1603 Canons, but with no specific mention of the colours to be used. The Laudians and Nonjurors continued this rather precarious survival, but most Anglican clergy preferred the surplice, scarf and academic hood. The second, more liturgically-focused phase of the Oxford Movement in the nineteenth century assured liturgical colours a firm place in Anglican practice once more, but Evangelicals continued to avoid them because of their similarity to Roman Catholic custom.

In the twentieth century the Liturgical Movement inspired a new approach to colours which perhaps drew on a more consciously psychological approach, that is colours which seemed best suited in the imagination to the tone of the particular celebration: drab colours for penitential seasons, white and gold for festivals, red for martyrs, green and yellow for growth and renewal. Much Anglican practice now follows the simplified pattern established in the 1969 Roman Catholic *Ordo Missae*, although local uses survive, often based on the medieval use of Salisbury, for example blue instead of violet in Advent, unbleached linen in Lent, and the use of red on some Sundays after Trinity. Some parishes also follow the custom, mentioned in both the *ASB* and *CW*, of rose colour on the Third Sunday of Advent and the Fourth Sunday of Lent, connected with the more joyful tone of the medieval Masses for those days. Black as an expression of mourning also survives in Anglican use for funerals and requiem Eucharists, although violet (penitence, forgiveness) and increasingly white (resurrection) are more common. All these possibilities are included in the notes on liturgical colours in both the *ASB* and *CW*. Not mentioned, however, is the increasingly common use of 'year round' textiles which are not confined to particular seasons or feasts, thus avoiding the need for constant change, and which perhaps allow for greater artistic freedom. It may be argued, though, that this practice lessens the visual emphasis on the observance of the Calendar which a full scheme allows.

It was significant that *ASB* was the first official, authorized Anglican liturgy to set out a scheme, and this is continued in the latest revision, with some further options which reflect the revised Lectionary or changes to the Calendar. As in the *ASB*, nothing in the new provision is mandatory, although colours, like vesture, have ceased to be the party issue they once were, and are becoming increasingly widely used.

The comparatively new discipline of liturgical theology (as opposed to the study of liturgical history), particularly in North America, has drawn attention to the context of liturgical celebration and the significance of the visual as well as the spoken as expressions of the inherently performative nature of liturgy. Liturgical colours are one element in this. The *General Instruction on the Roman Missal* of 1969 declared that they give 'effective, outward expression to the specific character of the mysteries of the faith being celebrated and, in the course of the year, to a sense of progress in the Christian life'. In this sense, then, liturgical colours are an aspect of the common pilgrimage of the Church in response to God's call, and the pilgrimage of the individual towards spiritual growth and maturity. Worship is the corporate and individual response to the mystery of God, and a place of its showing forth in creation. Colour is a factor in the animation of creation, a gift to the senses which assists the human capacity to encounter beauty and see in it the hand of the creator. In this way it has a place in worship, where creation's loving response to the creator is most typically expressed. This suggests that where liturgical colours are used, careful consideration ought to be given to context and quality, lest what has the potential to be a powerful sign of the interplay of human and divine love become an empty piece of ritual.

D. THE CALENDAR IN THE LIFE OF THE CHURCH

A commentator on the *CW* Lectionary and Calendar has said that 'Many Christians will instinctively view the calendar as high church flummery . . . and a cycle of saints' days as absolutely off the wall – perhaps even a sign of the terminal irrelevance of Anglicanism in the modern world' (Michael Vasey in Lloyd *et al.*, *Introducing the New Lectionary*, 1997, pp. 4–5). Yet as its history and liturgy make clear, the celebration of the seasons and festivals of the liturgical year has, at least by official intention, always been an integral part of the life of the Church of England. The degree and manner of actual use of the Calendar has reflected the differing strands of Anglican self-understanding, and yet the authorized liturgy of the Church has always assumed the Calendar to be of prime importance. The *BCP* is meticulous in setting out the manner in which the Calendar and Lectionary are to be used, and how they are to inform and animate the daily prayer of the people of God around the inseparable tables of Word and sacrament. Subsequent revisions of the Calendar have certainly not sought to undermine this foundation. The latest of these reflects in a balanced, rich and imaginative way the historical, theological and pastoral factors that have shaped the Church of England. In so doing, it presents the opportunity to rediscover the seasons and feasts of the Christian year, and through them, to be drawn deeper into the mystery of salvation.

The Sanctification of Time

The advent of the third Millennium has drawn attention to the human fascination with time, and the Calendar as a means of giving it order and structure has also been the subject of popular interest. The Christian understanding of time is grounded in the Hebrew Scriptures, and their interpretative accounts of the intervention of God in human history. Key events in this history, such as the exodus, became occasions of regular celebration, but not only in terms of remembering, and certainly not in the form of dry historical re-enactment. Instead, they were occasions of shared celebration of and commitment to the involvement of God in the life of the community of his chosen. The Christian community has also ordered time in a way that expresses belief in God as Lord of time, although there have been differences of theological emphasis and liturgical expression. The Christian Calendar is therefore an interface between God and Church, and between Church and world. Critically linked to the Lectionary, it is also an interface between Bible and Church. The Christian ordering of time is therefore something dynamic, not lifeless or mechanistic. Nor need it be seen any longer as the preserve of a particular theological tradition.

The Mystery of Salvation

Participation in the Christian year is not simply a pious historical reflection on the life and acts of Jesus Christ, but a celebration of the one mystery of God in Christ, which allows the Christ of faith to grow in us and in the Church. It is a celebration not of what Christ did or said, but of Christ himself. The mystery is accessible to us through many different lenses, whether in Scripture or in the sacramental life of the Church and of our daily lives. We cannot yet acknowledge its entirety. We celebrate the saving acts of Christ because we are not whole, but seek to be through his mercy and love. Each season and festival is a window on to God, a view through a glass darkly, and the celebration of each an aspiration to see him face to face. In the words of Thomas Merton, liturgical time is 'humanly insecure, seeking its peace altogether outside the structures of all that is established, visible and familiar, in the shape of a kingdom which is not seen' (*Meditations on Liturgy*, 1976, p. 40).

Using the Calendar

In view of this rich theological context, there ought to be many opportunities in the life of the Church to use the Calendar imaginatively and creatively as a tool for the further life and growth of the people of God. As the Liturgical Commission's preface to the Calendar says, 'The Christian year, with its cycle of seasons, provides the Church with its most compelling way into the mystery of faith' (*CLC*, p. 7). This suggests that the Calendar should be seen as an essential context for the worship and witness of the Church, rather than an optional extra. It will be up to each community to use the material according to its own perceived priorities, but four headings may be useful as starting points for revisiting and revitalizing the seasons and feasts of the Christian year as an integral part of their common life: Vision, Mission, Liturgy, and Spirituality.

Vision

Every Christian community needs to be prepared to re-examine itself in the light of the gospel and of the society in which it is placed, in order that the individual and collective response to God's love is vibrant and appropriate. This will involve a certain amount of vision, an ordering of priorities, and an honest assessment of the gifts that are needed to further the work of Christ in the parish, hospital, school or other pastoral setting. The Calendar can be used in this process as a framework of celebration and spiritual discovery. The seasons, with their recurring themes of death and rebirth, penitence and forgiveness, darkness and light, act as a mirror in which can be glimpsed the redeemed humanity God calls us to be. The lives of the saints and holy ones of God down the ages provide further lenses in which are focused both the fragility and the potential of our response, and offer the hope that broken lives may be remade in God's image. The Calendar offers the Church daily reminders of the ultimate goal of every Christian, the vision of God and the joy of the life eternal. In this way it can have a sacramental function, because it can reveal in our lives the work of God, and alert us to the action of the Spirit in drawing us closer to the life of heaven.

Mission

A consequence of a community's renewed vision must be a renewed concern for mission. The Calendar makes present in the Church and is itself a witness to God's creative and redemptive activity. Christian communities and those who exercise leadership and other ministries within them can use the Calendar as a vital means of celebrating and sharing the good news with others. For example, the many catechetical courses now available for new Christians and for all in need of nurture and spiritual growth can be offered in the context of the seasons. This is already true of the Roman Catholic Rite of Christian Initiation of Adults, which builds the progress of the candidates into the Lent–Easter cycle and thus declares their exploration and profession of faith to be a function of God's saving work in Christ's death and resurrection. Other programmes encourage such an approach, but with imagination all can make use of the opportunities the Calendar offers to mark particular stages in people's lives as human beings and as Christians. Of course, this can also be done outside the context of particular programmes, but can be given the same high profile in the life of the community that conveys the significance of associating God's activity in the world with challenge and change in the lives of his people.

For many years, the season of Christmas has been a time of heightened contact with those who do not normally actively participate in the life of the Church. Occasions such as Christingle and 'Crib services' have become popular fixtures in the 'local' Calendars of many parishes and other communities in connection with the celebration of the birth of Jesus. The feast of Christmas itself has in this way become very elastic, bursting out of 25 December and reaching back at least into early December. There are many who find this frustrating, and who wish to see a more accurate observance of late Advent that is less pre-empting of the actual feast for which it prepares. However, the nature and structures of our society cannot be ignored. For example, school and university terms end in some cases well before 25 December, and it would seem churlish to deny those closely defined communities the chance to celebrate Christ's birth before they depart for the vacation. This makes the point that mission and Christian celebration are geared towards communities as well as individuals, and use of the Calendar in mission must always acknowledge this, even if it means departing from the strict letter. There is a place for the imagination, and a necessity to recall that no amount of order and structure on the part of human beings can confine the God who reaches out to us in love and compassion.

Liturgy

Interlinked with the vision and mission of Christian communities is the celebration of the liturgy, and here the Calendar finds its main focus, for it colours and defines the nature of liturgical celebration in both Word and sacrament. It will be for each community to decide what its pattern of celebration will be, day by day and week by week, and yet a renewed appreciation and use of the Calendar can enrich existing opportunities for worship and suggest others that may give shape to the vision and enhance the mission to which the Church is called. Many parishes and groups of all traditions have rediscovered the daily offices as a way of offering structured daily prayer, and the Calendar offers the essential background to this, as it informs the Lectionary, and the mood and manner of the celebration. Many communities celebrate a daily Eucharist, and here again the full potential of the Calendar can be released, although priority should probably be given to restoring the daily office as the public daily prayer of the people, as opposed to a private devotion of the clergy alone.

Spirituality

The spiritual potential of a full celebration of the Calendar is vast. In one of the resources published in support of the *CW* Calendar, Robert Atwell notes that the annual commemoration of the saints 'must have been an extremely moving event in the life of a Christian community. It precipitated within the consciousness of the Church a powerful sense of solidarity, of a belonging in Christ which transcended death. This awareness is something recent generations seem largely to have lost' (*Celebrating the Saints*, 1998, p. iii). Atwell argues rightly that a restored sense of communion with Christ through the remembering and celebration of his holy ones would encourage 'prayer in which the whole Church shares, living and departed, commending one another to the mercy of God' (*ibid.*, pp. vi–vii). This assertion may trespass on the theological sensitivities of some, and yet it remains true that the sense of the continuity and solidarity which the Calendar by its very nature encourages is a valuable tool for prayer and a deepening spirituality which has closeness to Christ and union with God as its goal. As Thomas Merton further commented, 'In the cycle of the holy year, the Church rhythmically breathes the life-giving atmosphere of the Spirit, and her bloodstream is cleansed of the elements of death. She lives in Christ, and with him praises the Father' (Merton, 1976, p. 33).

Daily spiritual reading guided by the Calendar can feed this process, as can the publication in parish magazines and weekly newsletters of notes on the saints celebrated that month or week, seasonal meditations linking up with the Lectionary, and suggestions for daily prayer arising from persons and themes occurring in the Calendar. Relatively simple efforts of Christian teaching like these can pay large dividends in fertilizing the soil of spiritual growth, and contribute to the maturity of the community in faith and shared witness.

References and Further Reading

On the history of the Calendar:
Adolf Adam, *The Liturgical Year*, Pueblo, New York, 1981.
Peter Cobb, 'The History of the Christian Year' and Kevin Donovan, 'The Sanctoral', in *The Study of Liturgy*, C. Jones, G. Wainwright, E. Yarnold and P. Bradshaw (eds), revised edn, SPCK, London, 1992, pp. 455–84.
Roger Greenacre and Jeremy Haselock, *The Sacrament of Easter*, Gracewing, Leominster, 1995.
J. C. J. Metford, *The Christian Year*, Thames and Hudson, London, 1991.
Kenneth Stevenson, *Jerusalem Revisited*, Pastoral Press, Washington DC, 1988.

On individual saints:
Paul Burns (ed.), *Butler's Lives of the Saints*, new edn in 12 volumes, Burns & Oates, Tunbridge Wells, from 1995.
D. H. Farmer (ed.), *Oxford Dictionary of Saints*, 4th edn, Oxford University Press, Oxford, 1998.

On liturgical colours:
G. Cope, 'Colours, Liturgical', in *A New Dictionary of Liturgy and Worship*, J. G. Davies (ed.), SCM Press, London, 1986, pp. 178–80.
W. H. St J. Hope and E. G. C. F. Atchley, *English Liturgical Colours*, SPCK, London, 1918.
C. E. Pocknee, *Liturgical Vesture*, Mowbray, London, 1960.

On time and calendars in general:
D. E. Duncan, *The Calendar*, Fourth Estate, London, 1998.

On the CW Calendar:
Michael Perham, *Celebrate the Christian Story*, SPCK, London, 1997.
Kenneth Stevenson, *All the Company of Heaven*, Canterbury Press, Norwich, 1998.

Daily spiritual readings, with introduction:
Robert Atwell, *Celebrating the Saints*, Canterbury Press, Norwich, 1998,
Robert Atwell, *Celebrating the Seasons*, Canterbury Press, Norwich, 1999.

Other works:
T. Lloyd, P. Moger, J. Sinclair and M. Vasey, *Introducing the New Lectionary*, Grove Worship Series 141, Cambridge, 1997.
T. Merton, *Meditations on Liturgy*, Mowbray, London, 1976.

Chapter 4

A Service of the Word

A. HISTORY

Early Christian Worship

The earliest form of a Service of the Word within the Christian tradition was almost certainly based on contemporary synagogue practice. The exact content of these services however remains something of a mystery. Nevertheless, by the middle of the second century we know of A Service of the Word combined with the celebration of the Eucharist on Sundays, and by the third century there is evidence for Services of the Word on Wednesdays and Fridays afternoons, connected with the custom of fasting on those days as well as signs of daily assemblies for the instruction of new converts at least at some times of the year.

Daily morning and evening worship in the fourth century did not usually include readings from Scripture. But the regular services of the Word observed in the previous century continued alongside it. In the monastic office which began to develop at about the same time, however, scriptural readings were added to the reciting of Psalms. It was only when these two traditions were later combined that daily worship began to contain the three elements of praise, prayer and Bible reading, with which we are familiar in Services of the Word today. Since such services were in Latin and only rarely attended by lay people, they did not offer much edification to the majority of church members.

The Reformation Period

At the Reformation there was a movement to reinstate the importance of services focused on the reading of Scripture in the vernacular, and on preaching, which were separate from the Eucharist. This was true both during the week and on Sundays; although the extent to which the laity ever regularly attended weekday services in England is unclear. Certainly the Preface to the 1549 BCP encouraged the laity to join in Morning and Evening Prayer 'that by daily hearing of the Scriptures read in church they should continually profit more and more in knowledge of God and be the more inflamed with love of his true religion'. Unlike similar services in Luther's Germany and Calvin's Geneva, these offices made no official provision for a sermon even on Sundays.

although the combination of Morning Prayer, Litany and Ante-Communion, which became the staple Sunday diet of many Anglican parish churches, was usually accompanied by sermons and often quite lengthy ones too.

This is reflected in the development during the Elizabethan period of elaborate pulpits with sounding boards to help the congregation hear better in an age before the invention of the sound system. The length of this combined service also led to the development of pews, at least for the wealthy, so that they could sit out the three hours or more spent in church on a Sunday morning in relative comfort. Free pews for the ordinary man and woman were uncommon until the nineteenth century, when the work of the Incorporated Church Building Society and others meant that many parish churches now began to provide seating for the entire congregation in return for a grant towards church repair and re-ordering. In many places, the morning service was usually attended by the better off, while their servants and tenants were allowed to attend Evening Prayer on Sundays, once their work was done.

Since those who attended church only on Sundays found themselves faced with a disjointed pattern of Scripture reading, having missed six out of the seven portions prescribed for the week, a set of specific Sunday readings was authorized for use in 1559. Permission was also granted at this time for the singing of hymns at the beginning and at the end of the service. Hymn-singing elsewhere in the service, however, was not finally legalized for another 300 years.

During the Puritan ascendancy in the mid-seventeenth century the trend towards the importance of Word rather than sacrament was strengthened still further. In the Westminster Directory of 1645 provision for A Service of the Word was of prime importance. Its purpose was to enable the public reading of the Word of God and also to teach about the Old and New Testament by means of a sermon. This exposition on the Word was to be preceded and followed by prayers. These are not prescribed, although there is a list of suggestions in the Directory as to what might be included. This Presbyterian experiment in public worship, however, did not, at least within Anglicanism, survive the restoration of Charles II to the throne.

The Eighteenth Century

The worship in the average parish church in the eighteenth century took the form of a long combined morning service at 10 a.m., with an afternoon service at 3 p.m. The country was divided, however, into 'single' and 'double duty' regions. In the north the habit of regular churchgoers seems to have been to attend divine service in both the morning and the evening, while in the south the tendency was to attend only once a day, often (as was sometimes) according to social class. The pattern of quarterly Communion also seems to have been well established by this date, although there were a few dioceses in which a monthly celebration of Holy Communion was more common.

Complaints about this state of affairs were widespread, especially amongst more Evangelical clergy who were concerned that the Church of England was not really meeting the masses with the pattern of worship described above. John Jones, Vicar of Alconbury, in his *Free and Candid Disquisitions* (1749) complained about the amount of repetition in the usual combined service of Morning Prayer, Litany and Ante-Communion, and believed that Morning Prayer by itself was sufficient. He also requested that more topical prayers might be added to the Prayer Book. Convocation, responsible for formulating any changes to worship, responded conservatively by adding to the prayers printed in the *BCP* in 1759. One of the prayers concerned the cessation of distemper amongst cattle, a subject on which Jones had expressed concern!

In the second half of the eighteenth century the Church of England was faced with a new challenge in the guise of Methodist preaching services. It was the intention of the Wesley brothers that these should supplement the weekly worship of the parish church, and indeed the early Methodists were encouraged to receive Holy Communion in their parish church regularly. However, as all those who have read George Eliot's *Adam Bede* will know, the draw of the early Methodist preachers was considerable. They talked in a way that related Scripture to life. The reading of Scripture and the sermon was accompanied often by nothing more formal than extemporary prayer. Moreover, since it was illegal for more than 12 people to meet for worship in any building other than a church or licensed dissenting chapel, from which more often than not the Methodists were excluded, the meetings took place in the open air. This was in itself a draw to those who found the barrier of crossing the church threshold difficult. Matters came to a head with a survey of religious observance contained within the 1851 census. This proved that a large proportion of the population of the United Kingdom was essentially unchurched, and that there were millions who no longer counted themselves as belonging to the Church of England, or indeed to any of the other mainstream denominations.

The Nineteenth Century

How was the Church of England to respond to this? As early as 1854 a committee of the Convocation of Canterbury was appointed to consider if any change in the rules of worship was necessary. It reported in July of that year and advocated permission for occasional services compiled from Prayer Book materials. Three years earlier Lord Shaftesbury had worked tirelessly for the repeal of the law prohibiting gatherings for worship of more than 20 people except in a licensed church building. This latter action opened the floodgates for using theatres and other public buildings for the holding of mission services, designed to bridge the gap between the Church of England and the populace at large. Since these services were directed at the unchurched and unconfirmed, they were essentially both non-eucharistic and much simpler than the normal Anglican Sunday morning or evening services of the day.

Many of the services were very creative liturgically. The Anglo–Catholics trawled the medieval office of Compline and also the baptism service for material. One such service, the 1869 *Book of Mission* evening service, consisted of a Scripture reading drawn from Evening Prayer, Psalms 151, 120, collects, the Lord's Prayer and a sermon, followed by a form of renewal of baptismal vows. Another at St Thomas's, Regent Street, made use of Gregorian chant and a metrical litany, although how popular this proved to be is not recorded. Occasionally Anglo–Catholics stepped outside the authorized services, the *BCP* or medieval services for their inspiration. Father Dolling, one of the best-known Anglo–Catholic clergy of the late nineteenth century, favoured an informal structure in his 'little dissenting services', which consisted of hymns, an informal talk and extemporary prayer, to which the congregation added hearty 'Amens'. On the whole, however, it was the Evangelicals who were most adventurous in their choice of material. The vicar of St John's, Portsea, in 1857, introduced an experimental service in a former circus building. This included the singing of the national anthem, the reading of edifying portions of the newspapers, the singing of a hymn, a reading from Scripture, a second hymn, then prayers, and finally a doxology. At much the same time in the Iron Room at Christchurch, Barnet, William Pennyfather introduced a service of prayer, singing and preaching, to which he added an occasional Communion service according to the rites of the Church of England.

These various offerings were marked by their innovation. However, their impetus was marred by a complete lack of co-ordination among those churches hosting them. Part of the reason for this was because no one was really sure what was needed to attract the unchurched masses. Some saw the way forward as being through occasional mission services. Others saw the need to introduce a permanent Third Service, complementary to the statutory services, which might nevertheless be less unwieldy than the forms of Morning and Evening Prayer in use at the time. There was also disagreement as to how much should be prescribed by the Church in any Third Service, and how much left to the minister's discretion.

Changes in official policy were slow. It was not until 1872, in the Act of Uniformity Amendment Act, that due recognition was given to the fact that when the morning service took the form of Morning Prayer, Litany, and Holy Communion, it was not only long and wearisome but also contained a considerable amount of duplication. Permission was therefore granted to treat these as three separate services. An even more significant development was permission for a Third Service to be held on a Sunday, supplementary to the statutory services of Morning and Evening Prayer. Authorization was also given at this point to the practice, already widely adopted, of replacing the metrical Psalms with the hymns of such writers as Wesley, Cowper and Watts. With a place for them in the liturgy, hymn-writing in the English language now began to mushroom.

The 1872 Act made provision for beginning to change the face of Sunday morning worship dramatically. While the Anglo–Catholics continued to move inexorably towards a sung Holy Communion as the main Sunday service, many middle-of-the-road and Evangelical parishes moved towards an 8 a.m. Holy Communion and an 11 a.m. service of Morning Prayer. Meanwhile the Third Service, where offered, became by far the most popular service among the churchgoing poor. The content of such services, however, was considerably more closely regulated than that of the mission services. Such Third Services were permitted to contain (apart from hymns and anthems) only words from Scripture and from the BCP. This was clearly not enough for some. An anonymous writer in the *Church Quarterly Review* for 1876 reminded the Church that finding one's place in the Prayer Book was still enough to baffle those unfamiliar with its mysteries. There was, he said, a need for simply constructed and flexible services for Sunday use which might permit almost any degree of modification.

A greater concession was made in 1892, when provision was made for use within the Third Service of material 'substantially in agreement' with Scripture and the BCP. This was allowed so long as the Third Service really was a Third Service, additional to, rather than replacing, the statutory services of Holy Communion and Morning and Evening Prayer. Despite the experiments of the twentieth century, this remained the legal position until 1993, when the General Synod authorized A Service of the Word as an official alternative to Morning or Evening Prayer.

The Third Service and the mission service then can both be seen as antecedents of the popular family service of the 1960s and 1970s, or of the all-age worship of the 1980s and 1990s. However, the family service also has another distinguished ancestor in the Sunday School services of the late nineteenth and early twentieth centuries. The Sunday School Movement had originally been founded as a way of providing a basic education, including the ability to read the Scriptures, to those children who spent the other six days of their lives working in the new factories of industrial England. It was intended that the children who attended Sunday School should participate in the worship of the parish church. However, the length of the church services of the day meant that many Sunday Schools began to hold their own services. These varied in content, and also in competence, depending on the abilities of those who led them. They usually included a collect, prayers, Bible reading and hymns. To help those who were not comfortable with constructing worship for themselves, in 1932 *Church Teaching from the Kindergarten* was published, consisting of a draft order of service for every Sunday of the year. This was followed in the 1940s by *The Children's Church*, produced by the Church Book Room Press, containing a simplified version of Morning Prayer, which was later to become the basis upon which the CPAS built their own *Family Service* in the 1960s.

The Twentieth Century

Despite these efforts at making worship more popular (a movement not confined to the Anglicans but also involving Methodists, Baptists and Presbyterians), at the outbreak of the First World War there were millions of people who were still entirely unchurched. The evidence for this was provided by a survey of churchgoing habits amongst soldiers, carried out by the British army in 1915, which deeply shocked the churches and questioned any complacency concerning the spiritual health of the nation. For Anglicans, although the separation of the Communion Service from Morning Prayer and the Litany in 1872 had done something to address the problem of length, the net result was that the churchgoer was confronted with the choice between a service of Holy Communion and Morning Prayer, while the non-churchgoer remained baffled by the language and complexity of the liturgy.

As part of the movement to try and address this, Walter Frere in *Principles of Liturgical Reform* (1911) had already pleaded for a shorter combined service incorporating both the Office (normally Morning Prayer) and Holy Communion, without returning to the repetitive and overlong combined service in use before 1872. The 1928 Prayer Book, in the drafting of which Frere himself was heavily involved, took these ideas a step further by suggesting omissions which might be made from Morning Prayer if this was to be followed immediately by another service such as Holy Communion. These included omitting the penitential introduction to Morning Prayer, and ending the service after the Second Collect. Further flexibility was given to Morning and Evening Prayer by the addition of seasonal introductory sentences and the provision of a greater variety of Occasional Prayers to supplement the State Prayers. Special Psalms and lessons were also provided for Sundays, recognizing fully at last the distinctiveness of the Sunday congregational service in the life of the Church.

These changes were widely used in the worship of the English parish church. Yet they had no formal authority until the Prayer Book Alternative and Other Services Measure was passed in 1965. This authorized, from 10 June 1966, on a limited basis variations for experimental use, including the shortened Morning Prayer. This was to be followed by the Eucharist. However, several other features proposed in 1928 were abandoned, including introductions to the Psalms and the supplementary prayers. Overall, Series 1 Morning and Evening Prayer was a very conservative revision, especially for Sunday use. Slightly less conservative were the provisions of Series 2 Morning and Evening Prayer, authorized for use from 1968. A shorter penitential introduction, based on that in the Series 2 Communion Service, was provided. The *Benedictus* and *Te Deum* were transposed, and the *Gloria in Excelsis* was permitted as an alternative to either. There was also now, for the first time, official provision for a sermon at Morning and Evening Prayer on Sundays. Consideration was also given for the first time to typography and layout, with the use of italics to mark out the congregation's part.

For some, these changes were simply not far-reaching enough. Many parishes, especially more Evangelical ones in the cities, found that even after the revisions of Series 2 (Revised), Series 3 and the *ASB*, Morning Prayer was still too long and unwieldy to be used as the main diet of Sunday worship.

Without authorization, many parishes began to shorten the Psalms at Morning Prayer and to reduce the number of canticles, replacing them with choruses and worship songs. The more *avant garde* parishes also began to shorten the confession and to omit the Creed.

The Development of Family Services

Some attempt at standardizing practice was made by the CPAS, which issued its *Family Service* in 1968 and revised it again in 1976. This was based on a shortened form of Morning Prayer, with hymns and choruses in place of Psalms and canticles, a sermon called 'The Talk', intercessions and a simple credal statement offered as an alternative to the Creed itself. This proved to be immensely popular and was used in churches of all kinds up and down the country. Yet it did not have any official status and therefore could legally only be used as a Third Service. In practice, however, it was often used as the main, or indeed the only, worship in many churches on Sundays. Other material initially written for local use also came into the public domain at about this time. This included work done by Michael Botting, Chairman of the CPAS, at the time when he was Vicar of St Matthew's, Fulham. He published *Reaching the Families* (1969) and *Teaching the Families* (1973). Another noteworthy effort was *Family Worship* (1973), later revised as *Church Family Worship* in 1986 and 1988. The latter contained, in addition to the *ASB* services of Morning Prayer and Holy Communion Rite A, a eucharistic prayer for use in other denominations (but often used unofficially in Anglican parishes), together with 800 hymns and worship songs and more than 700 prayers, all contained within the covers of one book. As such, it was the first step in the move away from a set text to a menu of different choices. At the same time, the JLG's daily office was also being billed as suitable for Sunday use and designed 'to meet the needs of the large number of people on the fringes of Christianity who were either totally non-churched or who had lapsed in their churchgoing habits'.

The appearance of these resources worried those concerned with church order. Ronald Jasper, Chairman of the Liturgical Commission at the time, pleaded in 1965 for the Church of England to produce its own authorized family service materials, distinct from the provisions made in Morning and Evening Prayer. The plea was made on the grounds that many Church of England clergy were either using the CPAS materials (which were competent, even if unauthorized), or were composing their own, also unauthorized and often less competent, materials. In response to this, the Archbishops asked the Liturgical Commission to prepare a report on the whole issue of informal services, to include both family services and other occasional acts of worship such as harvest services and services for Mothering Sunday.

The task was undertaken by John Wilkinson, who reported his findings to the Archbishops and to the Liturgical Commission in February 1966 and to the House of Bishops in April 1967. At the same time, he wrote a small booklet of good practice entitled *Family and Evangelistic Services* (1967). This was not an official publication of the Liturgical Commission but came with a Foreword by its then Chairman, Ronald Jasper. Wilkinson's proposals were based around a fourfold structure of Adoration, Confession, Thanksgiving, and Supplication. He proposed the use of an Opening or Introduction, followed by the main text of the office, then some prayers and finally a Conclusion. The report was concerned to provide a liturgy where young people would be welcomed into church rather than be sent out to engage in their own 'special' activities. It also spoke of the need for careful planning of such family services and for the need to avoid the worship leader becoming little more than a compère presiding at an entertainment. Involvement was hailed as a key concept of such services, and to that end responsorial Psalms and readings were commended. Following the presentation of the report to the House of Bishops, it was intended that it should be commended by each bishop to his own diocese. However, for reasons of pressure of work or conservatism, and despite the elements of good practice which it contained, the report seems to have almost entirely disappeared from view and played little or no further part in the development of family services or all-age worship.

In spite of this setback, good work was continued throughout the 1970s. Ronald Jasper himself engaged with the Joint Liturgical Group on the question of how and why family services worked, how they could and should be regulated, how they might be adapted to various styles of churchmanship, and what problems they raised (*Getting the Liturgy Right*, 1972). However, the group saw the so-called family service as being no more than a bridge from non-attendance into full participation in the worshipping life of the Christian community. Their general approach therefore was that these services must not be allowed to diverge too greatly from traditional forms, lest they failed in their purpose of bringing people into the full worshipping life of the Church. As such they were seen as mission services.

More conservative members of the Church needed much convincing that these new family services were necessary or even desirable. A report on family services from the Chelmsford Diocese (*For Families: Report of Bishop's Working Party on Non-statutory Worship Within the Diocese of Chelmsford*, 1986) did little to allay some of these fears. While it accepted that family services were popular and often well planned, it was also concerned that some of them were also banal, stilted, uncreative, inhibited and boring. Concerns were also expressed that some of the prayers which passed for confessions and absolutions were not confessions and absolutions at all, while some of the credal statements in use were hailed as verging on the heretical.

At the other end of the spectrum, the report of the Archbishop of Canterbury's Commission on Urban Priority Areas, *Faith in the City*, had made a plea, as early as 1975, that formal liturgy must be complemented by more informal and spontaneous acts of worship (Section 6:110–111) and spoke of how involving families in worship had paid dividends in some situations

(Section 4.20). This same report also put in an appeal for short, functional service books and cards, which could be easily understood by a variety of people, young and old alike, and pleaded for the language used in worship to become more concrete and less philosophical, and also for a greater use of meaningful symbols.

Moving Towards A Service of the Word

By the mid-1980s, the Liturgical Commission had become convinced of the need to look at the whole issue of family services, and more widely, services of the Word in general, and to make some concrete proposals to the General Synod and the House of Bishops as to their authorized provision and use. The work done was originally dubbed a 'Directory' of resources, but the title was changed just before publication in 1989 to *Patterns for Worship* (PW) (GS 898), because of the questions which the word 'Directory' raised about the nature of Anglican worship and its necessary components. The finished work was a resource which could be used in a flexible way but which in the end would ensure a well balanced rite. In addition to skeleton outlines for a Service of the Word and for the Eucharist (a Form of Holy Communion, Rite C), a wealth of material was provided, including recommended confessions, absolutions, and affirmations of faith, together with forms of intercession, thanksgivings, blessings and other endings. In putting these resources together the Commission was anxious for it not to result in enforced uniformity. However, they also recognized that there was a need to set boundaries to the proposed freedom through the safeguarding of certain elements within Anglican worship, including a recognizable structure; an emphasis on reading the Word and on using Psalms; the use of liturgical words repeated by the congregation, some of which, like the Creed, would be known by heart; the use of a collection and of the Lord's Prayer in every service; a concern for form, dignity and the economy of words; and an acknowledgement of the centrality of the Eucharist within Anglican worship (see also the relevant sections of Chapter 2 above).

This publication represented a major step in the concept of Anglican worship, seeing it as based upon the idea of a recognizable shape in which some elements are mandatory and others optional, rather than upon any necessary and always following of set texts. This position was later confirmed when the Service of the Word provisions were finally authorized for use in 1993. It is notable, however, that before the 1993 authorization the 'menu' approach to the Eucharist proposed earlier had been abandoned. Instead, in *A Service of the Word and Affirmations of Faith* an alternative table was provided for the use of the Service of the Word with Holy Communion, complementary to the tables already provided for the combination of Rite A Holy Communion with Morning and Evening Prayer in the ASB. Some of the other resources from the original report which were not published in the 1993 text have since reappeared in the commended edition of PW (1995) in a revised and often extended form.

As authorized, *A Service of the Word* was unique as a Church of England service, since apart from the basic menu 'consists almost entirely of processes and directions, and allows for considerable local variation and choice within a common structure' (p. 4). This was deliberate, since it was felt that the needs of parishes would be met, not by a group of experts at the centre laying down the services, but by creating a new environment with clear guidelines and only a few authorized or prescribed texts. In this way a new generation of worship leaders might grow up, capable of generating liturgy which is both local and culturally relevant while still observely part of the liturgy of the Church as a whole.

This basic menu, with notes and help for constructing the service, was re-authorized in 1999 for inclusion in *CW*. However, at this point provision was also made for including within *A Service of the Word* an outline form of *A Service of the Word with a Celebration of Holy Communion*, *BCP* Morning and Evening Prayer and two new forms of Morning and Evening Prayer to be used on Sundays. Two forms of Night Prayer, one contemporary the other traditional, although coming within the provisions of *A Service of the Word*, were nevertheless separately commended for use by the House of Bishops. A number of canticles also appear, as do a wealth of optional prayers, and several authorized confessions and absolutions, creeds, and affirmations of faith, and the litany. It is with this rich diet at its disposal that provision for all-age worship, especially on Sundays, after more than a century of experiment, has now come of age in the Church of England. Parish worship committees can tap in to material, which is both flexible and usable while still being essentially Anglican, as the Church enters upon the new challenges which the twenty-first century will bring.

B. COMMENTARY

A Service of the Word is an authorized structure, rather than a set text, and allows for the development of locally relevant, participatory services which are in tune with the culture, society, and spiritual life of the local church community. It permits considerable flexibility and freedom while maintaining the principle of Church of England worship being 'that which is authorized or allowed by Canon'. Underlying all the provisions is the understanding that the 'primary object in the careful planning and leading of the service is the spiritual direction which enables the whole congregation to come into the presence of God to give him glory' (Introduction). So the choice of which words and texts are used is only part of the required preparation. Equally important are the vision of what worship is, the use of the worship space colour and symbol, and the structure, shape, flow, and action in the service.

The authorized structure of *A Service of the Word* is to be used in conjunction with other resources, in order to allow flexibility and foster creativity. These will include material within *CW*, other provision by the Liturgical Commission, such as *PW*, seasonal material (including *BHG* and *LHWE*), texts and forms that are locally devised, and commercially produced resource material. A Service of the Word gives requirements, guidelines and parameters for the use of different resources. Any material used should be 'neither contrary to, nor indicative of any departure from, the doctrine of the Church of England in any essential matter' (Notes), as is required by the Canon Law which relates to the use of discretion by a minister.

As its name suggests, this service has the ministry of the Word at its centre. The Preparation sets the context for the Liturgy of the Word, the Prayers flow from it in response, and it ends in a Conclusion or leads into a Eucharist. However, a cautionary Note states that A Service of the Word with a Celebration of Holy Communion 'requires careful preparation by the president and other participants, and is not normally to be used as the regular Sunday or weekday service'.

Preparation

> The minister welcomes the people with the **Greeting**.
> **Authorized Prayers of Penitence** may be used here or in the **Prayers**.
> *Venite, Kyries, Gloria*, a hymn, song, or set of responses may be used.
> The **Collect** is said either here or in the **Prayers**.

A clear beginning to the service is one of the features of A Service of the Word, enabling the congregation to gather together, and turn their thoughts and attention to the worship of God. So a liturgical greeting is required, although its form can vary, and it can come before or after an opening hymn, informal introduction, and opening prayer. A prayer of penitence, with a confession and an absolution, and the collect, may be part of the Preparation or part of the Prayers later in the service. However, the traditional position for the collect, before the first reading, is required when it is being used as the first part of a Communion service.

As the Preparation provides the context for the Liturgy of the Word, it can be thematic, seasonal, or general in the choice of words used. It can begin a dialogue with God which continues in the content of the readings or in the focus of the sermon. The mixture of praise and prayer within the Preparation needs to be planned to have a meaningful shape and flow. This will normally consist of a call to worship, whether informal, liturgical, or in song, a sentence of Scripture as a reminder of whom we come to worship and why, and an opening prayer. Through the Preparation the congregation is enabled to be more open to hear God's Word so that they may better respond to him.

Prayers of Penitence
The position in which these are used can vary. They can be early in the service as part of the Preparation, or later as response to the Liturgy of the Word, or in preparation for approach to Holy Communion if the Service of the Word is

forming the first part of a Eucharist. The positioning will affect the approach to confession and the choice of wording, as will the season, theme and occasion of the service. The Prayers of Penitence can be omitted, except at the principal service on Sundays and Principal Holy Days.

Only authorized forms of confession and absolution are to be used. Note 2 allows for the use of any authorized forms, such as those in the *BCP*, authorized seasonal and thematic material, forms used elsewhere in *CW*, and those authorized forms which are printed at the end of the Service of the Word section (see the commentary on these below).

The variety of authorized prayers allows for confession along many different lines. Used as part of the overall flow and conversation of the service, their potential for encouraging a time of openness and honesty before God is considerable. Linked to this is the encouragement to incorporate silent reflection as part of this time. Consideration needs to be given to the way confession is introduced, the posture encouraged, and the use of silence or music, as well as which text is chosen.

Hymns, canticles and songs

By their use in this part of the service, the sense of flow and the dynamic of a developing dialogue with God can be expressed. Thus, the *Venite* or other appropriate canticle or a song can be used as a call to worship; the *Kyries* can be used on their own as a humble approach to God, rather than as a form of confession; or there can be praise in response to the assurance of forgiveness that we receive in the absolution, expressing our thanksgiving at the extent of God's mercy and at what God has done through Jesus Christ. The praise can take the form of a canticle, the *Gloria in Excelsis*, a song, or a responsive acclamation or responsive Scripture. A scriptural song may also be used on occasions as an alternative. Greater use of canticles can be found in the forms of Morning and Evening Prayer for Sundays (see Chapter 11 below).

Collect

This is the same as that allocated for the Eucharist. It will be as prescribed for the day itself on a Sunday, Principal Holy Day, or Lesser Festival, or that provided for Commemorations according to the designation of the person being commemorated (e.g. bishop, martyr). On all other occasions it will normally be that provided for the previous Sunday or Principal Holy Day (see Chapter 8 below). When the Collect of the Day is used to sum up the prayers later in the service, a thematic collect based on one of the readings may be used here before the readings. When the Service of the Word is used with the Eucharist, the collect is said after the Prayers of Penitence and before the Liturgy of the Word. Where the Morning or Evening Collect is also used, it should be placed at the end of the service immediately before the Closing Prayer or Blessing. These two collects can be found at the beginning of the section called 'Prayers for Various Occasions'.

The Liturgy of the Word

This includes:

- readings (or a reading) from Holy Scripture
- a Psalm or, if occasion demands, a scriptural song
- a sermon
- an authorized Creed or, if occasion demands, an authorized Affirmation of Faith

This is the heart of the service, and the Introduction makes the point that this must not be so slight a section that it becomes an insignificant component with other parts of the service. The opportunity for creative liturgy, and a flexible approach to the communication of the Word is considerable. The primary concern is for a ministry which will enable the Scriptures to be understood as the Living Word of God. The most effective communication varies in different situations and on different occasions. A Service of the Word does not prescribe a particular approach but encourages appropriate and imaginative use of the Scriptures.

Readings

Note 5 states that two are preferred, but that there may be occasions where one reading is more appropriate. The choice of readings will be governed by the authorized Lectionary, which allows flexibility at some times of year. While the Lectionary must be used at least from Advent 3 to The Baptism of Christ, and from Palm Sunday to Trinity Sunday, at other times it may be adapted or abandoned. When A Service of the Word forms the first part of the Eucharist on Sundays and Principal Holy Days, the Lectionary readings are normally used. The sense of the whole Church telling its story as it follows the seasons is maintained by adhering to the Lectionary provision (see Chapter 9 below). For occasional services there is more freedom, with a choice of readings arising from the occasion, festival or theme of the service.

With the creative scope allowed in A Service of the Word, it is helpful to think of how a passage can best be communicated. Some passages may readily lend themselves to a dramatic reading or to an acted version. Resources are available to make such dramatizations simple. Other passages are better communicated by one reader. They may be enhanced by the use of visual aids, in slides or overhead transparency processes or with banners – perhaps made by the Sunday School or a church group. Sometimes a responsive reading is appropriate, or a time of discussion immediately after the reading, which can open up a passage, perhaps by asking a simple question as to why this passage is in the Bible. The quiet playing of music may enhance a reflective passage. A balance between creativity and simplicity needs to be held, so that services do not become too busy and complicated and so distract from the reading of the Word rather than elucidating it. Consideration of the flow of the liturgy, time, and appropriateness also need to be addressed.

In addition it is important to address the way in which a straight reading of Scripture can be improved. Reading of the Scriptures is reading the living Word of God. This reader ministry is an unusual one, for it is both to speak the written words with clarity and also be used to deliver what is potentially a life-changing communication from God through his Holy Spirit. In a liturgical context the reading of Scripture is a corporate activity, as the faith community reacts to and engages with and rejoices as the readings of God to his people; it is also an individual... as God's Holy Spirit ministers through the Word to each soul who is open to... receive. Both the corporate and individual dimensions are important.

Some aspects of good ministry in Scripture... such as... audibility, through the skills of reading, adequate volume..., sound system... projection... and provision of loop system for the... of hearing. Training in voice production, projection and delivery can make a big difference, and to give attention to... Equally important is the need that the passage to be read is within understanding, appropriate inflexion and expression, and to balance between lively reading and a serious delivery of God's Word. Preparation is essential for this to be possible which will mean plenty of notice for the reader to allow... time to... the close understanding, and possibly some explanation of the passage with the preacher and others... in this section.

Some congregations make use of copies of the whole Bible or of the daily readings, so that the passage can be followed. The practice of handling one Bible can develop familiarity over time, although it can also be intimidating practice for newcomers. Provision for today's readings allows for them to be taken away, and consequently has the potential for re-reading and remembering the subsequent sermon. Removing physical barriers that distance the hearer from the reader can also be helpful. For example, the lectern can be moved toward, or a portable lectern used nearer to the congregation, and the practice of having a Gospel procession and reading in the nave brings the Word to the people. But reading from a specifically defined place, rather than simply from where the reader happens to be, helps to focus the importance of the reading. Listening engagement with the text can also be encouraged by allowing a time of silence after the reading for reflection.

Psalms

As Chapter 10 below indicates, Psalms are part of the ancient tradition of the Church. They are therefore duly seen as a consistent element in a Service of the Word, although there is flexibility in the form in which they are used. They may be sung or spoken in the tradition of ways, but most commonly in a metrical rhythm version, or in responsive form or paraphrased. On occasions they can be replaced by a song, canticle or a canticle (see Chapter 11 below).

It is worth noting that a great deal of new material is now being composed and published for the congregational use of Psalms. It is recognized that

Anglican chant, while still being very popular in traditional churches, is not found to be helpful in some situations. Alternatives for singing Psalms include responsive settings, usually providing a sung refrain for the congregation with the text being carried by a cantor or the choir. Some sung settings of Psalms use a traditional format for the text, but slightly adapted so that it forms repeatable units, which can be easily sung by a whole congregation. This is somewhere between a chant and a metrical (hymn) version. Singing Psalms aids their memorization, which can form an important part of people's devotional life. If Psalms are said, it is again possible to use a refrain which is said corporately while a reader uses the main text, or the Psalm can be said responsively in alternate verses (either between leader and congregation, or between different sections of the congregation).

Sermon

This term is used to cover a variety of ways of bringing the Scriptures which are read to engage with the lives of the congregation (see Chapter 5 below). It must not be omitted on Sundays and Principal Holy Days. As in other parts of A Service of the Word, the emphasis is on allowing the sermon to be creative, culturally relevant, and engaging the whole person. For example, it is possible to use drama to bring out the message in a vital and lively way. Visual aids provide images that can help the message to be clear and to be memorable. Integration of the sermon with the service in an interactive way can enhance the understanding of, and response to, a passage. Discussion, in buzz groups or in come-back with the preacher, encourages personal engagement with the content. Several small talks interspersed with songs, silence, drama, or prayers, can be more engaging than one longer sermon 'slot'. The application of a passage can be reinforced by giving examples, not just in illustrative stories, but also by using testimony, or interviews. For example, members of the congregation can tell how they understand being a Christian in the workplace, or how they have faced a crisis, or have learned something. A time of silence after the sermon, or a quiet reflective song, can give the opportunity for the challenge presented to be faced.

The sermon may come after either of the readings, or before or after the prayers. It should be seen as integral to the whole flow and movement of the service. For example, the prayers can prepare for listening to it or be part of the response to it. A careful choice of an Affirmation of Faith or Affirmation of Commitment after the sermon can give the opportunity for verbal expression of renewal. Or the alternative later position for the Prayers of Penitence can be used to enable response.

A Creed or an Affirmation of Faith

This is seen as an appropriate response to hearing the Word and to understanding it through the sermon (in whatever form those are offered). In essence it forms a climax to the Liturgy of the Word. One of the historic

Creeds is normally used on Sundays and Principal Holy Days, except at a non-statutory service, when one of the authorized Affirmations of Faith may be used instead. Both may be omitted on other days.

The Affirmations of Faith should not be regarded as definitive and comprehensive statements of faith. They generally express part of the Christian faith rather than trying to encapsulate the totality of it, as the historic creeds have attempted to do. Most of them are not the product of centuries of debate, agreement and fine tuning, but are selections of and excerpts from the Scriptures, which are appropriate for corporate or responsive readings. A few of them are significantly different forms of the traditional creeds (see the section of this Chapter on Creeds and Affirmations of Faith below).

Prayers

These include:

> intercessions and thanksgivings;
> the Lord's Prayer.

The Prayers continue the response to the reading of the Word and the sermon, and form part of the conversation of liturgy. They therefore need to flow from the preceding sections and lead on to the next. The Introduction again encourages creativity and variety of form. Some ways of enriching the prayers include using pictures on the overhead projector, praying in small groups, encouraging extemporary prayer, allowing times of silence, using processional prayers, using responsive forms, or accompanying the prayer with music – such as a Taizé chant. The Introduction also suggests collect-type prayers and intercessions led by groups as well as individuals. Intercessions should normally be concerned with the whole Church and the world, although it may also be appropriate at times to focus on more local need.

Thanksgiving is seen as an essential part of these prayers, forming a climax to the service, and a whole thanksgiving section may be included. This would consist of word – in readings or testimony; music – in songs and hymns; and a selection of prayers. Four Thanksgivings are included in the *CW* main volume – for the Word, Holy Baptism, the Healing Ministry of the Church, and the Mission of the Church.

A small selection of prayers is included in the section, 'Prayers for Various Occasions', and the Litany is printed in both modern language and *BCP* form (see the section on the Litany below). A vast number of resources are also available for leading prayers, both in other Church of England provision, such as *PW* (1995) and seasonal resources, and also in commercial publications. *PW* (pp. 214–16) gives examples of ways that intercession can be led, and some warnings as to what to avoid. Its helpful checklist underlines the importance of looking at the day's readings and discovering the theme of the service, including co-ordinating with the preacher; finding out about particular needs, events

more suitable to use this in some circumstances, and especially in ecumenical situations.

Conclusion

One of the basic principles of A Service of the Word is that it should have a clear ending. This can be a blessing, dismissal or other liturgical ending. To this end a few blessings and endings are provided in 'Prayers for Various Occasions', although a great many more can be found in *PW*, *LHWE*, *PPEE*, *Enriching the Christian Year* and other resources.

The Liturgy of the Sacrament

When the service forms the first part of a service of Holy Communion, the Prayers are followed directly by the Peace and then the Preparation of the Table. The eucharistic prayer has to be one which is authorized, and the Lord's Prayer is used in its usual eucharistic position and not in the Prayers of A Service of the Word.

C: PUTTING A SERVICE TOGETHER

Form and flow

With such choice and rich resources, the task of putting together a service calls for care and understanding. There is an excellent introduction in *PW* (especially pp. 20–6). This, together with the relevant sections in its commentary and its sample services, explain how A Service of the Word can be used well. The potential is considerable, but so is the opportunity for a disjointed service which throws together a multitude of styles, words, activities and ideas. Teamwork, consultation and an integrated approach to A Service of the Word is therefore important. Consideration should be given to the theme, the type, the resources, the facilities and the gifts and resources of those involved. The style will depend on the occasion.

The order will depend on the structure of the service and its flow. For example, does the service follow the congregational structure, and flow well from one part to the next? Does it have all the required elements of a clear beginning and preparation, ministry of the Word, prayers and praise, and a clear end? Does it progress and have a point of climax – in Holy Communion or in the sermon and response to it, or in an act of thanksgiving? Does it involve the congregation and give opportunity for response, action and engagement with God?

A Service of the Word is not only concerned with words and structure. Action should also be a constituent element of it. This is used in many a profound way in a service. Consider decide changing the lighting to change the mood, or using movement in conjunction with a candle, or Bible, inviting the congregation to move physically in a procession, or to a focal point for prayer, or having symbolic actions such as signing oneself with the cross using water at the font during an act of Renewal of Baptism Vows.

The way in which a service sheet is put together can also affect the overall feel of a service. This issue is addressed in *PW* (pp. 233–7) and in Mark Earey's *Producing Your Own Orders of Service* (2000). The whole business of producing local liturgies has been made much easier with the growth of the use of desktop publishing and with the availability of dedicated software such as *Visual Liturgy*. Moreover, the advent of computer projection facilities opens up many possibilities for using the creative potential of *CW* and presenting clear and easy-to-read text and visual images. Guidelines on copyright considerations have also been issued. The Church of England's own website gives constant updates on current liturgy provision and resources (www.cofe.anglican.org).

Music and A Service of the Word

Until the late nineteenth century, hymns were not an authorized part of Morning and Evening Prayer. The only music allowed actually within the service itself, apart from the chanting of the Psalms, was the Anthem between the Third Collect and the prayers for King/Queen and the Royal Family. This state of affairs meant that the Anglican Church often lost out to the Methodists and Congregationalists, in whose worship music had always played a vital part. Once hymns were allowed within Anglican worship, the floodgates opened, especially after the publication of *Hymns Ancient and Modern* (1861) and its more Catholic counterpart *The English Hymnal* (1904). Until the 1970s these, together with the *Anglican Hymnbook*, formed the staple diet of most parish churches in terms of hymnody. In the 1960s and 1970s they were supplemented by publications such as *One Hundred Hymns for Today* (and *More Hymns for Today*), *English Praise*, *Youth Praise*, and by *Anglican Praise*. Yet times were changing. One change resulted from growing ecumenism. As Anglicans began to worship with other denominations, they began to experience a wider range of music both from the Roman Catholic *Celebration Hymnal* and from the Wesleyan *Hymns and Psalms*. At the same time Anglicans, like members of the other Christian Churches, also began to demand hymns which were more culturally relevant and politically correct. Finally, a great change was wrought by the charismatic movement, which began to use more praise songs, and by the growth of family services, where the need was for simple tunes and memorable words which could be easily learned and remembered. The result has been a positive explosion in song and hymn-writing over the last 20 years, with new hymn- and song-books appearing almost every year. Ecumenical gatherings have given rise to some of the new song-books, such as those associated with Spring Harvest. Some of the recent collections, such as *Mission Praise*, *Songs of Fellowship* and *The Source* have concentrated mainly on praise and renewal, but more traditional fare in new arrangements has also appeared, as in *Hymns Old and New* (which appeared in both an Anglican and a Roman Catholic edition), *Hymns for Today's Church*, *Church Family Worship*, and *Sing Glory* (2000).

So where does the worship leader go? Luckily, many hymn- and song-books contain a full thematic and biblical index which can be of tremendous help when constructing music for worship. Yet balance also needs to be struck in other areas, such as between traditional and new music, in taking note of both the doctrinal message of the hymn and its liturgical appropriateness, and of relating these to the needs and abilities of the congregation and local musicians. If the liturgy of A Service of the Word is rich in language and content, so too should be the music which forms such an integral part of the worship.

Hymns and songs are important, yet they are not the only way of making music in A Service of the Word. Reference has already been made to the availability of settings for the Psalms. Singing of the canticles, especially of the Gospel canticle at Morning and Evening Prayer, is also being encouraged, and new settings will be needed to help this to happen.

D. MORNING AND EVENING PRAYER

A Service of the Word does not just provide for an additional non-sacramental service on a Sunday or for occasional services on weekdays. It may also be used as an alternative to Morning and Evening Prayer, both on Sundays and weekdays. It therefore gives legal status to many existing forms of daily office, provided that they follow the structure of A Service of the Word, including regional office books, and other experimental forms. Furthermore, the Schedule of Permitted Variations to the *Book of Common Prayer* Orders of Morning and Evening Prayer, approved by the General Synod and included in *CW*, gives authority to many common practices related to those services which were not strictly allowed according to the text and rubrics of the 1662 *BCP*, and the *CW* main volume lays out these services in this modified form. It also includes worked-out examples, again under the provisions of A Service of the Word, of Orders for Morning and Evening Prayer for Sunday use in modern language, and Night Prayer in both traditional and modern language forms. (A history of the daily offices of the Church will be included in the second volume of this commentary.)

The modern forms of Morning and Evening Prayer in *CW* do not merely derive from the *ASB* services, but also from the office book of the Society of St Francis (SSF). During the 1970s SSF houses were being creative and experimental in their offices, and then later developed a new office book. This aimed at enriching the *ASB* provision, which was thought to be rather limited for daily use. The resulting hardback publication of *The Daily Office SSF* (1981) became popular far beyond the SSF houses, and many Church of England clergy and lay people used it regularly. It has a pattern of prayer four times a day, at Morning, Midday, Evening and Night. While based on the traditional formula of readings, Psalms and canticles, it has a different flavour to it, which is more akin to the so-called 'cathedral' offices of the early Church (i.e. those used in churches and cathedrals by clergy and lay people together, rather than those of monastic communities). In recognition of its richness and widespread use, the Liturgical Commission of the Church of England requested involvement in its further revisions. The subsequent office book had one version for SSF use and another independent publication adapted for general use, called *Celebrating Common Prayer* (*CCP*), which has become widely appreciated. Some of its distinctive features, such as the opening prayer, responsory after the Scripture readings and the rich and varied canticle provision, are recognizable in the services in the main volume of *CW*.

The Orders for Morning and Evening Prayer on Sunday are therefore a hybrid of the *BCP* services of Morning and Evening Prayer, which were themselves revised for the *ASB*, and material from *CCP*. According to the spirit of A Service of the Word, these examples are flexible in arrangement. The Introduction states that their central core is the ministry of the Word, interwoven with canticles to supply the response of praise, followed by intercessory prayer in one form or another. The response of praise is also underlined by the encouragement that some singing should be used during the service, especially of the Gospel canticle, which is 'the climax of the morning and evening praise for the work of God in Christ'.

Note 11 outlines an alternative arrangement of Morning Prayer as a commemoration of the resurrection, which is particularly commended for use in the Easter season. The idea is derived from the ancient early Sunday morning vigil of the resurrection observed weekly throughout the year by Christians in Jerusalem and elsewhere from the fourth century onwards.

Preparation

The suggested greeting at Morning Prayer is taken from 1 Timothy 1.2 ('Grace, mercy and peace . . .') and from Psalm 118.24 ('This is the day that the Lord has made . . .'). This is given as an alternative to the more traditional 'O Lord open our lips . . .' At Evening Prayer the two greetings are from Sunday Evening Prayer in *CCP*. The greeting may be followed at Morning or Evening Prayer by an adaptation from the opening paragraph from the *ASB* Morning Prayer ('We have come together . . .').

Prayers of Penitence

The introduction to the confession at both Morning and Evening Prayer comes from Matthew 4.17. Any authorized confession and absolution may be used. (For further details on those printed here, see the section 'Forms of Confession and Absolution' below.) The versicles and responses which conclude these prayers in the morning service are drawn from Psalm 28.7, 9.

Prayer of Thanksgiving

Such prayers were a new feature in *CCP*, although the idea was developed from forms of evening Thanksgiving for Light found in *PEC*, a practice popular in Roman Catholic circles today and based on the daily *Lucernarium* of early

Christians, when either at home or in church at dusk they would give thanks for the gift of the light of the day, of lamplight to lighten their darkness, and of the light of Christ to illuminate their lives. The prayers in *CW*, which are optional, are drawn from those in *CCP*, and their 'blessing' form echoes the style of Jewish prayers.

Opening Canticle

Another optional element, it is suggested that at Morning Prayer the *Benedicite* (A Song of Creation) in either its longer or shorter form be used in Ordinary Time, the *Jubilate* (A Song of Joy) in festal seasons, the Easter Anthems in the Easter season and the *Saulte* (A Song of Triumph) in Advent or Lent (Note 4). At Evening Prayer, the *Phos hilaron* (A Song of the Light) and/or verses from Psalms 141 or 104 are recommended (Note 6). (For these, see Chapter 11 below.)

Opening Prayer

This is optional and based on similar forms in *CCP*.

The Liturgy of the Word

This section is entitled 'The Word of God' in these orders, and has two possible shapes. The first places the Psalm(s) and Old Testament canticle at Morning Prayer, and the New Testament canticle at Evening Prayer together in a block, followed by either one or two readings, an optional responsory (or other song or chant), and the Gospel canticle (the *Benedictus* in the morning and the *Magnificat* in the evening). This is broadly the pattern of the traditional Benedictine office in the West and of the revised Roman Catholic daily offices. The alternative shape is that of the *BCP*, in which the first reading follows the psalmody and the second comes between the canticles. The former tends to emphasize the office as an act of praise, the latter makes the readings more prominent.

The sermon, which is compulsory if the service is the principal service on a Sunday or Principal Holy Day, may follow the readings or the Gospel canticle, or come at the end of the service before the Conclusion. The Apostles' Creed or authorized Affirmation of Faith, which ends this section of the service, may also be omitted when it is not the principal service on a Sunday or Principal Holy Day.

Thanksgivings

Some flexibility at this point in the service is provided by the provision of four optional Thanksgivings. These come after the sermon, where that follows the Gospel canticle. The Thanksgiving for Holy Baptism comes from *CCP* (398–9), and some of the material from the Thanksgiving for the Word also appears in *CCP* (240). Each of the Thanksgivings is self-contained as far as rounding off the service is concerned, as they contain, in addition to a Prayer of Thanksgiving, an Affirmation of Faith, a responsorial form of intercession, the Lord's Prayer (except in the Thanksgiving for Holy Baptism) and an appropriate liturgical ending. When the Thanksgiving for the Word is used, the Confession is omitted from its normal place as penitential prayers are contained within the Thanksgiving.

The element of action in all four Thanksgivings is strong. In the Thanksgiving for the Word, testimonies may be given, and in the Thanksgiving for Baptism the action takes place around the font and may include sprinkling the congregation with the water, or encouraging them to make the sign of the cross on themselves with water. In the Thanksgiving for the Healing Ministry of the Church, laying-on of hands and/or anointing may be included. In the Thanksgiving for the Mission of the Church a commissioning of all those willing to take on tasks in the name of the Church is included.

Prayers

Except where a specific form of responsory prayer is used (as in the Thanksgivings above), the form of intercession is very flexible. Intercessions should normally be broadly based and focus on the needs of the whole world, although particular need (as in the case of a local disaster) may at times call for a more local focus. One of the forms of the Litany in *CW* may be used here. The Collect of the Day should also be included here, but not the Morning or Evening Collect, which, if used, should come immediately before the Blessing or other ending (Note 10). The Lord's Prayer is always said in this section, and the canticle *Te Deum* may also be added at the end of the section (Note 7).

The Conclusion

Following the requirement in A Service of the Word for a proper ending, both Morning and Evening Prayer are to conclude with a suitable blessing, or with the Grace or the Peace. The exchange of the Peace was used by early Christians not merely in the Eucharist, but as the conclusion of common prayer, where it formed what they called 'the seal' to their prayers.

E. NIGHT PRAYER

The Order for Night Prayer originates from the monastic office of Compline, which derives its name from the Latin word *completorium* meaning completion. It disappeared as a service in its own right in England at the Reformation, although elements from Compline in the Sarum usage were incorporated into the office of Evening Prayer by Thomas Cranmer. Compline was revived in the Anglican Church as part of the 1928 Prayer Book provision and much used subsequently, albeit unofficially, especially during the season of Lent. The traditional form of Night Prayer in *CW* is based on that in the 1928 Prayer Book. The confession, however, has been moved from immediately before the final responses to the Preparation. The hymn, 'Before the ending of the day' has also been moved from before the *Nunc dimittis* to an earlier position and the Creed has been omitted.

The contemporary form of Night Prayer in *CW* is taken from Night Prayer on Saturdays in *CCP*. Of its readings, however, only one is derived from this source (Jeremiah 14.9). The other two are taken from Night Prayer on Thursdays (1 Peter 5.8–9) and Sundays (Revelation 22.45). In the Notes, provision is made for altering the psalmody at Night Prayer if desired, with a different Psalm suggested for each day of the week (Saturday: as set; Sunday: Psalm 104; Monday: Psalm 86; Tuesday: Psalm 143; Wednesday: Psalm 31; Thursday: Psalm 16; Friday: Psalm 139). In place of the suggested reading, the Gospel for the following day may be read, especially on Saturday evening and on the vigil of major feasts. The confession may be said in a different version or else omitted altogether.

Night Prayer is intended to be a quiet and reflective service at the end of the day. The Notes suggest that those who take part should depart in silence at the end. Any other business or notices therefore should always be given before, rather than after, the service.

F. PRAYERS FOR VARIOUS OCCASIONS

In the 1549 and 1552 Prayer Books, Morning and Evening Prayer end with the Collect of the Day, followed by the Collects for Peace and Grace in the Morning, and a second Collect for Peace and the Collect for Aid at Evening Prayer. In 1662 there was provision to add an Anthem 'In Quires and Places where they sing', followed by what have become known as the State Prayers, unless the Litany was to be said. The same prayers are allocated for both Morning and Evening Prayer. These are: A Prayer for the Queen's Majesty; A Prayer for the Royal Family; A Prayer for Clergy and People; and the Prayer of St Chrysostom.

The *CW* Prayers for Various Occasions are basically these same prayers, together with a number of others, some of which were in the *ASB*.

A Morning Collect is the Collect for Grace, thanking God that he 'has brought us safely to the beginning of this day . . .' This prayer dates at least as far back as the eighth century, being found in the Gelasian and Gregorian Sacramentaries. It was the ferial Collect for Prime in the Sarum Breviary and has been part of Morning Prayer in the Church of England consistently since 1549.

An Evening Collect is the Collect for Aid, 'Lighten our darkness, Lord, we pray . . .' It was also in the Gelasian Sacramentary for Vespers, and was the Collect for Compline in the Sarum Breviary, from whence Cranmer used it in Evensong in 1549.

A Prayer for the Sovereign is adapted from one that first appeared in Report 517 of the Convocation of Canterbury in 1919, and was put into the 1928

Prayer Book. It replaced another prayer for the Queen that originated in the 1559 Prayer Book.

A Prayer for the Royal Family has been in use since 1604, with minor changes along the way. It was possibly written by Archbishop Whitgift.

A Prayer for Those who Govern reflects the unity and diversity of contemporary Britain within its European context.

A Prayer for Bishops and Other Pastors is an ancient prayer from the Gelasian Sacramentary, which became the Collect for a Mass for an abbot or his congregation in the Gregorian Sacramentary. Cranmer used it in the Litany, taking it from the Sarum Litany. The titles for the ministry have changed: Cranmer adding 'curates'; 1928 substituting 'clergy'; and *ASB* changing it to 'bishops and other pastors', which *CW* continues, recognizing the wide variety of ministry in today's Church.

A Prayer of Dedication uses themes from Psalms 118.14 and 119.105, to pray for ourselves to follow God with his help and by the light of his Word. It was composed by Ronald Jasper at the request of the General Synod, for inclusion into Series 3 in 1975.

The prayers for the guidance of the Holy Spirit, for those who work on land or sea, for those engaged in commerce and industry, for the unity of the Church, for the peace of the world, for social justice and responsibility, and for vocations, are all taken from the Collects for Special Occasions: see Chapter 8 Section P, below.

A Text of the Lord's Prayer
The ELLC text of the Lord's Prayer is printed here as a resource. It is suitable for use in ecumenical situations. See the section on the Prayers in the Commentary on A Service of the Word above.

Prayers from the Book of Common Prayer
This contains the equivalent prayers to the previous selection, suitable for use with traditional forms of service, using the wording of the *BCP*. Those provided are: A Prayer for the Queen's Majesty, A Collect for the Queen (the second Collect for the Sovereign from the *BCP* Communion Service, which is not included in Order Two), A Prayer for the Royal Family, A Prayer for the Clergy and People, A Prayer of St Chrysostom, and a General Thanksgiving. A Prayer of St Chrysostom is from the Byzantine Rite and dates back to around the ninth century, appearing in both the Liturgy of St John Chrysostom and the Liturgy of St Basil. Cranmer included it in the 1544 Litany, and then in both the 1549 and 1552 Prayer Books. Despite its name, its authorship is

unknown. Bishop Edward Reynolds of Norwich wrote the General Thanksgiving and it was added to the Thanksgivings in the 1662 *BCP*. The scriptural basis is Psalm 51.15; Luke 1.75; and Colossians 1.27. It also has affinity with a prayer by Elizabeth I and with regulations for the construction of a eucharistic prayer in the *Directory for Public Worship* (1664).

Endings and Blessings

1. Known as 'The Grace', this sentence derives from 2 Corinthians 13.14, and has been used in liturgical greetings from the fourth century onwards. It introduced the Sursum Corda in many Eastern rites. It was also used as a reading in the office of Terce in the Sarum Breviary. In 1559 it concluded the Litany, and was put at the end of the State Prayers in 1662.

2. Ephesians 3.20–1 is the basis for this ending, used by Dean Milner-White in the 1930s, and then incorporated into Morning and Evening Prayer from Series 3 onwards.

3. This responsive ending has been in use since at least c. 800 in Gallican rites, and then in the Roman rite from c. 1000. It concludes Lauds, Prime, Vespers and Compline in the Sarum Breviary. The 1928 Prayer Book proposed it as an ending to Morning and Evening Prayer, but it was not officially adopted until Series 3 onwards.

4. The Aaronic Blessing, as it is known, is based on Numbers 6.24–6. Gallican and Anglo-Saxon missals used it and it was included in the Visitation of the Sick and the Commination (in a shorter form) in 1662. It was not until the *ASB* that it was in general use, Series 3 having confined it to the end of the Form of Thanksgiving for the Birth of a Child and After Adoption.

5. This form was prepared by the Liturgical Commission for Series 3 alongside the Aaronic blessing. It was also brought into general use in the *ASB*.

G. THE LITANY

The term 'litany' (in Greek, *litania*) refers to a distinctive style of prayer, made up of biddings and responses. The format itself is not specifically Christian, although Christian prayers based on it have been known since the early Church. The earliest form used *Kyrie eleison* ('Lord, have mercy') as the response. After initially spreading in the Byzantine liturgy, this form also became used in the West. The earliest record in Rome is of a litany translated from Greek by Pope Gelasius (492–6), although litanies were not a consistent feature in Western liturgy until later.

The form which was to be dominant in the West was introduced by Pope Sergius I (687–701). It became known as the Litany of the Saints, because of its second section, and consisted of:

An introductory *Kyrie*, followed by invocations of the Trinity, with the response 'Lord, have mercy on us';

The invocation of the saints;

The deprecations – supplications for deliverance, with the response 'Deliver us, Lord';

The obsecrations – supplications through various events of Christ's life, with the response 'Deliver us, Lord';

The intercessions – just one in the original, with the response 'We beseech you to hear us'; and

Concluding devotions to the Cross, and to Jesus Christ as the Son and Lamb of God.

This basic form underlies subsequent litanies, although the weighting and content of the various sections varied. At times as many as 200 saints were invoked! Litanies were used both as devotional prayers and as part of the liturgy of the Church. In the medieval period priests would use one as part of their private preparation for Mass. Processional litanies were popular and were used on Rogation Days, at the Easter Vigil, Ordinations, the Visitation of the Sick, the Consecration of Churches, during Lent and at times of emergency, and in some places they were used before the ordinary Sunday Mass.

Cranmer's litany was the first that was officially produced in the vernacular in England, and it signalled the start of the liturgical expression of the Reformation. In line with established practice to pray a litany at times of crisis, processions were ordered by Henry VIII in 1544 as he was about to invade France. For this Cranmer produced a new litany, which was based on that in the Sarum rite, but was heavily edited and had other material added. A privately produced English litany had already been circulated by one William Marshall in the second edition of his primer called *A Goodly Primer in English*. He had used Luther's litany of 1529 as the basis for it, and Luther's litany is also reflected in Cranmer's version, along with the processional litany of the Sarum rite, a litany from the office for the Visitation of the Sick, and other material.

This litany of 1544 began with invocations of the Trinity, which are repeated by the congregation, and followed by 'have mercy upon us miserable sinners', supplementing the *Kyries* with a pronounced penitential tone. The invocation of the saints was reduced to one to Mary, one to the angels, and one to the saints, omitting around 50 named saints. (This section was deleted altogether in the 1549 *BCP*.) The traditional sections of deprecations, obsecrations and intercessions are all included. However, Cranmer groups petitions together, rather than having just one petition between each response, and the responses are slightly changed, as for example adding 'Good Lord' to 'we beseech thee to hear us'. The intercessions end with petitions based on the *Agnus Dei* and *Kyries*, which are followed by the Lord's Prayer. After a collect and a final set of petitions, there are six further prayers, ending with what we now call a Prayer of St Chrysostom.

The litany came to be used more frequently as a devotional prayer than for processions, although that tradition remained – especially at Ordinations and on Good Friday. It was used in preparation for Holy Communion and then as an appendix to the daily offices, and was said or sung kneeling. The 1552 *BCP* puts it after Evening Prayer, with a rubric as part of its heading which says it is to be used on Sundays, Wednesdays and Fridays, or as commanded by the Ordinary. In 1662 this was clarified to read that it was to be said or sung after Morning Prayer on these days. This arrangement gave rise to the pattern of Morning Prayer, Litany and Holy Communion, that became the norm. The sequence was frequently terminated after Ante-Communion, creating a non-eucharistic Sunday morning service which remained standard until the eve of the Parish Communion Movement at the end of the nineteenth century.

In 1662 the final six prayers became separated out from the litany altogether and supplemented to form an enlarged section of Prayers and Thanksgivings upon Several Occasions, to 'be used before the two final Prayers of the Litany, or of Morning and Evening Prayer'. In *CW* these specific intercessory prayers are not provided. The expectation is that appropriate prayers of intercession and thanksgiving would be adopted by local churches from a wide variety of sources (see the section on Prayers in the Commentary on A Service of the Word above).

In the twentieth century the litany is not in widespread use, although it was revised for Series 3 and the *ASB*. In the latter, the only occasion on which it was invariably used was at an Ordination, but it could be used at Morning and Evening Prayer, replacing everything after the Apostles' Creed and ending with the Lord's Prayer, Collect of the Day, and the Grace, and parts of it were also offered as alternative forms of intercession for Holy Communion Rite A.

CW offers two versions of the litany: the first is that of the *ASB* with two minor changes; and the second is that of the *BCP* without any changes. The more modern form has seven sections, and when it is used, selections may be made from sections II–VI, but sections I and VII must always be used.

I   Simple invocations to the Father, Son, Holy Spirit and the Trinity.

II   The deprecations (supplications for deliverance). There are five of them expressing all manner of sinfulness and dangers of the world, from which we need deliverance.

III The obsecrations (supplications through the events of Christ's life). There are four of these, in which we remember Christ's birth, life and ministry, death on the cross, and resurrection and ascension, expressing our belief that the same Lord has power to save.

IV   Intercessions for the Church. The fourth *ASB* petition to 'enlighten your ministers with knowledge and understanding . . .' now includes the opportunity to name the local bishop.

V   Intercessions for the world: prayers for the leaders of the nations, for Queen and Parliament, the administration of law, and for all God's people and families. The fifth petition of the ASB has been changed to reflect growing ecological concerns, a sense of our global responsibility, and a less human-centred view of the world. 'Teach us to use the fruits of the earth to your glory, and for the good of all mankind' (ASB) has become 'Give us the will to use the resources of the earth to your glory, and for the good of all creation.'

VI   Intercession for those in need. In the petitions we ask for God's mercy on those suffering in a whole variety of ways and we remember those who have died.

VII   Conclusion. A very simple form compared with the collects and final set of petitions in the Litany of the BCP.

H. FORMS OF CONFESSION AND ABSOLUTION

Authorized confessions and absolutions include those contained in the BCP, those found throughout the various services in the CW main volume, and others in this separate section towards the end of the Service of the Word provision, which can be used as alternatives to those in the main services. In this section the resources are given under different thematic headings to aid the choice of appropriate material. It is a collection from a wide variety of sources. Some were first authorized in 1993, when they accompanied the first authorized form of A Service of the Word.

Confessions
There are three basic forms of confession:

Responsive forms
A simple phrase is repeated by the congregation, in response to the leader specifying particular things for which forgiveness is sought. That on the theme of Incarnation and Christmas is a responsive form written by Kenneth Stevenson. Five of the other responsive prayers come originally from Church Family Worship (ed. Michael Perry, 1986): on Cross, Failure in Discipleship (an expanded Kyrie form); on Resurrection, Heaven, Glory, Transfiguration, Death, Funerals; on Creation, Harvest; and on City, World and Society; and the first of two responsive General Confessions, 'God our Father . . .' The other responsive General Confession has as the response the Trisagion, an Eastern text which appeared occasionally in the West. The origins of this form lie in an anthem popular in medieval Germany, and taken up in the Canadian BAS.

Corporate prayers
Several are based on short passages of Scripture, arranged by Stuart Thomas: on Psalm 51 – Lent, Penitence; on Luke 15 – Reconciliation; and on Hosea 6 – Love, Peace. The prayer on the theme of Trinity, Mission, is again from Church Family Worship. Of the five corporate General Confessions, the first, 'God our Father . . .', was written by Bryan Spinks; two are confessions from the BCP revised by the Liturgical Commission, and two are from In Penitence and

Faith: Texts for Use with the Alternative Services, compiled by David Silk (Mowbray) one of which, 'Almighty God, long-suffering ...' was adapted from one first published in *My God, My Glory*, Eric Milner-White.

Kyrie confessions

These are short thematic or seasonal sentences between the petitions of the *Kyrie*. These sentences can link confession to the theme and message of the service. The texts in this section can be used as they are, or as a pattern for short sentence confessions that can be written locally. Provided they are followed by an authorized absolution and are penitential in nature, they can replace other confession. Of those offered in A Service of the Word, the first two, on the theme of Spirit and Word, have come from use at Portsmouth Cathedral; the fourth one, on the theme of City, came from use at Holy Trinity, Weald-stone ... were authorized in 19... . Some had used one phrase with *Kyries* as part of a response to the reading of the Ten Commandments in ... (canticle rite 1662), 'O Lord, have mercy upon us and incline our hearts to keep this law.' Others have also used ... between the traditional repetitions, but the extent of these is developed in these authorized confessions, and the choice opening a wide range of possibilities. Item ...

Absolutions

The introductory notes state that ... is possible for an absolution should be chosen which reflects the style ... or language and length of the confession. Some even written as matching patterns and are then capable of ... being systematic. However, any such pairing is not for itself ... Those persons choosing the form will need to make a judgement ... of their confession and absolution to use together. The absolutions are not as clearly affirmed as relating to particular aspects of life, season, or situation as the confessions. The frequency of the 'us/our' alternatives ... in the absolutions shows the expectation that these prayers will very often be used by lay people, with the declaratory style of the 'you' form being said only by bishops and priests.

They are from similar sources to the confessions, with the addition of three others. 'May the God of love and power ...' is adapted from the Scottish Liturgy of 1982, and the second and the prayers are from *PHG*. The first prayer is by Kenneth Stevenson; the third from *Church Family Worship*; the fifth and seventh by the Liturgical Commission; the sixth from *In Penitence and Faith*; the eighth and ninth by Stuart Thomas; the eleventh by Bryan Spinks. The remaining two are traditional.

1. CREEDS AND AFFIRMATIONS OF FAITH

The basic texts of the three creeds, the Nicene, Apostles' and Athanasian Creeds, are to be found as part of the main services in CW and BCP. This section of the volume offers some alternative forms and wordings.

The Nicene Creed

A responsive form is offered as well as an alternative corporate form. The latter omits the phrase 'and the Son' when speaking of the Holy Spirit (the '*Filioque* clause'), as ecumenical occasions need to be sensitive to the historic debate which has led to a division of opinion over whether this phrase should be used. These two versions of the Creed are given in 'we' form, which is as the original Council formulated the profession. There is also good reason for recognizing the corporate nature of the Eucharist and therefore declaring the faith of the Church as one when we meet as the Body of Christ, to share in communion with him and one another. (See Chapter 6 for a commentary on the Nicene Creed.)

The Apostles' Creed

The versions from the *BCP* and *ASB* are both given. These are in 'I' form, reflecting the origin as a baptismal creed, in which an individual profession of faith is made. In this context a short, simple, Trinitarian declaration of faith was made and a common shape for this began to emerge, maybe as early as the second century. Although the present form is from the eighth century, it clearly has earlier antecedents on which it relies. It appears to reflect a threefold questioning of the candidate.

In Anglo-Saxon times in Britain it was used as a personal devotion at Prime and Compline. In 1549 Cranmer made it part of Morning and Evening Prayer. It was learned in the vernacular throughout the medieval period, but Cranmer did not expect it to be recited by all in 1549: the minister would say it, and the Lord's Prayer, 'in a loud voice'. In 1552 the people were to join the minister in saying both. In 1662 it was given its acquired title, The Apostles' Creed.

The text in the *ASB* was from ICET. In *CW* it is given in three forms:

1. The ELLC text, except that *CW* did not accept the ELLC wording, 'Jesus Christ, God's only son', but retained 'his only son'. The major change here from the earlier ICET version is the substitution of 'who was conceived by the Holy Spirit' for 'He was conceived by the power of the Holy Spirit'. This simplification is an older and more literal translation. There is no reference to 'power' in the Latin, but it was added to avoid giving the impression that sexual activity took place. The wording was reversed because it was then felt that another impression was given, of Mary being overpowered by the Spirit and therefore not exercising her free consent. The relative pronoun 'who' stops the Creed from just being a whole string of statements.
2. The traditional wording of the *BCP*.
3. The ICET text, divided into three sections, each said in response to a prompting question, as in *PW* 0F3:58. The same format has been

used in *CW* Holy Baptism, but with the adapted ELLC text as the response to the three questions. This version gives expression to the Trinity in its threefold format as well as in the words of the questions. In the Baptism service the Trinitarian motif is carried through to the threefold action of dipping or pouring of water. The use of this profession therefore has profound links with the baptismal promises.

The Athanasian Creed
Reference is simply made back to the *BCP* for this, no text being given in *CW*.

Authorized Affirmations of Faith
1. Adapted from the alternative Profession of Faith in the *CW* Baptism service, by making the response a corporate 'we' rather than the personal 'I'.
2. This responsive form of the Athanasian Creed was modernized by the Liturgical Commission for *PW* (2F4:59). This adaptation is too far removed from the original to be called a creed, and is therefore put with the Affirmations of Faith.
3. This affirmation takes the form of a hymn by Timothy Dudley-Smith, published in *A Voice of Singing* (1993).
4–7. These last four affirmations are passages of Scripture which express aspects of the Christian faith (Philippians 2.6–11; 1 Corinthians 15.3–7; Revelation 4.8, 11; 5.9; 22.17; and Ephesians 3), all formerly published in *Church Family Worship* and *PW* (2F6; 6F7; 0F8; 0F9).

A Form for the Corporate Renewal of Baptismal Vows
As a profession of faith arises from a baptismal context, so there is good reason to focus particularly on the renewing of baptismal vows on occasion. A form is authorized for this, and is recommended for use no more than twice a year, preferably at Easter, Pentecost, or the Baptism of Christ in the Epiphany season, or at the start of a new ministry. Water can be used, by sprinkling or by signing oneself with the cross using water from the font. Symbolic action of this kind can enhance the sense of recommitment, but is not the custom of all Anglican churches. The form includes the Decision and the Profession of Faith (the Apostles' Creed in response to three questions) from the Baptism service. This is followed by a prayer, and can include the Affirmation of Commitment, which comes from the Canadian *BAS*, was in *PW* (0F10:62), and is now part of the *CW* Baptism service. It can also be used after any authorized Creed or Affirmation of Faith at any service.

References and Further Reading
Michael Botting, *Reaching the Families*, Church Pastoral Aid Society, London, 1969.
Michael Botting, *Teaching the Families*, Church Pastoral Aid Society, London, 1973.

Colin Buchanan, *The Lord's Prayer in the Church of England*, Grove Worship Series 131, Nottingham, 1994.

Timothy Dudley-Smith, *A Voice of Singing*, Hodder & Stoughton, London, 1993.

Petà Dunstan, *This Poor Sort: A History of the European Province of The Society of St Francis*, DLT, London, 1997.

Mark Earey, *Producing Your Own Orders of Service*, Church House Publishing, London, 2000.

Faith in the City, Church House Publishing, London, 1985.

Family Worship, Church Pastoral Aid Society, London, 1973.

R. C. D. Jasper (ed.), *Getting the Liturgy Right*, SPCK, London, 1972.

Trevor Lloyd, *A Service of the Word*, Grove Worship Series 151, Cambridge, 1999.

F. C. Mather, 'Georgian Prayer Book Reconsidered: Some Variations in Anglican Prayer Book Worship 1714–1830', *Journal of Ecclesiastical History* 36, 1985, pp. 255–83.

Eric Milner-White, *My God, My Glory*, SPCK, London, 1954.

Michael Perham (ed.), *The Renewal of Common Prayer*, SPCK/CHP, London, 1993.

Michael Perry (ed.), *Church Family Worship*, Hodder & Stoughton (for Church Pastoral Aid Society and Jubilate Hymns), London, 1986 and 1988.

Paul Roberts, David Stancliffe and Kenneth Stevenson, *Something Understood*, Hodder & Stoughton, London, 1993.

David Silk, *In Penitence and Faith: Texts for Use With the Alternative Services*, Mowbray, London, 1988.

David Stancliffe, 'Is There an Anglican Liturgical Shape?', in Kenneth Stevenson and Bryan Spinks (eds), *The Identity of Anglican Worship*, Mowbray, London, 1991, pp. 124–34.

John Wilkinson, *Family and Evangelistic Services*, Church Information Office, London, 1967.

Chapter 5

Preaching

Introduction

Behind the simple word 'sermon', is an expectation of God's activity through the ministry of preaching, by the Holy Spirit working in the hearts and minds of those who gather to hear and receive his holy Word. Throughout the history of the Church, preaching has accompanied the reading of Scripture as an intrinsic part of its worship. Although the Scripture itself is primary, its explanation, exposition, application, and the encouragement to engage with it in personal and corporate response has been fundamental to the practice of the Church.

The prologue of John's Gospel states the incarnational principle, that the Word was made flesh and dwelt among us (John 1.14). Jesus, the living Word of God, made God known in his ministry and in the witness of his life, death and resurrection. The Church is given the commission to continue the work of making God known, through its life, witness and work – by the power of the Holy Spirit. Preaching is understood as an integral part of this vocation.

But as well as being the Word, Jesus also preached the Word. He saw his words as being spirit and life (John 6.63). His understanding of the need for people to hear the words of the kingdom and receive them is vividly expressed in the parables. By the Spirit the Church is to continue to offer the good news of the gospel (Romans 10.14–15), and the words of life. The living Word of God brings life (1 Peter 1.22–25) and hope (Romans 15.4). It cuts through to the very centre of soul and spirit, and judges the thoughts and attitudes of the heart (Hebrews 4.12). It teaches, rebukes, corrects and trains, and equips for service (2 Timothy 3.14–17). The Word of God is living and active and is God's means of speaking to humanity. Preaching is part of the process of disseminating this living Word, so it is potentially life-changing and transformational. It interprets and applies the Scriptures, making connections between God's Word and the time, place and daily lives of the hearers.

A. HISTORY

No single thread of development can be traced through the history of preaching, but an historical overview shows how the sermon has related to the liturgy over the centuries. From such a survey, albeit a brief one, it is possible to identify types and styles which have come to the fore. This lays the foundation for thinking about what approach should be taken to the sermon in *CW* services.

The New Testament

Apart from Jesus' peripatetic ministry, which clearly demonstrates a life dedicated to proclaiming the kingdom, making God known, and offering the words of salvation, we have evidence for a variety of approaches to preaching in the New Testament.

As is described in the chapter on the Sunday lectionary later in this volume (Chapter 9), the systematic reading and exposition of Scripture was well-established Jewish practice in New Testament times. Both Jesus (e.g. in Mark 1.21; 6.2; Luke 4.15–21; 13.10) and Paul (e.g. in Acts 13.13–16) continued the Jewish pattern of teaching in the synagogue, possibly based on a given reading of Scripture. We also have examples of more thematic preaching such as in Thessalonica, when Paul reasoned from the Scriptures about Christ (Acts 17.2–3).

In the early Christian fellowships we see that instruction took place within a context of worship (Acts 2.42), and Paul teaches about the importance of the reading of Scripture, teaching, and prayer (1 Timothy 4.13). It is possible that the Gospels of Matthew, Mark, and John, and the book of Revelation, reflect the practice of a systematic and lectionary-type approach to teaching within the Christian community. Paul's epistles were read to the gathered church and were then circulated to others (1 Thessalonians 5.27; Colossians 4.16), which formed the basis of some of the teaching in the early years of Christianity.

Paul, Peter and others preached frequently in public. They taught in public meeting places, preached at times of miraculous healings, spoke in their defence after arrest or opposition, and debated with religious leaders, to give a few examples (Acts 17.13, 17–34; 21.37–22.22; 2 Corinthians 2.12; 10.16). His cry from the heart, 'How shall they hear without a preacher?' (Romans 10.13–15), underlies his drive to take the good news of the gospel to the Israelites.

The Early Church

Early extra-biblical documents also show that teaching and preaching were an important part of a gathering of believers. The *Didache* (probably first century) implies that the Church in Syria had a daily preaching ministry, with a large number of teachers. Justin Martyr in Rome (*c.* 150) records that the Scriptures are explained in the context of a Eucharist, and believers are exhorted to imitate godly ways, 'for as long as time allows'.

Centres of learning developed in which there was often daily preaching, such as in Alexandria where Clement (*c.* 150–215) was a renowned teacher. Some of the daily ministry was specifically for the catechumens during Lent. Churches had a variety of liturgical provision. For example Caesarea, to which Origen (*c.* 185–254) moved later in his ministry, had Sunday services with short sermons following the readings, two midweek services, and daily morning prayer with an hour-long sermon on the Old Testament. It is clear, therefore, that there was preaching at both eucharistic and non-eucharistic services. Instruction in the faith and the building up of the Church were given high priority. However, it is equally clear that this waned over subsequent centuries.

The Medieval Church in England

Preaching in the Middle Ages was of an inconsistent standard. Some sets of homilies were circulated, for example those of Aelfric (*c.* 955–1020), Abbot of Eynsham, which included sermons on liturgical feasts, doctrine and church history, for preaching in the common language at the Mass. There were some notable examples of good preaching, but in general the parish clergy rarely preached on Sundays except on special occasions. If there was a sermon it was usually catechetical, giving teaching on the central truths of the faith.

The Reformation

In the Reformation the ministry of the Word, in reading and preaching, regained a more central place. The Reformers' emphasis was on personal relationship with God, so preaching often focused on an individual's response to God. Sermons were once again seen as having life-changing potential. Services and the sacraments were considered to be of limited meaning without an accompanying emphasis on the Word of God. Luther advocated Mattins at 4–5 a.m. and Vespers at 5–6 p.m., with semi-continuous readings and preaching, showing a return to the early Church pattern of daily instruction. Other Reformers had a similar commitment to the preaching of the Word to ordinary people on a regular basis. At one point Thomas Cranmer's draft for Morning Prayer gave the option of omitting the rest of the service from the *Te Deum* onwards in order to make room for preaching, but this is not part of either the 1549 or 1552 Prayer Books.

In England a Book of Homilies was produced to ensure good teaching on important aspects of faith, by providing authorized texts for those who did not have the learning or ability to prepare their own sermons. The 1542 Convocation agreed to its preparation, and 12 homilies were issued in 1547 under Edward VI. Cranmer wrote five of them, on Scripture, salvation, faith, good works, and against the fear of death. Others were written on Christian love and charity, the misery of mankind, against whoredom and adultery, and against swearing and perjury. Twenty-one more homilies were authorized in 1571 under Queen Elizabeth. The homilies emphasized New Testament teaching and were all based on the Bible in the vernacular.

In the 1549 and 1552 Prayer Books the Lord's Supper was to include the preaching of a sermon or the reading of a homily. (The 1549 *BCP* was alone in allowing its omission on a 'workday' or in private houses with the sick.) In 1549 the rubric specifically states that if the people have not already been exhorted to 'receive worthily' in the sermon, then the exhortation is to be read. The need for people to understand what they were doing, and why, so that they could make sincere and serious response, was paramount. The preaching, exhortations, and the general didactic nature of liturgy were part of this overall strategy. It is perhaps surprising that there was no sermon explicitly included in Morning and Evening Prayer, given the renewed concern for teaching. Cranmer's unfulfilled expectation of a more frequent Communion may be responsible for this apparent omission. In the 1662 *BCP* there is the direction that the curate will teach the Catechism to children and others after the Second Lesson at Evening Prayer, but this is the nearest there is to putting a sermon into the Offices. In 1552 this teaching had been required half an hour before Evensong on Sundays and Holy Days. (See the rubric following the Confirmation Service in 1552 *BCP*, and the rubric at the end of the Catechism in the 1662 *BCP*.)

In the Counter-Reformation preaching was also emphasized. The Council of Trent in 1545 underlined its importance, calling for two sermons on Sundays, and for the better teaching of clergy to this end.

Post-Reformation

Sermons became an important reason for going to church. They began to be published, and people read them for pleasure. Preachers developed distinctive styles and emphases and even had their own followers, becoming well-known personalities. This passion for preaching and listening to sermons often came at the expense of an appreciation of the sacramental aspects of worship. The sermon could be very long, anything from one to three hours. Notes were taken and used in teaching households, and even children were expected to memorize them.

Increasingly there was a tendency to see worship as a supporting context for the sermon, rather than to see the sermon as an integral part of a wider activity. So Archbishop William Laud (1573–1645) found it necessary to say that the sermon was a limited tool for God in comparison to the presence of Christ in the sacrament. Although it tended to be the Puritan preachers who overvalued the sermon, some of them had a broader vision for worship, as the Puritan Thomas Adams shows:

> all our preaching is but to beget your praying; to instruct you to praise and worship God . . . Beloved, mistake not. It is not the only exercise of a Christian to hear a sermon; nor is that sabbath well spent that despatcheth no other business for heaven . . . God's service is not to be narrowed up in hearing, it hath greater latitude; there must be prayer, praise, adoration . . .

In the Commonwealth period the *Westminster Directory* (1645) gave instruction on how to preach the Word. After a prayer, a chapter of the Bible was read, as part of a systematic and continuous progression through Scripture. Singing followed, and then a long prayer preceded the sermon. After the sermon there was thanksgiving and the Lord's Prayer. The preaching was the focus of the meeting, with its power to transform lives and edify. But it was to be followed by the Lord's Supper, which was to happen 'frequently'.

The 1662 Prayer Book restored the liturgical worship of the pre-Commonwealth services, and so the sermon was once more officially in the context of Holy Communion. Nevertheless, the services of Morning and Evening Prayer had a sermon unofficially attached to them, and these, together with the infrequent celebration of the Lord's Supper, became the predominant pattern for most people for many years. Church design frequently reflected this by the prominent position given to the pulpit. Morning and Evening Prayer did not have provision for a sermon within the set liturgy until the revisions of the 1960s.

Eighteenth-Century Revival
Revival in the eighteenth century challenged the dryness and lack of spiritual depth, which became apparent as rationalism developed. Preaching had become a highly intellectual pastime. Emphasis centred on the responsibility of listeners to think, judge and act according to logic and reason, and to behave in a moral and rational way. In contrast, the revival preaching was a passionate challenge to personal faith. The field-preaching and peripatetic ministry of John Wesley (1703–91) and his brother Charles (1707–88), George Whitefield (1714–70), and others who followed them, reached thousands who did not normally go to church. The style was animated, and the attendant enthusiasm for God, and accompanying phenomena, even led to derision. The format was an exposition, with prayers and some singing. From this ministry there later arose a non-eucharistic preaching service, which became the foundation of Methodist and much Nonconformist worship. It comprised prayer, hymn, prayer, text, sermon, hymn, prayer, hymn, and blessing.

Revival also occurred in Anglican churches, with a renewed commitment to biblical exposition and preaching that called for a personal response of faith. A good example of this is the ministry of Charles Simeon (1759–1836). His expository preaching was based on a daily habit of rising at 4 a.m. for four hours of private prayer and devotional study of the Scriptures, along with a commitment to the liturgy and spiritual discipline of the Anglican Church.

Victorian Preaching
The Oxford Movement (from 1833) called for the Church to renew its spiritual life and reassert its spiritual authority in the nation. The Church was challenged to reform its structure and its worship. The commitment to the *BCP* remained firm but was accompanied by a desire to use its provision fully. As the movement developed, so did the recovery of the concept of non-verbal

aspects of liturgy as a powerful means of communication. There was an increased emphasis on the way the faith was expressed in form, ceremony, ritual, architecture, music, vesture, and colour, particularly in relation to the Eucharist. These aspects were seen as leading to an appreciation of the sacred mystery of God and a sense of the holy. In this, as in other matters, appeal was made to the early Church for the re-validation of practices lost in the Reformation. This idea of the liturgy being 'a sermon in action' was eagerly picked up by the later Tractarians and subsequent ritualists and the ecclesiologists of the Cambridge Camden Society.

Thus the two major trends which had been in evidence in the Church of England since the Reformation developed further. One was towards a sermon-based form of weekly meeting, and the other was towards a more sacramental approach. Although both used the *BCP* as the underlying form, the expression of Anglican worship was surprisingly diverse, and this led to tension. The sermon-based format led to concern that preaching had become a substitute for worship, rather than an integral part of it, and that the service of Holy Communion had become relegated to a minor role. Increasing ritualism led to concern at the prospect of returning to pre-Reformation theology and practice.

Word and Sacrament in the Twentieth Century

The advent of the First World War brought the sharp realization that both Word and sacrament were important. The Church was shocked at the extent of the ignorance of religion reflected by the troops. Along with other proposals, there was a call to establish Holy Communion as the central service on Sundays and to improve the teaching of the faith. Different patterns were tried. For example, in 1931 Archbishop William Temple proposed an 8.45 a.m. said service of Mattins up to the *Benedictus*, a 9 a.m. sung Holy Communion, and an 11 a.m. Sermon of at least 30 minutes with hymns and short prayers. Despite such attempts, practice remained divided into two main approaches. Where there was a non-eucharistic service with longer sermon, the Communion tended to be marginalized, and where the Communion Service was central, a limited role was given to preaching. As the Parish Communion Movement grew in strength, throughout the century but particularly in the post-war years, a number of churches embraced the service of Holy Communion and struggled with the pressure it put on the preaching ministry.

The emergence of the Liturgical Movement in the Roman Catholic Church on the Continent brought a renewed focus on the importance of both Word and sacrament. Among other emphases, there was a rediscovery of the Bible and of the importance of liturgy being in the vernacular. This movement later received its formal expression in the Second Vatican Council (1962–65), which underlined the intimate connection between words and rites, and decreed that there should be more reading from holy Scripture, that the ministry of preaching was important and should be biblically based, and that Bible services should be encouraged.

The liturgical revision of the 1960s in the Church of England similarly sought to establish the importance of both Word and sacrament. The expectation behind the structure of the Series 2 Holy Communion service, with its clear identification of the ministry of the Word, was that there should be 30 minutes for the ministry of the Word, including 15 minutes for the sermon, and 30 minutes for the celebration of the sacrament. However, to those committed to a preaching ministry, 15 minutes seemed restrictive, and the tension has not been entirely resolved. The broad nature of the Church of England is reflected in a continuing diversity of attitude towards the relation of Word and sacrament. While all agree on the importance of both, in practice the relative emphasis varies.

B. THE PURPOSE OF PREACHING

The history of preaching shows the existence of different emphases, which demonstrate a wide range of purposes. The use of the sermon in *CW* services will continue to reflect this range. Deciding on how to preach from the Lectionary provision will include decisions on purpose and style.

For example, when the Church gathers to praise God, we remember his mighty acts, throughout all history and most especially in his Son. So preaching can be *proclamatory*, as the historical events and their meaning are declared, and it can be *doxological*, as it points to the glory and majesty of God, drawing us to give him praise and honour. Preaching can also *explain* and *expound* the Word, so we can receive it with understanding. In *exhortation* we are encouraged to make a response, as we are challenged and convicted of the need for greater commitment and greater conformity of our lives to the will of God for us. When we come to meet with God in Holy Communion, the preaching can be *devotional*, to prepare us for the spiritual encounter and encourage a right attitude of heart, mind and spirit.

We meet for mutual encouragement and to support one another in the pains and joys of life. Hence preaching can be *pastoral*, applying the Scriptures to the issues and situations we face, as a community or as individuals. It can both arise out of, and speak into, the real-life world of the congregation. Such preaching may express God's mercy and his power to act, to bring liberation, redemption, healing, and love. It can nurture and sustain us, as we are brought comfort, assurance of God's promises and insight into God's perspective on our situation.

We meet for the building up of the faith community, and to be equipped for the work and witness of the kingdom. In preaching there can be *doctrinal instruction*, teaching the central truths and building up our knowledge and love of God through the Scriptures. The values and vision of the faith community are communicated and reinforced, fostering corporate response to God as he deals with his people. Preaching can also *equip for service*, and bring a challenge to do God's work, encouraging and inspiring disciples to go out into their daily lives, showing God's love, and offering the life of Christ through the Spirit.

These various purposes have led to different types of preaching, which have tended to handle the Scriptures in different ways. This in turn affects the shape and flow of services. Of course, any one single sermon may incorporate more than one type of approach.

Expository Preaching

Expository preaching draws out the meaning of a passage of Scripture, by examining its context, message and application. This is best brought out when recognizing the wider import of the relevant biblical book. Therefore expository preaching is usually done in conjunction with readings which continue from one service to another, in a systematic and comprehensive way. In the early Church this approach was often associated with daily preaching, a practice briefly revived by some Reformers. More frequent now is a weekly pattern, which carries a series of sermons on a particular book of the Bible. Because of the need for continuity in the readings, expository preaching tends to dictate the content of the rest of the service. The *CW* Sunday Lectionary has the principle of semi-continuous readings, giving some continuity in the Scripture reading from one service to another, but having some gaps and breaks. This opens up the possibility of expository preaching.

In expository preaching the starting point is always the text of the passage, the meaning of which is then elucidated and the application drawn. Through careful and consistent exposition there is the opportunity for building up a knowledge of God's Word and applying its truths to one's life. It requires commitment on the part of the congregation, for its consecutive nature means that regular attendance makes the best use of the teaching being given.

Thematic Preaching

This emphasis allows teaching needs to dictate the choice of Scripture to be studied. It is a didactic and doctrinal approach. The topic to be addressed is brought to the light and wisdom of God's Word, for guidance on how to deal with the issue being examined. Thematic preaching can affect the rest of the service by offering a ready-made theme for the other components of the liturgy. We see thematic preaching in the ministry of both Jesus and the apostles, as they taught central truths of the faith and used the (Old Testament) Scriptures in their message.

Most recently we see thematic preaching encouraged in the *ASB*. Although the weekly eucharistic Lectionary readings were chosen to be appropriate to the season, there was a supplementary section which suggested themes for each week of the Christian year. Originally envisaged as a helpful guide, in practice the themes quickly came to dictate the whole direction of the service and were specifically expressed within the sermon. At first this thematic approach was widely appreciated, opening up the opportunity to preach on important areas of faith and doctrine. The Lectionary, with the supporting collects, seasonal sentences, and post-communion sentences, gave the services a good, cohesive feel. This was to be commended. But the recurring cycle became restrictive and repetitive. It forced Scripture into being read through the lens of a particular application, which was sometimes inappropriate to the passage.

Festal or Liturgical Preaching

The Christian year has its own integrity as a programme of instruction for the building up of the Church. Reading about and preaching on the major events of Christ's life – birth, death, resurrection, and ascension – and the associated major doctrinal truths, provides a foundation course in Christianity. This has been understood throughout the Church's history, and is a primary cause for the formation of lectionaries. It is a kerygmatic (gospel-centred) programme of teaching.

However, the addition of less central festivals, which then displace other teaching, has been a cause of concern at various times in history, as it was in the Reformation. Some even saw the radically pruned Reformation Calendar as too restrictive. For example, the Puritans tended to downplay the importance of the Church year, feeling the need for greater freedom in teaching and preaching than it afforded. Preaching with the *CW* Lectionary illustrates the tension between a consecutive teaching approach and a festal-based approach. It tries to combine the two and only its continued use will prove how well it has managed the task.

Catechetical Preaching

It was common practice in the early Church to instruct candidates before and after baptism, giving rise to the particular genre of catechetical preaching. For example, the *Didache* sets out a syllabus for what is important for a candidate to learn before being baptized, in how to live life as a Christian and as a child of the light. The catechetical sermons of Cyril of Jerusalem (*c.* 315–86) also demonstrate a comprehensive and serious period of preparation, accompanied by discipline and self-examination on a daily basis over the period of Lent. This type of preaching is now effectively replaced by baptism preparation and confirmation classes, Alpha and Emmaus courses, and similar programmes. Liturgy relating to these has been suggested, such as prayers for those starting the courses and staged rites associated with initiation services. If these are eventually implemented, then catechetical preaching may regain a place in the Church's practice.

However, a similar type of preaching is the teaching of the faith to the whole congregation, as a refresher course for mature Christians and an introduction for newer attenders. For example, preaching through the Creeds, Ten Commandments, Lord's Prayer, or Beatitudes would revive the sense of their importance as basic building-blocks of faith, and would give an excellent coverage of the central Christian truths.

Topical Preaching

The necessity for topical preaching can arise for a number of reasons. There can be particular pastoral needs in a congregation which need addressing, or particular events – local or global – which focus issues or provoke serious questioning as to how to respond. Jesus used topical situations in his preaching, such as the actions of Pilate and the collapse of the tower at Siloam (Luke 13.1–5). The immediate experience of the congregation or the community can be addressed in a reflective way, offering the love and power of Christ and a biblical perspective on the situation. The choice of Scripture for such sermons will depend on the message envisaged. The manipulation of the set readings is not usually helpful as it risks distorting the real meaning of the passages.

Important though this kind of preaching is, a regular topical approach can be dominated by the preacher's agenda, and regular selectivity can leave large and important sections of Scripture unread and unexplained. Topical preaching needs to be balanced against the benefits of systematic teaching. The relationship of topical preaching to the rest of the service also needs consideration. In some circumstances it may be appropriate to allow the whole service to be governed by it, for example in the choice of hymns, the call to penitence, the intercessions and the Propers used in a Eucharist. But again, the regular use of this approach carries dangers of being too narrow.

Missionary Preaching

In response to the call to take the gospel to all nations, preaching can be proclamatory and kerygmatic, putting forward the truths concerning Christ. It can be apologetic, defending orthodoxy and defending belief itself. Or it can be exhortatory, offering a way forward for personal response to Christ. The relationship of this kind of preaching to worship raises an interesting question. Is it appropriate to ask or expect a non-believer to express the Christian faith in hymns, prayers, or other responses? There are five basic approaches to this.

1. The gathered community is the witnessing community. Coming into an environment of belief and sensing the reality of God's presence within the Body of Christ can lead to a desire to know him for oneself. Baptism and the Eucharist demonstrate the gospel truths and act as both a testimony to what is the core of Christian faith, and as an invitation to come into that faith, and into the family of faith.

2. The worshipping community has a responsibility to make the faith accessible to any who seek after God. This approach is usually linked with non-eucharistic services. The emphasis is on worship forms and content that are easy to use and in which everyone present can readily participate. This includes preaching a sermon which is accessible to all, both fringe visitors as well as church members, with the more concentrated teaching taking place on other occasions. Another approach

along the same lines is the recognition of the importance of invitation – reaching out to particular sectors of society or spheres of community life and specifically inviting them to a service devised for their needs.

3. The Church meets people where they naturally go for other purposes. There are a growing number of 'church plants', using schools, community halls, and other secular venues. This avoids asking people to come into a building and an environment which is strange to them. Traditional services and formats are seen as part of the barrier to faith, so these churches use all the liturgical flexibility offered over recent years to make services relevant and accessible. Dynamic and interactive models of preaching may also be appropriate in such venues.

4. There is the possibility of 'alternative worship', in which services and preaching are planned within an entirely different cultural framework. The language, ritual, and non-verbal aspects of the liturgy are radically evaluated, and only what is relevant to the specific social and cultural grouping is used. These services often use several media at once, and rely on indigenous creativity.

5. Presentations are made rather than holding services of a more traditional kind. An example would be mission services, sometimes now known as 'seeker services'. The aim is to provide specific occasions when the gospel message is communicated to non-believers in tailor-made events, combining music, drama, preaching, and simple prayer, and requiring the minimum of faith to participate.

It follows that different understandings of the purpose and role of preaching within liturgy, and different types of preaching, lead to different ways in which the sermon relates to the rest of the service. Thus, the various parts of the rite will be used in different ways. For example, the extent and content of the preparation section beforehand, and the nature of the response sections afterwards, will vary according to the aim and focus of the message. The occasion on which the sermon is delivered and the context to which it is addressed will either affect, or be affected by, the liturgical setting. By careful consideration of the balance and flow of the service, the sermon and liturgy work together towards enabling a whole encounter with God.

C. PREACHING WITH THE *COMMON WORSHIP* LECTIONARY

The *CW* Lectionary is radically different from that of the *ASB*. The pattern of semi-continuous reading of Scripture opens up the opportunity to expound books of the Bible on a week-by-week basis, to hear the great stories of the Bible read over several weeks at appropriate times of year, and to examine foundational events and doctrines over shorter periods using readings from different books.

The way the sermon relates to the rest of the service is also different, as the ready-made cohesion of a thematic approach is no longer provided. The Holy Communion collects, post communion prayers and other material are now governed by the season, and may not necessarily link with the message of the sermon. The theme of a service is likely to emerge from the reading on which the preaching is based, so co-ordination, consultation and communication within a church team have become even more necessary. For example, hymns cannot be picked months in advance to go with a set theme.

Outside particular seasons of the Church's year, the readings at any service are chosen to run independently of one another, as part of separate series that run through several weeks, rather than relating to a common theme on one day (see Chapter 9 on the Sunday Lectionary). After many years of theme-related readings in the *ASB*, this is going to confuse preachers who try to guess what theme it is that ties all the readings together. There may be some common ideas which are related to season, or emerge by coincidence, but the readings are not primarily intended to link together. The preacher therefore needs to view them over a period of weeks or months.

Where several people preach, some measure of co-ordination is required, and opportunities to study together or discuss the biblical book can be very helpful. Ministers will need to consider the requirements of the congregation, the balance of systematic exposition with seasonal preaching, and the balance of Old Testament and New Testament books covered. Overall planning of preaching will also need to take into account the requirement that all eucharistic services must have a Gospel reading. In a church with a varying service pattern, this will affect the choice of whether the principal, second service, or third service readings are followed. Many resources are being commercially produced to foster good preaching with *CW*. However, only local leaders can take decisions about what is most appropriate in their situation.

Permission is given in *CW* to alter or even opt out of the official Lectionary provision, within certain parameters. Departure from the Lectionary may be desirable for pastoral, preaching or teaching reasons, and this is allowed with PCC approval, apart from specified periods. From Advent 1 to the Presentation of Christ in the Temple and from Ash Wednesday to Trinity Sunday and on All Saints' Day, the Lectionary should be followed, at least at the principal service (Lectionary Note 7). However, it is also acknowledged that there may be reasons for having even greater flexibility when using A Service of the Word. So there the Notes allow for the protected period to be slightly shorter – from Advent 3 to the Baptism of Christ, and from Palm Sunday to Trinity Sunday. Although there are distinct advantages to staying with the Lectionary, opportunities to do a thematic series of sermons, or a catechetical series, or exposition on another part of the Bible, may be welcome in a local situation.

CW, especially in the Service of the Word, also encourages a creative and dynamic approach to communicating the Word of God. The sermon may be delivered by more than one person, or involve the use of drama, or be divided into parts to allow for greater engagement with, and response to, God's Word (see the section on 'Sermon' in Chapter 4).

The new Lectionary puts the integrity of the Scriptures at the heart of the ministry of the Word. It opens up the possibility of the congregation hearing them read and explained as they were written – with stories told and teaching given as they occur in their context, and arguments worked through systematically. Re-discovering the cohesion of the Bible will help in its understanding and application.

Any preaching can be a catalyst for engagement with God. In our worship we encounter God, and through the preached message the Holy Spirit can awaken awareness of him, stir the conscience, and provoke a response. The response may be corporate or individual. It can be immediate, with the liturgy providing the vehicle for that response, and it can go on in subsequent days as we allow ourselves to be shaped and formed by what we have heard. Consequently there is a need to see the liturgy of the Word as a climax in a service, especially in a Service of the Word, the Introduction to which directs that it 'not be so lightly treated as to appear insignificant compared with other parts of the service'.

References and Further Reading

William Challis, *The Word of Life*, Marshall Pickering, London, 1997.

Martin R. Dudley (ed.), *Like a Two-Edged Sword: The Word of God in Liturgy and History*, Canterbury Press, Norwich, 1995.

Donald Gray (ed.), *The Word in Season*, Canterbury Press, Norwich, 1988.

John Leach, *Responding to Preaching*, Grove Worship Series 139, Cambridge, 1997.

Hughes Oliphant Old, *The Reading and Preaching of the Scriptures in the Worship of the Christian Church*, 3 vols, Eerdmans, Grand Rapids, 1998–9.

Tim Stratford, *Interactive Preaching: Opening the Word and then Listening*, Grove Worship Series 144, Cambridge, 1998.

T. Thomson, *Preaching as Dialogue*, Grove Pastoral Series 68, Cambridge, 1996.

William H. Willimon and Richard Lischer (eds), *Concise Encyclopedia of Preaching*, Westminster/John Knox, Louisville, 1995.

Chapter 6

Holy Communion

A. HISTORY

Jewish Precedents

Many religions have included among their practices the consumption by worshippers of food sacrificed to a deity. In doing so, fellowship is established, not only with the deity, but also among the offerers. But early Judaism was distinctive in that all meals were seen as religious occasions, and so were not to be conducted without prayer. Thus, by blessing God for his bounty, pious Jews continually reminded themselves that all they had were the gifts of God.

At meals such as that on the Sabbath, the focus of the week, wine would be drunk and the blessings were said corporately. All would first wash their hands ritually and then the person deemed most senior would stand, and, holding the bread, would bless God for it on everyone's behalf. They in turn would respond 'Amen'. Then he would break and distribute it. The meal would be eaten, and concluded with a final cup of wine, which, after a blessing similar to that used over the bread, would be passed around the table.

The wording of the prayers used was not prescribed until a later period, but they had their origin in two types of Jewish prayer. One of these is the *berakah*, an example of which is found in Genesis 24.27, where Abraham blesses God for finding a wife for Isaac. The format involved an opening blessing, a descriptive phrase, and a clause indicating the reason for the blessing. Thus there is remembrance of gifts given, a confession or acknowledgement that it is God's action, and a proclamation of the same to anyone else present. Similar to this was the *hodayah*, in which the passive opening formula ('Blessed be God') was replaced by a more active, first-person clause ('I/we confess to you, O God, that . . .'). An example can be found in Isaiah 12.1. When prayers of this type were translated into Greek, the verb *eucharisteo* ('I give thanks') began to be favoured, and thus a note of gratitude crept in to the formula.

At the annual Passover feast, the meal involved the eating of a lamb which had been sacrificed in the Temple, and of special foods, such as unleavened bread and herbs. The youngest person present was supposed to ask about these traditions, which ensured a re-telling of the Exodus story, thus again enabling the recollection, acknowledgement and proclamation of what God had done. Furthermore, there was also a sense of a continuing involvement in these salvific acts of the past, as the ritual encouraged all Jews to consider themselves as having personally taken part in the Exodus. And there was also the expression of hope for a Messianic deliverance and a consummation of God's kingdom.

The First Century

The Synoptic Gospels tell us that the Last Supper was a Passover meal. John's Gospel disagrees, indicating that Jesus died as the Passover lambs were being sacrificed, which would suggest the previous day for the meal. At any rate, the Last Supper took place within the context of the Passover season, even if it were a day early. This means that we can know a little more than the evangelists tell us about that final meal.

It is reasonable to presume that Jesus followed traditional ritual to some extent, although we are told that he offered a new interpretation, relating the bread and wine to his own body and blood, and invited his friends to remember him in this way (Matthew 26.26–29, Mark 14.22–25, Luke 22.14–20, 1 Corinthians 11.23–26). Owing to a discrepancy in Luke, it is not entirely clear in which order the bread and wine came, nor indeed whether there is anything to be inferred from a possible reversal of the order.

Nevertheless, had the Christian Eucharist been merely a reworking of the Passover meal, it would presumably have become only an annual rather than a weekly event. The Gospels describe many occasions when Jesus ate with his disciples and others during his lifetime, and several of his post-resurrection encounters with them are said to have taken place in connection with meals, and on the 'first day' of the week (e.g. Luke 24.30f). This suggests that the Eucharist was as much a continuation of the regular meal fellowship the disciples had enjoyed with Jesus as it was a remembrance of the Last Supper and of his death. In its celebration, they were assured of his living presence with them and looked forward to the coming of the kingdom and the heavenly banquet, of which the Eucharist was a foretaste.

These early Eucharists were probably complete meals eaten by the Christian community on the evening of the first day of the week ('the Lord's day'), and involved the familiar Jewish rituals, but now directed in remembrance of Jesus. The thanksgivings soon began to refer explicitly to Jesus and to what God had done through and in him (1 Corinthians 11.26). The meal itself was a shared event, with contributions brought by everyone, and although they would meet in someone's home, that person was not the host in the sense of being the provider of all the food. In this respect, and in the informal ministry of the Word that might follow the meal, first-century Christian practice was similar to some Jewish fellowship meals.

The Second and Third Centuries

As Gentiles became Christians, this very Jewish eucharistic practice came under pressure. Culture clashes and misunderstandings arose, and St Paul certainly found the need to complain about practices in Corinth (1 Corinthians 11.17f). Persecution also occurred sporadically, making meetings and catering difficult and dangerous. Thus, by the second century, when Justin Martyr describes the Christian practice known to him, several things had changed. No longer was the Eucharist a complete meal in the evening, but it took place as an act of worship, apparently in the morning. Meals did continue in Christian circles, but were now distinct from eucharistic services.

In the second century we also find that the eucharistic action was preceded by a liturgy of the Word with prayers, not unlike contemporary synagogue practice. There would be readings from the Old Testament and from writings that would eventually form the New Testament, and then the president (as Justin calls him) preached. Intercessions followed, and a kiss of peace was shared before the bread and wine (the latter mixed with water according to usual Eastern custom) were brought forward. Sometimes this ministry of the Word would be replaced by baptisms of new converts.

The Eucharist proper would then begin. The president would take bread and wine and give thanks over both. The prayer(s) for this were not yet definitively prescribed, as Justin says that the president gave thanks as best he could, and the others responded 'Amen'. Then came the breaking of the bread, and both bread and wine were distributed to everyone present, and, if necessary, taken to any who were unable to be there.

Tertullian and Cyprian, writing in the third century, tell us that any who were not yet baptized or who were under some disciplinary measure were dismissed from the room before the Christian community began its prayers, and that the communicants each brought some bread and wine for the service, and were allowed to take it home afterwards for ritual consumption during the week.

The Fourth Century Onwards

As we move through time, more and more evidence of liturgical practice becomes available and geographical influences and traditions become discernible. A key change came with the Constantinian adoption of Christianity as the Roman religion, which meant that the celebration of the Eucharist now became a more public event, and this new status admitted the influence of Roman court ceremonial to the liturgy. The unbaptized were no longer dismissed after the ministry of the Word, and further prayers, in addition to the intercessions and the eucharistic prayer, were gradually added. Eucharistic prayers themselves were expanded to include such elements as the *Sanctus* and an account of the Last Supper (usually called the institution narrative), as well as taking on a greater intercessory dimension, with prayer being offered not only for those receiving the sacrament, but also for any for whom its benefits were desired.

Sociologically, the context of Eucharist had changed, and the number of those attending had grown considerably, altering the close community feel that it had in the second century. The Eucharist remained a community event in which Christ's presence was experienced, but greater emphasis was now being placed on his presence in the elements themselves. A specific petition for the consecration of bread and wine, praying that they become the body and blood of Christ, began to be added to eucharistic prayers. In Eastern rites this was brought about by expanding the *epiclesis* (a petition for the descent of the Spirit) in the latter part of the eucharistic prayer; in the Roman rite, the petition for consecration was inserted prior to the narrative of institution. Thus two different theories arose: that the bread and wine were consecrated either by *epiclesis*, or during the recital of the institution narrative. The West came to hold the latter view, while the East believed that both were necessary.

It became appropriate for 'all mortal flesh to keep silence' in the presence of Christ in bread and wine. This reverential approach brought about significant changes in practice: an increase in gestures and expressions of adoration, and a decline in the frequency of the reception of communion among the laity. Church leaders thought that many of the new converts were behaving inappropriately in church, and while they tried to encourage a more reverent attitude towards the sacrament, many people were made to feel unworthy and were deterred from reception altogether. The altar table, which had customarily been placed in the midst of the people, with the president behind it, was gradually moved away and placed in an enclosed 'sacred space' at the end of the building, and later concealed behind a screen.

Medieval Rites

Sacrifice is a theme at the heart of the Eucharist. The notion that Christ is the Passover Lamb slain for all appears very early on (e.g. 1 Corinthians 5.7), and insofar as the Eucharist is a memorial of his sacrifice, it is not surprising that it is itself described as a sacrifice in subsequent centuries. In the medieval period, however, the ordinary people came to see the Mass as a *new* sacrifice offered explicitly for the living and the dead, with the priest officiating at this sacrifice.

In the earlier tradition, it was rare for a priest to preside at the Eucharist, which was the bishop's prerogative. Priests and deacons would be present and would take their proper roles, but as Christianity spread, it became more common for a congregation to experience the ministry of no more than a single priest, and episcopal High Mass became something of a rarity. The priests also began to conduct the liturgy not so much *with* the people as *for* them. Indeed, even if there were nobody present, the prayers of the priest were deemed to be spiritually effective for them. This led to the development of the 'private Mass' from the eighth century onwards, and since it was believed that the more Masses were celebrated, the better the benefit for the soul (particularly the departed soul), unattended Masses began to proliferate.

By the end of the Middle Ages most communicants were receiving the sacrament only about twice a year, and were passive observers at the Sunday Mass for the rest of the time. Certain parts of the eucharistic prayer were held by the clergy to be sacred, and were now recited in secret, inaudibly. The practice of kneeling for prayer and reception of communion was adopted, with bread and wine being fed directly into the recipient's mouth. Eventually, for fear of spillage of the sacred blood, the congregation was denied the chalice altogether, and with the increased use of special unleavened bread, the practice of bringing gifts for the offertory also died out. The laity became spectators and hearers of an event that took place behind a screen, and was conducted in Latin, a language they did not speak. A bell was rung at significant moments, when they would look up from their private devotions to observe the elevation of the bread and wine.

There was, however, some connection between priest and people. Between the ministry of the Word and the eucharistic prayer might come a vernacular element known as 'Prone', which comprised a sermon, intercessory biddings and instruction on the Ten Commandments, and this did at least admit of some variety and interest.

The Reformation

In opposition to medieval theologians, the sixteenth-century Reformers maintained that there was no offering of Christ to the Father in the Eucharist, only the sacrifice of oneself, with thanks and praise, through Christ to the Father. They also insisted there should be no eucharistic celebration at which both clergy and people did not receive communion, in the form of both bread and wine. However, they debated the nature of the presence of Christ in the Eucharist, and there was some disagreement among them over this question.

Martin Luther rejected the traditional doctrine of transubstantiation, inherited from Thomas Aquinas, but still retained belief in the real, objective presence of Christ in the bread and wine. This, for him, amounted to consubstantiation, in which the substance of bread and wine remained along with the substance of body and blood. Luther was not so radical, therefore, as some other Reformers, preferring to simplify the eucharistic rite and translate it into German, replacing the eucharistic prayer and its reference to the sacrifice of the Mass with a straightforward recitation of the institution narrative.

Ulrich Zwingli in Zürich disagreed with Luther, denying his idea that Christ could be both ascended and glorified, and also in the bread and wine. For Zwingli, Christ intended the eucharistic elements merely to *signify* his body and blood in the midst of an act of memorial. True 'communion' in this context was between God and believer independently of the reception of bread and wine. The Eucharist was an aid to devotion, but not itself the means of grace. Thus it need not be celebrated frequently, and, when it was, it was almost as a supplement to the ministry of the Word.

John Calvin, in Geneva, rejected Luther's position, but was not as extreme as Zwingli. For him, Christ offers himself in communion, and is received in faith. Calvin's orders of service were not dissimilar from Zwingli's, but inasmuch as the Eucharist was held to be an instrument of grace, Calvin preferred a weekly celebration. Ultimately though, across the Reformed Church, a rarer celebration of the Eucharist became the norm.

The Reformation in England

Thomas Cranmer's blend of the views already mentioned formed the basis of the Church of England's eucharistic theology. He rejected transubstantiation and the sacrificial nature of the Mass, maintaining that the bread and wine remained as such before, during and after consecration. Yet, when received in faith, Christ becomes really present in that reception.

His first step along the road to reform was in 1547 with the stipulation of the use of English for the readings, Creed, Lord's Prayer and Commandments. Later in the same year, Parliament directed that communion be received by the people in both kinds, and in March 1548 a set of suitable communion devotions for insertion into the Latin Mass appeared.

Only a year later, the Latin went, and the first full English eucharistic rite was authorized. Notwithstanding the English text, altar and vestments were retained, and so the service might have looked like a mere translation to the ordinary worshipper. There were differences though: the 'offertory' became a focus for almsgiving; there was to be no elevation of the bread or wine; and any references to the sacrifice of the Mass were expunged from the new text. An offering of oneself, and of praise and thanksgiving, was included; and the eucharistic part of the service was not to proceed if no one was willing to receive with the priest. The practical consequence of this was that, since reception of communion had become a rare event for most people, the Sunday service began to feature only Morning Prayer, the Litany and Ante-Communion.

1549 did not go far enough for some, and another revision appeared in the Prayer Book of 1552. Now there was to be no ambiguity over the theology expressed: the eucharistic rite became an explicit manifestation of the belief that it was intended as the eating of bread and wine in grateful remembrance of Christ's Passion. The word 'Mass' was abandoned and clergy were instructed to wear only cassock and surplice, and to stand at the north side of a linen-covered wooden table set up east–west in the chancel. The Ten Commandments were added near the beginning, and this, together with its sparse content, gave the rite a strongly penitential flavour. There was to be no singing, except for the *Gloria in Excelsis*, which was moved to the end of the service as an expression of the praise that those who had received communion were now made worthy to offer.

The structure was also rearranged in other ways (see Figure 6.1). The intercessions were moved out of the eucharistic prayer, and placed earlier in the service, followed by confession and absolution. The eucharistic prayer itself evolved into a prayer for fruitful reception, with the petition to bless the elements replaced by the request that those receiving the bread and wine might be partakers of Christ's body and blood. The prayer now terminated abruptly

1549	1552
Lord's Prayer	Lord's Prayer
Collect for Purity	Collect for Purity
Introit Psalm	
Kyries	Ten Commandments
Gloria in excelsis ————————	
Collect of the Day	Collect of the Day
Collect for the King	Collect for the King
Epistle	Epistle
Gospel	Gospel
Creed	Creed
Sermon	Sermon
Exhortation to Communion———	
Sentences and almsgiving	Sentences and collection of alms
Taking of bread and wine	
	➤ Prayer for the Church
	➤ Exhortation to Communion
	┌ Invitation
	│ Confession
	│ Absolution
	└ Comfortable Words
(Eucharistic prayer:)	
Sursum corda	Sursum corda
Preface and Sanctus	Preface and Sanctus
Prayer for the Church ———	➤ Prayer of Humble Access
Prayer of Consecration————	➤ Prayer for Worthy Reception
Prayer of Oblation ———————	
Lord's Prayer ———————	
Peace	
Invitation	
Confession	
Absolution	
*Comfortable Words*___	
Prayer of Humble Access ———	
Communion (and Agnus Dei)	Communion
Scriptural Sentences	
	➤ Lord's Prayer
	➤ Prayer of Oblation *or*
Prayer of Thanksgiving	Prayer of Thanksgiving
	➤ Gloria in excelsis
Blessing	Blessing

(Elements in italics in the first column indicate material drawn from the 1548 'Order of the Communion')

Figure 6.1
A comparison of the structure of the eucharistic rites of the first two English prayer books.

after the institution narrative, and the communion followed immediately, with what had been the final part of the prayer deferred until afterwards as the prayer of oblation. Ordinary bread and wine were to be used, and the leftovers were for the priest's own use. What was distributed was to be placed in the communicants' hands, while they knelt, and the priest's words entreated them to remember that Christ died and shed his blood for them, rather than making explicit any theology of a real presence.

The 1559 *BCP* made some small changes, among them the combination of the 1549 and 1552 words of administration, and the addition of some (perhaps deliberately) vague instructions about vestments. During the Elizabethan period it was also permitted to put the table where the altar would have stood when it was not being used for the eucharistic service, and unleavened bread was reintroduced for the communion.

1662 and After

By the seventeenth century many clergy were reverting to wearing more than a surplice at the Eucharist, and to placing the table in the 'altar' position. The Scottish rite of 1637 attempted to be a bit more 'catholic' than the 1559 book had been, and thus, after the Restoration of the Monarchy in 1660, the high-church party sought to bring the Scottish rite to bear on the proposed revisions. There was little desire for change in Parliament, however, and Puritan influence was still strong. Thus the changes were few, and are mostly found among the rubrics. The word 'offertory' returns, and a new mode of offering alms in a dish to the priest (rather than placing them in a box) was introduced. The priest received these offerings and placed them on the table, with the bread and wine. The departed are again commemorated, but there was no direct prayer for them, nor any mention of the saints. Directions for taking the bread and wine into the priest's hands during what was now called 'The Prayer of Consecration' were added to an unchanged text. A rubric about the reverent consumption of leftovers was added, and one about kneeling to receive the elements, omitted in 1559, was restored.

In 1927/8 there was an attempt to revise the Prayer Book. For many, the 1662 eucharistic rite did not reflect their own theological position, and so a number of changes were proposed. Among them were that the priest was no longer to be required to stand at the north side of the table; in place of the Commandments, Christ's Summary of the Law could be substituted; the Creed and *Gloria* could be omitted on weekdays; and in the intercessions, prayer for the departed returned. At the heart of the debate, however, lay the Prayer of Consecration, and a form closer to that of 1549 was proposed, with the Prayer of Oblation restored after the institution narrative and an *epiclesis* inserted in this latter part of the prayer, bringing it into line with many ancient rites.

This revised Prayer Book was, however, ultimately rejected. Evangelicals disliked the inclusion of self-oblation before communion, and Anglo–

Catholics disliked the new *epiclesis* because it appeared to deny the efficacy of the institution narrative. And although parts of the book were used unofficially, its Communion Service was not generally adopted. Instead, the so-called Interim Rite came into use among those who wanted a revision of the service. This re-ordered parts of the 1662 service into a more classical shape: the Prayer of Humble Access was placed before the *Sursum corda* and *Sanctus* rather than after it, and the Prayer of Oblation and the Lord's Prayer were located after the institution narrative, but without the addition of the *epiclesis*.

Nevertheless, desire for official revision remained. In an increasing number of parishes the main service on a Sunday morning was now a Eucharist, and something other than the 1662 rite was called for there.

Alternative Services and the ASB

In 1965 the first series of Alternative Services included a Communion Service similar, but not identical to, that proposed in 1928. Old Testament readings were introduced, and three options were allowed for the eucharistic prayer: 1662 unchanged, the Interim Rite, and a version of the Interim Rite in which the actual self-oblation was removed from the Prayer of Oblation and placed after the communion. The service, which also included prayer for the departed in the intercessions, was authorized in November 1966, only just securing the necessary majority in the Church Assembly.

At the same time, the newly created Liturgical Commission was working on a more drastic revision, Series 2, which appeared in first draft in 1965. This offered a service with a distinct pre-eucharistic shape of readings, sermon, Creed, intercessions and penitence, leading into a eucharistic rite which clearly distinguished the four actions of taking the bread and wine, thanksgiving over them, the fraction and the sharing of communion. Gregory Dix's book, *The Shape of the Liturgy* (1945), was influential in providing an historical rationale for such an approach to revision. The rite was enthusiastically received, and so the Commission produced a completed draft in 1966, which was authorized from July 1967 and widely adopted.

The next stage was to introduce a rite in contemporary language. Around this time, the ecumenical International Consultation on English Texts (ICET) produced *Prayers We Have in Common* (1970), a set of English texts, including the Creed, the *Gloria in Excelsis* and the Lord's Prayer, in modern language. Thus by 1971 the ground had been prepared for Series 3, which was radical in language and format. After some revision, it was authorized for use in November 1972. The rite introduced several new features, including congregational acclamations in the eucharistic prayer after the institution narrative and at the end of the doxology, together with an unusual form of the dialogue before the *Sursum corda*, 'The Lord is here/His Spirit is with us'. The ICET proposals were adopted with some minor changes, and there was a much greater amount of seasonal material for Proper Prefaces, introductory and post-communion sentences, and blessings.

This rite was very popular, but Series 2 also continued to be widely used, and so a revised version, combining both the Series 1 and 2 rites into a single form, was authorized in July 1976. This followed the Series 2 structure with the addition of various optional texts from Series 1, notably the intercessions, the eucharistic prayer and the post-communion prayer. Together with more flexible rubrics and material in the appendices, this produced a service not dissimilar to variations of 1662 that were being commonly used.

Finally, it was decided to undertake a full revision of the Series 3 service before the publication of the *ASB*. The Liturgical Commission's proposals contained no radical changes, but a host of minor improvements. For the first time, rubrics permitted the use of the penitential material either at the beginning of the service or after the intercessions, and versions of the Series 1 and 2 eucharistic prayers were added. The General Synod submitted a large number of amendments to the detail of the service, so that this was perhaps the most revised and considered service in the entire *ASB*. The principal changes in the Synod included the addition of another eucharistic prayer based on that in the *Apostolic Tradition* of Hippolytus, and an appendix containing a form of the rite following the pattern of the 1662 Prayer Book. This service was included in the *ASB* as Rite A, and the Series 1 & 2 revised service as Rite B – the only service in the book in traditional language.

From ASB to CW

In 1991 the General Synod asked that new eucharistic prayers suitable for use when children were present be prepared, and the Liturgical Commission returned with five prayers, though none of these was exclusively for use when children were present. Nonetheless, the Synod asked the House of Bishops to proceed. The House responded by introducing two of the prayers to the Synod in October 1994, and the Revision Committee adopted four of the five original proposals, together with two of their own, one of which had been drafted in collaboration with the Board of Education and was for use with children. In February 1996 these prayers failed to receive 'Final Approval' in the Synod, because the necessary two-thirds majority was not reached in the House of Laity (the voting was: Bishops 25–10, Clergy 164–44, Laity 135–81). These prayers had been seen as the first stage of revision for the 2000 book, and it was anticipated that they could be used immediately with Rite A, and form part of the revised rites being worked on.

In spite of this setback, the Commission published its proposals for revision in July 1996, *Holy Communion Rites A & B Revised* (GS 1211), which omitted any texts for the Rite A eucharistic prayers and Lord's Prayer. The Commission put forward a conservative revision of Rite A, judging that people were generally happy with that rite. For Rite B, however, it essentially proposed a traditional language version of Rite A, with the same structure, and the same choices at the same points. While the Revision Committee of the General Synod was at work on these proposals, the Commission published separate proposals entitled *The Prayer Book as Used: Additional Work for the Current Revision Committee on Holy Communion Rites A & B Revised* (GS Misc 487), and as a result of this, the Committee reorganized the revised Rites A and B as Order One in modern and traditional language forms, added a version of the Eucharist in the 1662 Prayer Book as commonly used as Order Two, and adapted the *ASB*'s conclusion to Rite A 'according to the pattern of the *BCP*' as a complete modern language version of Order Two.

Meanwhile, in January 1998 the Commission published six new eucharistic prayers for trial use in selected parishes, under the terms of the new Canon B5(a). Because of the restriction in the Standing Orders of the General Synod preventing an identical text being reintroduced within the lifetime of the same Synod, these had to be different from the previous six which had failed to be authorized. A revised version was published in June 1998 as GS 1299 and introduced into the Synod, which then added two more prayers as part of the revision process, one of which was substantially the same as one of the failed six and the other was drafted at a late stage to meet popular demand in the General Synod for more congregational participation – so strong a demand as to cause Synod procedures to be varied to allow for such a late addition.

The text of one line of the Nicene Creed occupied a considerable amount of time in the Synod, and the Creed was eventually taken as a separate item for authorization. The contentious issue was the translation of the Greek word *ek* before the words 'Holy Spirit' and 'the virgin Mary' in reference to the incarnation. In 1980, the Synod had preferred to render the word as 'of', rather than ICET's 'from'. In 2000, ELLC (ICET's successor) had decided to accept 'of', but now the Synod voted for 'from'. Finally, however, all the pieces were in place, and the Holy Communion Service received the necessary two-thirds majorities in each of the three Houses in February 2000.

B. ORDER ONE

The Title

The service of Holy Communion has been known by a range of titles, and some of these are retained in the title used in *CW*. The New Testament refers to 'the breaking of the bread' (Acts 2.42), 'communion' (1 Corinthians 10.16) and 'the Lord's Supper' (1 Corinthians 11.20). Justin Martyr and others in the second century refer to the 'eucharist' (meaning 'thanksgiving'), and by the fourth century the 'sacrifice' and the 'offering' appear. In the East the term 'The Liturgy' became the principal name, while in the West 'Mass' became dominant. This originally referred to the dismissal at the end of the service (Latin, *ite, missa est*).

In the 1549 Prayer Book the rite is called 'The Supper of the Lord and the Holy Communion, commonly called the Mass', and in 1552 this became 'The Order for the Administration of the Lord's Supper, or Holy Communion', a title which was continued in 1662. The title 'The Eucharist' was used in the

Episcopal Church in the USA from 1804 onwards and this usage spread widely. In the *ASB* the service was called 'The Order for Holy Communion also called The Eucharist and The Lord's Supper', and despite attempts to change the order to put 'Eucharist' first, this has remained as the composite title (with the addition of the words 'the Celebration of', to emphasize the distinction between the title of the whole rite and the act of receiving the eucharistic elements).

The Gathering

In the first section of the service the congregation gathers together and prepares for worship. In essence it may be very brief – no more than the greeting and the collect – but the addition of other elements helps both gathering together to form a community and preparation to listen to the Word of God and celebrate the Eucharist.

The service may begin with a formal entry of the president and other ministers. Only with the legalization of public Christian worship under the Emperor Constantine was an opening procession introduced. Earlier, the ministers would have simply taken their place among the congregation, but by the fifth century a formal procession of the ministers, together with the book of the Gospels and perhaps preceded by candles and incense, was established, in a manner similar to that used by civil officials on state occasions. From the time of Pope Celestine (422–32) the procession was accompanied by the singing of Psalms and congregational antiphons. This lengthy procession was severely curtailed in places where there was a smaller building, fewer ministers, and little or no choir. In the Sarum order, the entrance rite was reduced to an antiphon, just one verse of a Psalm, *Gloria Patri*, and a repetition of the antiphon. The 1549 *BCP* provided an introit Psalm (or portion of a Psalm) followed by the *Gloria Patri* for all Sundays and other feasts. These disappeared in 1552, but in the reign of Elizabeth I hymns and anthems were permitted to be sung at the beginning and end of any rite. Series 2 permitted a hymn or Psalm as an introit, and Series 3 added optional seasonal scriptural sentences. In *CW* specific sentences are not included, but Note 4 allows suitable sentences to be used to accompany the president's greeting.

The entry may be accompanied by a hymn, and 'a Bible or Book of the Gospels may be carried into the assembly' (Note 6). The service may also begin with the Trinitarian formula. Occurring in Matthew 28.18, it came to be the universal formula associated with baptism. Its first appearance in the Mass was as the opening of the medieval office of preparation, to be said by the priest in the vestry or at the foot of the altar. It was not included in the 1549 *BCP* or any subsequent English revision, although the 1928 proposed book did provide an act of devotion for use before the service which began with the invocation of the Trinity. In the current Roman rite this opening invocation is mandatory, but in *CW* it is optional and deliberately printed in a lighter typeface in response to the desire of the General Synod to give less weight to some options.

Greeting

From at least the fourth century, if not earlier, the Eucharist began with a greeting, although in later Western practice it did not occur until just before the collect. This was its place in 1549. It was, however, omitted in 1552, and not restored there until the twentieth-century revisions. The *ASB* put it back to the beginning, where it remains in *CW*, with an alternative form based on 1 Timothy 1.2; 2 Timothy 1.2; 2 John 3. The resurrection acclamation, which was to be substituted for the greeting during the Easter season in the *ASB*, has been made supplementary to it in *CW*. Other words of welcome or introduction may be added.

Prayer of Preparation

Previously known to Anglicans as the Collect for Purity, this prayer has been re-named to avoid any possible confusion with *the* collect of the service. Its composition is attributed to St Gregory, Abbot of Canterbury *c.* 780, and it is perhaps reminiscent of Psalm 51. It appears in the eleventh-century Leofric Missal, and in the Sarum rite it is part of the priest's private devotions before the start of the service. It survived there together with the Lord's Prayer in the 1549 and subsequent Prayer Books. Until Series 2, both prayers were to be said by the priest. Series 2 had the ambiguous rubric 'Then may be said', making the prayer itself optional and leaving the identity of the speaker unclear, and Series 3 had the same rubric, but printed the text in bold type as a congregational prayer, a practice continued in the *ASB* and in *CW*.

Prayers of Penitence

In the Church of England it was the *ASB* which first placed the Prayers of Penitence in this position. Earlier Anglican orders had placed confession after the intercessions.

Penitential prayers at the start of the service derive from the private devotions made by the Pope in Rome. This later developed throughout the Western Church into mutual confession and absolution by the priest and other ministers, said privately before the service began. There is also some evidence by the eleventh century of a vernacular confession and absolution just before receiving the communion. In the sixteenth century the continental Reformers adapted these latter forms, and in England Thomas Cranmer followed suit in his 1548 Order of Communion, which was to be inserted into the Latin Mass at the point of reception of communion. It contained exhortations to communion, an invitation to confession, the prayer of confession itself, an absolution, the 'Comfortable Words' and finally the Prayer of Humble Access, to be said by the priest alone, before communion was received.

In 1549 this was slightly rearranged: the exhortations came after the sermon, while the rest remained before the communion, with the preamble to the absolution altered. At the start of the service the *Kyrie eleison*, 'Lord, have mercy', was said in ninefold form after the introit Psalm. In 1552 the *Kyries* were replaced by the Ten Commandments, with an expanded *Kyrie* as a congregational response to each commandment. The other elements came after the intercessions, except for the Prayer of Humble Access, which followed the preface and *Sanctus*. The exhortations were revised in 1662, but the rest remained unchanged.

The 1928 proposed revision placed the exhortations in an appendix and moved the Prayer of Humble Access to follow the Comfortable Words. The Decalogue could be replaced on most occasions by the Summary of the Law or the *Kyries*. In Series 1 the Prayer of Humble Access became congregational and permitted in either the 1662 or 1928 position. In Series 2, the Decalogue and its alternatives, still in an appendix, became optional; the invitation, confession and absolution were replaced by new, shorter forms, and the Comfortable Words and the Prayer of Humble Access were optional. Series 3 removed the Decalogue from the start of the service, leaving only the (optional) *Kyries*. But it allowed the penitential section to begin with either an expanded form of the Decalogue or the Summary of the Law. Further new forms were provided for the invitation, confession and absolution, and a slightly shortened form of the Prayer of Humble Access remained optional.

The *ASB* further developed the penitential material. It was permitted either at the beginning of the service or after the intercessions, and although the Comfortable Words were only printed at the later position, they were permitted at the earlier one too. The confession was again slightly revised, and alternative forms of the confession and the Prayer of Humble Access were provided.

The earlier position has become the norm in many places, and in *CW* the material only appears here, though Note 10 permits its use after the intercessions. The Prayer of Humble Access, however, is detached from the penitential section and restored as a prayer for worthy reception immediately before the communion.

Summary of the Law

The Summary of the Law from Matthew 22.37–40 was first used by the Nonjurors in 1718, and then in the Scottish Liturgy of 1764. The English 1928 book included as an option a synthesis of Matthew 22.37–40 and Mark 12.29–31. In Series 3 the Summary was divided and used to bracket the Decalogue, a suggestion of Michael Peck, Dean of Lincoln. The first part followed the first commandment and the second part followed the tenth, while the other commandments were also each provided with a New Testament verse as a Christian commentary or expansion. In the *ASB*, the Summary appeared in its Marcan form in the text of the rite, and this is unchanged in *CW*. Other forms of introduction to the penitential prayers may be used: the Commandments, the Beatitudes or the Comfortable Words. All this material also appears (together with the hymn 'Come, Holy Ghost', a very short exhortation and a form of confession and absolution) in a separate 'Form of Preparation' printed before Order One, which may be used by individuals on their own, or as a replacement for the Prayer of Preparation and the Prayers of Penitence in the eucharistic rite, or as a completely separate service.

The Invitation to Confession

The invitation in the 1548 order, and in 1549, was Cranmer's own composition, and invited the congregation to confess their sins not only to almighty God but also 'to his holy Church'. The people were asked to 'draw near', indicating a physical movement to the place of communion. In 1552 the confession was not to the Church but 'before this congregation', but this phrase was removed in 1662. 1662 also changed the invitation to 'draw near with faith', indicating a spiritual rather than a physical movement. 1928 and Series 1 provided a shorter form consisting of the second part, beginning 'Draw near with faith'. In Series 2 there was a briefer invitation, based on Hebrews 4.14 and 10.22, inviting the people to 'draw near with a true heart, in full assurance of faith'. (This form is provided in *CW* as the seasonal invitation on Ascension Day.) In Series 3 a further new form was composed, derived from three of the four Comfortable Words. This form continued in the *ASB* and is in *CW*. A range of alternative forms is provided in the section of Supplementary Texts and seasonal forms in the Seasonal Provisions. Note 4 also permits any other appropriate sentence of Scripture to be used.

Confession

Almost all of the confession in 1548 and 1549 is from Archbishop Hermann of Cologne. Cranmer omitted the reference to original sin, but added the phrase 'by thought, word and deed' from the Roman rite. Series 2 introduced a new short form of two sentences, the first from the old Roman rite, and the second an abbreviated version of Cranmer's conclusion. This was criticized for its brevity, and the lack of expression of contrition. The latter was corrected in Series 3, which also indicated more fully how we sin: 'through ignorance, through weakness, through our own deliberate fault', a phrase borrowed from the New Zealand rite. In the *ASB*, the phrase 'in the evil we have done and the good we have not done' was omitted and the word 'ignorance' was replaced by 'negligence'. *CW* has this as the first of two forms printed in the text, changing 'fellow men' to 'neighbour'. The second alternative derives from Series 2 Revised Morning and Evening Prayer, which in turn was mostly based on the JLG's *Daily Office*, and is found in Presbyterian books before that. Its final petitions are drawn from Micah 6.8b. Other authorized forms of confession may be used instead.

Kyries

The use of *Kyrie eleison* as a congregational response to a litany form of intercession can be traced to the fourth century in the East. Such litanies spread to the West in the fifth century, retaining the Greek response. Pope Gelasius

(492–96) introduced a litany at the start of the Mass. By the time of Pope Gregory the Great, *Christe eleison* had been added as a response to alternate petitions. On ferial days the petitions were omitted, leaving only the *Kyries*. By about 700, the *Kyries* had become an independent element at the start of the Mass, and increasingly elaborate musical settings were provided. The number of repetitions was controlled by a signal from the Pope. An extensive collection of musical tropes was developed, but this was suppressed by the Reformers and by Rome in the sixteenth century.

In 1549, Cranmer retained the *Kyries* in ninefold form. In 1552, a single expanded *Kyrie* was used as a response to each of the Ten Commandments 'Lord, have mercy upon us, and incline our hearts to keep this law'. In 1928, the *Kyries* were restored as a weekday alternative to the full Decalogue. In Series 1 the *Kyries* could be used on any occasion, and for a while the *Kyries* were regarded as a penitential and weekday alternative to the *Gloria in Excelsis*. In Series 3 the rubrics provided that the *Kyries* and *Gloria* were alternatives, but the *ASB* permitted both or neither to be used.

Beginning with *LHWE*, the *Kyries* started to recover their primitive role as responses, this time for use with brief and alternative forms of the confession. This provides a simple variation in the form of the confession, but as these are necessarily brief and may not express full contrition and repentance, a fuller form should normally be used on Sundays (see Note 10). If the *Kyries* are not used as part of the confession, they may instead be used in the sixfold or traditional ninefold form after the absolution.

Absolution

In 1548, Cranmer used the Roman absolution with a preamble declaring the authority of the Church to absolve sinners. In 1549 this preamble was changed to 'Almighty God, our heavenly Father, who of his great mercy hath promised forgiveness for sins to all them, which with hearty repentance and true faith, turn unto him: have mercy . . .' This remained in subsequent Prayer Books, until 1928 allowed the option of a shorter beginning: 'Almighty God have mercy . . .' Series 1 retained the two 1928 forms, but Series 2 had only the shorter, and in the final phrase, 'bring you to everlasting life' was changed to 'keep you in life eternal', resting on the Johannine witness that eternal life is a present reality as well as a promised destiny. Series 3 extended the opening words to 'Almighty God, who forgives all who truly repent . . .' This simplified form of Cranmer's preamble was retained in the *ASB* and *CW*. Other authorized forms may be used in its place.

Gloria in Excelsis

This office hymn of unknown authorship was first used as a canticle at the daily morning office in the East. It was introduced at the beginning of the Roman Mass on festive occasions by Pope Symmachus (498–514). By the time of Gregory the Great it had become customary on all Sundays except in

Advent, pre-Lent and Lent. Musical settings became increasingly elaborate, and reformers, both Protestant and Roman, were concerned to simplify the setting for congregational use. Some continental Protestants, including Luther, continued to use it at the entrance, while Zwingli placed it between the Epistle and Gospel.

In the 1549 service, the *Gloria* is said or sung after the *Kyries*, but in the 1552 book it appears at the end of the service as a hymn of praise. This use continued in subsequent books and meant that the service began on a penitential note and ended with the acclamation of the *Gloria*. The 1928 book made its use optional except on Sundays and holy days. Series 1 printed it at the end of the service but allowed its use at the beginning. Series 2, on the other hand, printed it at the beginning but allowed it to be used at the end. In Series 3 a note allowed it as an entrance hymn, or at the gradual or at the end, but in the *ASB* Rite A removed the option to use it at the end (except for the order following the pattern of the *BCP*, which retained it in that position). Order One prints it only as part of the Gathering, but Note 3 permits hymns and canticles to be sung at any appropriate point. In Order Two it only appears at the end of the service, where its use is normative, although there are suggestions for its omission in Note 29.

The Collect
The final part of the Gathering is the collect or opening prayer. Together with the Greeting, the collect is the only part of the Gathering which must be used on every occasion. The introductory notes emphasize that the ministry of the president serves to unify the liturgy and draw the congregation into a worshipping community. One expression of this is when the congregation is invited to pray silently for a few moments before the collect is said, which is encouraged in Note 8.

Liturgy of the Word
This section is entitled 'The Ministry of the Word' in the *ASB*, and the following section 'The Ministry of the Sacrament'. *CW* changes 'ministry' to 'liturgy' because the former is now widely used in contexts such as 'a ministry of healing' and 'personal ministry' which relate to functions exercised by individuals, rather than sections of a service. The word 'liturgy', on the other hand, implies more the common work of all God's people, rather than something 'ministered' to the people by 'ministers'.

Readings
The regular reading of portions of Scripture has always been part of Christian worship. From 1549 until the 1960s the English service included two readings, the first almost invariably from the New Testament, usually an Epistle, and the second always from the Gospels. With the gradual preference for a Sunday morning 'Parish Communion' rather than Morning Prayer, many

people heard only New Testament readings, and so Old Testament lessons were added to the eucharistic Lectionary in Series 1. Since then, English revisions have made provision for three readings, one nearly always from the Old Testament, one from the New Testament other than the Gospels, and one from the Gospels, with the option of omitting either of the first two.

The versicle and response at the end of the first two readings first appear in the post-Vatican II Roman rite. The words *verbum Dei* (literally, 'the Word of God') were suggested by Pope Paul VI. The more idiomatic translation prefixed with 'This is' is the work of the Roman Catholic English translators, taken up by ICET. The response *Deo gratias* ('Thanks be to God') was an ancient Roman acclamation of approval, in use by the eighth century. In the 1549 book nothing is said at the end of the reading of the Epistle, and not until 1662 was the reader directed to say 'Here endeth the Epistle'. Series 3 introduced the optional use of the ICET texts. Initial drafts for *CW* were 'The Word of the Lord', but the revision process reinstated 'This is'.

Psalmody

Psalms were used as part of the eucharistic liturgy of the Word at least as early as the mid-fourth century. This Gradual Psalm was an integral part of the Lectionary and, unlike the use of psalmody elsewhere in the service, was not followed by the *Gloria Patri*. 1549 removed the Gradual Psalm (though an introit Psalm remained until 1552), and psalmody was not restored to the service until Series 2 allowed its use. Series 3 appointed two optional passages of psalmody for every occasion, and suggested that they could be used at the entrance and/or between either of the readings, though they might be used at other suitable places too. In *CW* the Psalms are again an integral part of the Lectionary, and in particular are a response to the first reading (see Note 12).

Gospel Reading

The Gospel reading is the climax of the Liturgy of the Word, and this is marked in various ways, including standing to hear the reading (Note 1), a different introduction and response from that used with the other readings, and the optional singing of the Alleluia or other acclamation. Standing for the Gospel is at least as old as the fourth century, as is preceding it with a joyful Psalm sung responsorially, a cantor singing the verses and the congregation singing Alleluia in between. As with other psalmody, this was eventually reduced to a single verse, preceded by two Alleluias and followed by a third. Later other scriptural, and even non-scriptural, verses were used on occasion. In the East, the Alleluia is always used, but in the Roman rite it was replaced before and during Lent by a non-responsorial tract. The revised Roman rite provides that during Lent the Alleluia is replaced by words such as 'Praise to you, O Christ, king of eternal glory', and this pattern is followed in the various seasonal versions provided in *CW*.

The 1549 book directs that the Gospel be announced with the words, 'The holy Gospel, written in the . . . chapter of . . .', to which the 'clerks and people' answer 'Glory be to thee, O Lord', a response originally common in the East and in the Gallican rite and which eventually made its way into the Roman rite. The 1552 book eliminated this response, and it was not restored until the 1928 proposed revision, together with the response at the end of the reading, 'Praise be to thee, O Christ', which appeared in the low Mass of the Roman rite. Series 1 continued these forms, together with an alternative response at the end of the Gospel, 'Thanks be to thee, O Christ, for this thy holy Gospel', a variation on words which appeared in the Scottish Book of 1764. This alternative did not appear in Series 2. Series 3 introduced different modern language forms: 'Glory to Christ our Saviour' at the announcement, and 'This is the Gospel of Christ/Praise to Christ our Lord' at the end. The older forms had been addressed directly to Christ, a custom continued in the English version of the Roman rite, but these forms had been felt in the 1970s to be inelegant. *CW* restores in a modern form the traditional wording, a direct acclamation of Christ present in his Gospel: 'Glory to you, O Lord' and 'This is the gospel of the Lord/Praise to you, O Christ', the vocative 'O' being judged sufficient to soften the perceived inelegance of the current Roman Catholic form.

Sermon
See Chapter 5.

The Creed
In origin a baptismal statement used in Jerusalem, the Nicene Creed was adopted by the Council of Nicaea (325) in the fight against Arianism (emphasizing that the Son is of the same essential Being as the Father), and further amplified at the Council of Constantinople (381) to combat Apollinarianism. This Niceno–Constantinopolitan Creed was adopted at the Council of Chalcedon (451) as the profession of Constantinople. By the late fifth century it was in use in the Eucharist at Antioch, and spread through the East. At the Council of Toledo (589) the Visigoths, converted from Arianism to orthodoxy, incorporated the Nicene Creed into the Eucharist. This usage spread to Gaul, to the Anglo-Saxons, and then, perhaps under the influence of Alcuin, to Charlemagne's court at Aachen. Not until the eleventh century did its use reach Rome, where it was restricted to Sundays and Festivals. Originally recited in the plural form ('We believe'), it came to be said by the priest in the singular ('I believe') as congregational participation diminished.

By the thirteenth century, the Creed was said after the Gospel and before the sermon, and the Reformers generally kept it in this position, although many preferred the use of the Apostles' Creed. Cranmer in the 1549 order not only retained the Nicene Creed, but made it mandatory on all occasions. This continued until the 1928 book allowed its omission except on Sundays and Holy Days, and subsequent rites have followed the same usage.

As elsewhere, Series 3, followed by the *ASB*, used the text from ICET; and with only two exceptions, *CW* follows the most recent revision from ICET's successor, ELLC. Significant features of the translation include:

Line 5: 'seen and unseen'. This qualifies the preceding line 'all that is'. It does not refer to present and future acts of creation, but to all that exists in heaven and earth.

Line 6: 'We believe'. Though not in the Greek, the repetition is implied by the sense and is found in several early creeds.

Lines 8–23: In the Greek the verbs in this section are expressed as a series of participles hard to reproduce in that form in Latin or English.

Lines 7–11: 'begotten'. This word appears three times in the Greek and describes the Son's relationship with the Father, not the process of physical birth. The translation omits the word in line 7, 'the only begotten Son', retaining it in lines 8 and 11. This safeguards against any suggestion that the Son was created in time; rather the Son exists eternally alongside the Father. Yet paradoxically, the relationship is one of Father and Son, and the explanation is that the Son's generation is an eternal process, outside time.

Lines 9–10: 'from'. The Greek preposition *ek* is translated as 'from' here. In line 8 it is translated as 'of'. Line 9, 'God from God' is not found in the original Chalcedonian form, but is retained in conformity with the usual Latin and English versions.

Line 12: 'of one Being'. This translates the Greek philosophical term *homoousios*, and safeguards the unity of the Godhead. The argument is that the Son is not made but begotten, and so shares the same uncreated Being as the Father.

Line 13: 'through him'. 'Him' refers to the Son, the Father's agent in creation. See John 1.3, Hebrews 1.2.

Line 14: 'For us'. The word 'men' is omitted, because it is increasingly seen as referring only to one sex. 'Us' refers to the whole human race, not just those present or to Christians alone.

Lines 15–16: ELLC discarded the ICET/*ASB* rendering of these lines in favour of a new translation from the Greek: 'was incarnate of the Holy Spirit and the Virgin Mary/and became fully human'. In both these lines *CW* does not follow the ELLC text (see above p. 108). The important point in line 15 is that 'of/from the Holy Spirit' refers to the agency of the Spirit in the action of the whole Godhead in the Incarnation; and 'of/from the Virgin Mary' emphasizes that Christ was conceived and born from a woman, taking our real and actual human nature into his person. The familiar text 'and was made man' was preferred to 'and became fully human' in line 16, since in English 'human' can be used as an adjective (= 'humane'). The Greek *enanthropesanta* carries no male overtones at this point.

Line 18: 'suffered death'. The Greek *pathonta* carries the notions of both 'suffering' and 'death'.

Line 20: 'in accordance with'. A better translation than Cranmer's 'according to', which might seem to suggest that Scripture says one thing, while other authorities say something different.

Line 22: 'is seated'. This is preferred to 'sits', to emphasize the permanence of Christ's position of honour.

Line 26: 'the Lord, the giver of life'. These are two distinct phrases, both applying to the Holy Spirit. They avoid the possible misunderstanding of Cranmer's version, 'the Lord and giver of life', which might suggest 'the Lord of life' and 'the giver of life'.

Line 27: 'and the Son'. This, the *Filioque* clause, the 'double procession' of the Spirit, was not part of the original Greek, but was introduced in the West, at the Council of Toledo (589). A version of the Creed without this clause is provided elsewhere in *CW* for use on suitable ecumenical occasions. The problem is not so much the truth of the phrase, as the authority for inserting it into the Creed.

Line 29: 'prophets'. In ICET, followed by *ASB*, this word was capitalized, either by oversight or a printing error, and this is now corrected.

Line 30: 'We believe in one holy'. The word 'holy', present in the Greek and omitted by Cranmer, is restored. The *ASB*, not following ICET, printed this as a new paragraph, but in *CW* it is more properly printed as a continuation of, and subordinate to, the paragraph on the Holy Spirit.

Prayers of Intercession

Justin Martyr records that general prayers were offered at the Eucharist, and that these were the prayers of the faithful; that is, that praying with the Church was restricted to those who had been baptized. By the fourth century such intercessions in the East were usually in the form of a litany, but they might also be included in the eucharistic prayer itself. Pope Gelasius introduced the litany to Rome in the fifth century, placing it at the very beginning of the rite, with the *Kyrie* as a response to each petition (see above). This seems to have replaced the earlier intercessions in the Roman rite, which took the form of a series of biddings, each followed by a period of silent prayer and a concluding collect, a practice which has survived down to this day only on Good Friday. By the time of Gregory the Great (590–604) the Roman rite included intercessions within the eucharistic prayer and the introductory litany had disappeared, leaving only the *Kyries*. As the eucharistic prayer came to be said inaudibly, so the rite was left without audible intercessions either, and this attracted the attention of the Reformers. Possibly influenced by the office of Prone, several of the Reformers placed the intercessions between the sermon and the eucharistic prayer.

The 1549 *BCP* provides for the Litany to be said before Mass on Wednesdays and Fridays, and also placed intercessions between the *Sanctus* and the institution narrative, the position occupied in the Roman rite by prayers for the living. Prefixed with the bidding 'Let us pray for the whole state of Christ's church', prayer was offered for the Church, the king and Council, the clergy, the people, those in need, the congregation, praise for the saints and commendation of the departed. The prayer is a pastiche, with elements from Scripture, the Roman canon and other sources. In 1552 the Litany was also required on Sundays, and the intercessions were moved to an earlier position in the service, after the collection for the poor and before the exhortations and confession. The words 'militant here on earth' were added to the opening bidding, and the final section praising the saints and commending the departed was omitted. Minor changes were made in 1662, omitting 'pastors', which had become associated with Puritanism, and restoring a commemoration of the departed. 1928 added a few phrases so that the prayer was not just for the Christian Church, while Series 1, providing both 1662 and 1928 forms, also allowed the long monologue to be broken into paragraphs with a congregational response after each.

Series 2 introduced a new form, derived from the ancient Roman bidding and collect form. Intercession was divided into four sections, each consisting of an optional bidding in the minister's own words, followed by silent prayer, a versicle and response, and a short fixed prayer. This format was further developed in Series 3 and the *ASB*, so that there were six sections in which prayer was offered. The *ASB* also included two alternative patterns of intercession in an appendix, as well as allowing other forms to be used. Since 1980, a considerable number of forms of intercession have appeared, in both official publications and privately produced books. As a result, the Church has become accustomed to a variety of patterns of intercession.

CW provides five different forms, and unlike the *ASB*, preference is not given to one particular form by including it in the main text of the service, but all appear in the Supplementary Texts. Form 1 is a slightly modified form of the intercession in the *ASB*'s Rite A. Apart from two minor changes of wording, the main change is in the final commendation, where 'ourselves and all Christian people' becomes 'ourselves and the whole creation'. Form 2 is a modernized form of the 'Prayer for All Conditions of Men', composed for the 1662 *BCP*. It appeared in an appendix to the Series 2 rite as an alternative intercession, divided into three separate prayers, each with the option to add further biddings, and each with its own 'Amen'. In Series 2 Revised it was printed as a single prayer with congregational responses between each section, and in this form it appeared in the *ASB* in modern language in the section 'Prayers for Various Occasions' and also as an alternative in the Eucharist.

Form 3 appeared as the first intercession in the *ASB*'s Rite B, and derives from the *BCP*'s 'Prayer for the whole state of Christ's Church', as modified in 1928 and Series 1. Its introductory sentence is replaced by the same one as is used by the other *CW* intercessions, and the ending is shortened, so that it may be followed by any of the collects and endings that are provided. Form 4 is a slightly revised version of the *ASB* Rite A second alternative form, which itself is part of the litany as it appears in the *ASB*. The Eastern introduction which it acquired there has been used to introduce all five forms of intercession in *CW*. Form 5 is a litany which derives from the American 1979 *BCP* and appeared in a slightly modified form in *PW*. It is based on the Great Litany from the Eastern liturgies of St Basil and St John Chrysostom.

The Supplementary Texts also provide collects and other endings for the intercessions. Five of these prayers are from the *ASB*, deriving in turn from prayers in the *BCP* since 1549. Prayers 1 and 8 are both versions of the Prayer of St Chrysostom, which can be traced to the ninth century in the Byzantine rite, Prayer 1 being the much freer rendering of the two. Prayer 2 is from the Gelasian Sacramentary, where it was a prayer for travellers. Cranmer adapted it for more general use in 1549. Prayer 3 was composed for the 1549 book, and is inspired by a variety of biblical images, such as Ecclesiasticus 1.5, Matthew 6.8 and Romans 8.26. Prayer 4 is a simplified version of another of Cranmer's 1549 compositions, similar to the collect of Trinity 23, which derives from the Gregorian Sacramentary, with echoes of Psalm 17.6 and John 14.13, 14. Prayer 5 derives partly from a prayer by David Silk based on Hebrews 12.1, 22–24. Prayer 6 is also adapted from Hebrews 12.22–24 and Prayer 7 from Luke 13.29, both by Michael Vasey and appearing previously in *PW*.

The Liturgy of the Sacrament

This second half of the rite is structured after the pattern of the action of Christ at the Last Supper, in taking bread and wine, blessing or thanking God for them, breaking the bread, and sharing both bread and wine with his disciples. These four actions, however, are not all of equal importance: we take in order to bless, and we break in order to share; and so the primary focus is on blessing/thanksgiving in the eucharistic prayer and on sharing in the act of communion.

The Peace

The exchange of a sign of peace derives from New Testament injunctions in Romans 16.16; 1 Corinthians 16.20; 2 Corinthians 13.12; 1 Thessalonians 5.26; and 1 Peter 5.14. Assimilation of a gesture of peace into the Eucharist is very early and widespread. Justin Martyr describes a greeting with a kiss prior to the presentation of bread and wine to the president. Origen and Tertullian also indicate that it served as the 'seal' at the end of the intercessions, while the New Testament injunction to be reconciled to one another before offering gifts at the altar (Matthew 5.23) later provided a scriptural basis for this position before the eucharistic action.

In fifth-century Rome and North Africa, however, the Peace is found placed after the eucharistic prayer, as a way of the congregation giving assent to what had been done, and the Roman tradition has continued this practice down to the present day. In this position it serves as immediate preparation for the reception of communion and has associations both with the petition, 'forgive us our sins as we forgive those who sin against us', of the Lord's Prayer and with the 'grant us peace' of the *Agnus Dei*.

The 1549 rite left the Peace in this Roman position, but in 1552 it was removed completely. It returned in 1928, as an option after the eucharistic prayer. In Series 2, still optional, it was placed in its ancient position before the eucharistic prayer, and a scriptural introduction from Ephesians 4.3 added. This arrangement became mandatory in Series 3, though with a different sentence, Romans 14.19. The use of a single sentence and a single interpretation were criticized, and so the *ASB* instead had a pastiche of Ephesians 2.14, 16, Matthew 19.20, 21, and 1 Thessalonians 5.13, together with five seasonal alternatives in an appendix. The rubrics allowed other introductions to be used, and *PW* provided some 29 such sentences. *CW* has no sentences in the main text, and the president may use any appropriate sentence or none (Note 4), but the section of Supplementary Texts contains seven suggested introductions for general use, and the Seasonal Provisions thirteen seasonal sentences. Note 1 directs that the people should stand for the Peace, and Note 16 permits the Peace to be moved either to be the opening greeting of the rite or to be placed in the Roman position at the fraction or to function as the dismissal at the end of the service.

Preparation of the Table and Taking of the Bread and Wine
Reference to the collection of alms in association with the Eucharist occurs in Justin Martyr, and he also states that the bread and wine were brought to the president at this point in the service, a practice continued in the later Christian tradition. At Rome this action later became very elaborate, accompanied by incense, hand-washing, processions and music. Each little ceremony associated with this preparatory act attracted prayers as time went on, some of which risked being confused with the eucharistic prayer itself.

Luther rebelled against this tradition, even describing the saying of prayers over the gifts as a form of idolatry. Cranmer also dispensed with these prayers in 1549, replacing them with Offertory Sentences, taken from Scripture. While these were being said, the people would enter the chancel to make an alms offering in the 'poor men's box', and then the communicants would remain there while non-communicants departed and the priest set the bread and wine on the altar without further ado. In 1552 this part of the service was even starker: the churchwardens simply gathered the alms from the people and placed them in the poor men's box, while the priest said the sentences. No reference is made to the bread and wine: most likely they had already been put on the table before the service began. In 1662 the word 'Offertory' reappeared, and the priest received the alms from the churchwardens and placed them on the table. He was then to set bread and wine there.

Series 1 gave the priest a choice: to place the gifts on the table as before, preceding the Prayer for the Church, or to do so just before the eucharistic prayer, in each case with a sentence from 1 Chronicles 29. Series 2 introduced a section called 'The Preparation of the Bread and Wine', which, although basic and silent, was nevertheless marked out, even if it could happen during the singing of a hymn. But significantly, the emphasis had shifted away from the offering of money to the presenting of bread and wine. Revisions of Series 1 and 2 restored the option of saying a sentence of Scripture, and Series 3, with the section entitled 'The Taking of the Bread and Wine' added the rubric 'The President takes the bread and wine'.

This Taking reflects the first of the four dominical actions and is derived from the ancient Jewish table custom in which the one presiding would take food and drink into his hands before blessing God for them. In later Christian practice the elaboration of Offertory ceremonies gradually obscured the distinctiveness of this action, and further 'manual acts' were introduced in the eucharistic prayer itself during the institution narrative. These were abolished in 1549, but restored in 1662 when both taking the bread and wine and breaking the bread at the appropriate points in the narrative were included. Series 3 and the *ASB* made it clear that the Taking was not to be confused with the Offertory, and the Taking again became an essential act in its own right before the eucharistic prayer (although the traditional manual acts were also allowed by a rubric).

CW permits a variety of practice. Specific thanks may still be given for the monetary offerings; and the option exists to use prayers such as the offertory prayers of the modern Roman rite, only alluded to in the *ASB*, but now included, with very slight modification, among 'Prayers at the Preparation of the Table' in the *CW* service. While some of these prayers relate specifically to the collection of money and others to the eucharistic elements, some are more general in character and look forward to the coming action. However, many would hold that any prayers giving thanks for the gifts of bread and wine are not only superfluous at this point but duplicate the function of the eucharistic prayer itself. The Taking is no longer mandatory at this point, but can take place instead during the institution narrative. It must, however, occur in one of these two positions (Note 17).

The Eucharistic Prayer

Recent thinking regards the eucharistic prayer as a unity, as a single act of praise and petition, itself set within the unity of the entire service. Thus, no individual part of it is to be thought of as 'consecratory', nor is there any single 'moment of consecration'.

It is now common in many churches to have more than one eucharistic prayer available for use, each of which has its own distinct emphasis. Rather than trying to say everything in one prayer, they offer a diversity of expressions and scriptural allusions. Order One contains eight different eucharistic prayers, recognizably distinct from one another in their overall style, imagery, language and length. Not all elements of eucharistic doctrine can be fully expressed in each prayer, but individual prayers are not 'party' prayers, and all of them are intended for use across the Church of England. Experiencing and praying at least some of their diversity is generally to be encouraged for all congregations, although certain prayers will be more appropriate for some occasions and situations than others. We will defer detailed consideration of the structure and contents of the individual prayers until later in the chapter (pp. 137–43), and merely note some common elements here.

Greeting and Sursum corda. These have been a regular part of eucharistic prayers since at least the third century. The greeting was omitted in the Church of England from 1552 onwards but restored in the twentieth-century revisions. The word 'spirit' is usually seen as a Semitic idiom meaning 'you', and the ELLC translation is thus, 'And also with you'. Series 3 introduced the alternative greeting, 'The Lord is here/His Spirit is with us', which alludes to the presence of the Holy Spirit among the eucharistic community in the eucharistic prayer. In the final response, ELLC changed ICET's 'him' to 'our'. This was not accepted in *CW*, but instead the pronoun was simply omitted, chiefly because there is no suggestion of a pronoun either in the ancient Latin text or in the *BCP* version.

Preface. Ancient Eastern eucharistic prayers have an unchanging preface, which usually includes a more extended reference to God's work of creation than is found in the West, where a very much shorter common preface eventually became the norm, with a number of Proper Prefaces for various occasions, each focusing on one particular aspect of salvation. Cranmer continued the Roman practice of a single common preface, which on its own contained no reference to any of the 'mighty acts' for which praise and thanksgiving were offered, but he reduced the Proper Prefaces to five, for Christmas, Easter, Ascension, Pentecost and Trinity Sunday. 1552 and 1662 retained this arrangement.

Series 1 increased the number to 14, while Series 2 cut back to four, but enlarged the common preface so that it gave thanks for creation, redemption, and sanctification. Series 3 kept this enlarged preface and added more Proper Prefaces, making a total of 11. The four eucharistic prayers of the *ASB* retained the system of a simple standard preface and interpolated Proper Prefaces which could generally be used with any of the prayers. In *CW* four of the five new prayers have a fixed preface (Prayers D, F, G and H), and the fifth (Prayer E) together with two prayers revised from the *ASB* (A and B) allow the option of the entire preface being replaced with a longer seasonal form rather than the insertion of a short Proper Preface in the traditional Western manner.

Sanctus. Derived from Isaiah 6.3, this was in use in Christian liturgy in the East by the fourth century, and in Roman rites by the sixth century. It was mostly accompanied by the *Benedictus*. In 1549 Cranmer retained this traditional form, although substituting 'Glory to thee, O Lord, in the highest' for the 'Hosanna' at the end of the *Benedictus*. 1552 omitted the *Benedictus* entirely, and substituted 'Glory be to thee, O Lord most high' for the 'Hosanna' at the end of the *Sanctus*. This remained unchanged in the 1662 revision. Series 1 restored the *Benedictus* for optional use after the *Sanctus*, but Series 2 separated it, placing it at the very end of the eucharistic prayer. Series 3 allowed freedom over where, if at all, both the *Benedictus* and the *Agnus Dei* might be used, but the *ASB* restored the *Benedictus* for optional use after the *Sanctus*, although still allowing an alternative use of it during the distribution of communion. Where the Eucharist is sung to lengthy settings, the latter makes practical sense, as it avoids a lengthy musical interlude in the midst of the eucharistic prayer.

The *Sanctus* is an integral part of the eucharistic prayer and should not be used as a pausing point, or opportunity for the congregation to change posture, especially in those eucharistic prayers where it comes not at the end of the praise section of the prayer but only part-way through it (Prayers D, F and G). Note 1 states that 'any changes in posture during the eucharistic prayer should not detract from the essential unity of that prayer', and thus, whether the congregation stands or kneels, it is preferable that the same posture should be retained throughout the prayer.

Institution Narrative. This is both a warrant for what is being done and also in itself part of the memorial and thanksgiving. In the medieval West it came to be regarded as the formula of consecration and associated with various 'manual acts' by the priest, who would, facing east with his back to the people, raise the bread and the cup above his head after the corresponding dominical words, so that the people might adore Christ present in the newly consecrated elements. The 1549 rite directed the priest only to take the elements into his hands and not elevate them, but in 1552 the manual acts were omitted altogether. In 1662 they were restored, and the priest was directed not only to take the elements into his hands but also to break the bread at the corresponding point in the narrative. Series 1 retained these manual acts, but Series 2 deferred the breaking of the bread until after the prayer was over. Series 3 removed all reference to actions during the prayer, preferring to focus on the 'Taking' before it began. They were not reintroduced in any of the *ASB* prayers, although a note did permit them still to be used, in addition to the separate 'Taking' before the prayer. *CW* is more permissive and, as indicated earlier, the bread and the cup may be taken into the president's hands either before or during the eucharistic prayer.

The wording of the narrative has varied greatly throughout Christian history, in no case conforming exactly to any one scriptural text. The four prayers in the *ASB* had identical wording for the narrative. In *CW*, Prayer D has different wording, and the other new prayers, while using the same form of the dominical words themselves, have slight variations in the rest of the narrative.

Anamnesis. Remembrance or memorial is at the heart of the eucharistic action. Jesus commanded his disciples to 'do this in remembrance of me', and the Church responded by continuing to celebrate the Eucharist. Although the whole eucharistic action is an *anamnesis*, the word is also used more specifically to refer to the part of the eucharistic prayer after the institution narrative which traditionally links the act of remembrance to what the Church understands itself to be doing in the Eucharist. In many ancient texts of this *anamnesis* section, remembering is combined with the notion of offering the bread and wine, and once the Western Church had come to think of the institution narrative as having already effected their consecration, such texts were then interpreted as meaning that the Church was here offering Christ to God.

Such a view of eucharistic sacrifice was rejected by the sixteenth-century Reformers, and so the 1549 rite avoided any explicit reference to offering and used the words, 'we do celebrate and make here before thy Divine Majesty with these thy holy gifts, the memorial . . .' In 1552 these words disappeared as the institution narrative was followed immediately by the distribution, with the words of administration clearly indicating that it is this reception which was the act of remembrance; and this arrangement was retained in 1662.

The 1928 book proposed a return to the 1549 form, but of course was never authorized. With Series 2, an attempt to adopt the ancient expression 'offer the bread and the cup' was rejected, but the agreed compromise, 'with this bread and this cup we make the memorial . . . We pray thee to accept this our duty and service . . .' (which is not very different from the form used in 1549), proved surprisingly popular and survived into the second eucharistic prayer of the *ASB* Rite A. The first prayer substituted the phrase 'celebrate with this bread and this cup his one perfect sacrifice . . .' The third prayer, although in other ways drawing upon the ancient *Apostolic Tradition*, avoided contention by using simply 'we celebrate this memorial of our redemption . . .' The fourth prayer used a traditional 1662 *BCP* phrase, 'we offer you through him this sacrifice of praise and thanksgiving . . .'

In *CW*, the first three prayers have stayed close to the *ASB* wording. Prayer D also uses simply 'with this bread and this cup', while Prayers F and H are even more reticent, with the words of remembrance leading directly into the *epiclesis*. Prayer E is more adventurous: 'in him we plead with confidence his sacrifice . . . Bringing before you the bread of life and cup of salvation, we proclaim . . .' The word 'plead' has been used across the spectrum of belief, by Evangelicals and Calvinists as well as by the Archbishops in their 1897 response to Pope Leo XIII's Bull against Anglican Orders. Prayer G also uses the expression 'we plead with confidence his sacrifice', but defers mention of the bread and wine until the *epiclesis*: 'Pour out your Holy Spirit as we bring before you these gifts of your creation . . .'

Acclamations.   In recent years Western Churches have experienced an increase in the number of congregational acclamations in eucharistic prayers. Traditionally in the West they were limited to the *Sanctus* (and *Benedictus*) together with the great 'Amen' at the end of the prayer. In the Byzantine tradition a further acclamation punctuated the eucharistic prayer, and some other Eastern Churches added still more. The CSI rite of 1951, reflecting something of the Syrian Orthodox tradition in India, divided a long Syrian acclamation in two, placing the first part after the institution narrative and the second after the *anamnesis*, forming a bridge to the *epiclesis*. Other churches soon followed the CSI example, but in the revised Roman rite only a single acclamation after the narrative was adopted. This had the unfortunate effect of further suggesting a consecratory character of the narrative alone, and of separating the narrative from the *anamnesis*, obscuring the close relationship between the two. The Roman rite provided a choice of four acclamations at this point, all preceded by the bidding, 'Let us proclaim the mystery of faith'. The words *mysterium fidei* were moved there from their older, but inexplicable, position as part of the institution narrative, where they referred to the chalice.

Series 3 followed suit with a single acclamation after the institution narrative. The proposals for *ASB* Rite A originally placed the acclamation after the *anamnesis*, but this proposal was defeated and the acclamations remained after the narrative in all four prayers. *LHWE* provided three additional forms of acclamation, identical to those in the Roman rite.

CW offers a variety of practice. Four 'standard' acclamations are provided, and each is given a distinct (but optional) bidding. In Prayers A and E, this acclamation is placed after the *anamnesis;* in Prayers B, C and G it comes after the institution narrative; while Prayers D, F and H do not use the standard forms at all. Prayers A, D and F also each have a series of acclamations or interjections through the prayer, though these are optional in A and F. Note 18 permits other acclamations to be used.

Epiclesis.   This word means invocation, calling upon God, in particular God the Holy Spirit. The roots of a petition of this kind seem to lie in the Jewish prayers of blessing/thanksgiving, which often also contained a petitionary element, asking God to continue his work among his people. In Christian usage this became eschatological, praying for the gathering of the Church into the kingdom at the end of time. But from early times some prayers address either Christ or the Holy Spirit directly, as in 'Come, Holy Spirit'; and in later texts this became a request for God to *send* the Spirit on his people. Over time the Eastern Churches began to regard the invocation of the Holy Spirit as effecting consecration and to add a specific request for the Spirit to come also upon the eucharistic elements. In the West, however, where consecration was linked to the institution narrative, a petition for consecration was placed before the institution narrative itself rather than in the second half of the prayer, and did not explicitly refer to the Holy Spirit.

In 1549 Cranmer added to the Roman petition the phrase 'with thy Holy Spirit and word' from the Eastern rite of St Basil, thereby combining the two traditions. The whole petition disappeared in 1552, being replaced with one for fruitful reception in line with Cranmer's theology of the Eucharist: 'grant that we receiving these thy creatures of bread and wine . . . may be partakers of his most blessed body and blood'. This was retained in 1662.

In the proposals of 1928 the role and position of an *epiclesis* caused controversy, and the replacement of the 1662 words by 'with thy holy and life-giving Spirit vouchsafe to bless and sanctify both us and these thy gifts of bread and wine that they may be unto us the body and blood . . .' proved unacceptable to many, and rendered any future discussion sensitive. Thus Series 1 reverted to the 1552/1662 form, and Series 2 made only a quite conservative change: 'grant that these gifts of bread and wine may be unto us his body and blood'. However, the position adopted in the 1971 Agreed Statement on Eucharistic Doctrine of the Anglican–Roman Catholic International Commission, that the bread and wine become the body and blood by the action of the Holy Spirit, eased the way for Series 3 to contain an *epiclesis* on the elements before the institution narrative and another separate *epiclesis* on those receiving after the *anamnesis*. The former asked God 'that by the power of your Holy Spirit these gifts of bread and wine may be to us his body and blood', and the latter prayed, 'as we eat and drink these holy gifts in the presence of your divine majesty, renew us by your Spirit . . .'

The *ASB* kept this double *epiclesis* in Prayers 1, 2 and 3, while Prayer 4, as in many other ways, maintained a position close to 1662, with a single *epiclesis* before the institution narrative: 'grant that by the power of your Holy Spirit we who receive these gifts of your creation, the bread and wine . . . may be partakers . . .' In *CW*, Prayers A and B retain the *ASB*'s double *epiclesis*, and Prayers C and E have a single *epiclesis* before the narrative. Prayers D, F, G and H, however, have a single *epiclesis* after the narrative and *anamnesis*, implying an Eastern rather than Western view of consecration.

Prayer for Fruitful Reception. As indicated above, early Christian petitions at this point in the prayer usually had an eschatological focus, praying for the gathering of the Church into the kingdom, but gradually into this supplicatory section came an increasing diversity of petitions and also a variety of objects of intercession, for whom the grace of the sacrament was sought. The 1549 rite continued this tradition, both with intercession for the whole Church and with petition for the forgiveness of sins and other 'benefits of Christ's passion' on behalf of the Church. In 1552 and 1662 this material was moved out of the prayer to form the intercessions before it and the Prayer of Oblation after communion, respectively, to eliminate any suggestion that the Eucharist was a propitiatory sacrifice. 1928 and Series 1 restored the Prayer of

Oblation to its former position after the *anamnesis*, a tradition continued in Prayer 4 of the *ASB* and Prayer C of *CW*. In contrast, Series 2 and all other subsequent prayers have included only relatively brief petitions for a fruitful reception of the sacrament. *ASB* Prayer 3 struck a more definite eschatological note, praying for the gathering of all communicants into the kingdom. This is continued in *CW* Prayer B, and a similar idea is expressed in Prayer G, while Prayers D, E, and F speak of sharing in the heavenly banquet. Prayer F alone, following its Basilean exemplar, also contains some more general intercession for the world, though Prayer G does include optional intercession for the Church.

Doxology. Most classic eucharistic prayers concluded with a Trinitarian Doxology, to which the people replied 'Amen', thus acknowledging and assenting to what has been done in their name. Even in medieval practice when the eucharistic prayer was virtually inaudible, if not silent, the priest would raise his voice towards the end, so that the congregation could respond with an affirmative 'Amen'. In Series 3, however, a new approach was taken by adding a further acclamation based on Revelation 5.13: 'Blessing and honour and glory and power, be yours for ever and ever, Amen.' This continued to be used in the first eucharistic prayer in the *ASB*, and has been included in Prayers A, D and G in *CW*. Prayer H has no 'Amen' as such, but uses the *Sanctus* as the congregational acclamation at the end of the prayer.

The traditional manual acts, permitted by rubric, undoubtedly include lifting the elements at this climactic point in the eucharistic prayer. In line with the view that the whole prayer is consecratory rather than there being a single moment of consecration, it is particularly appropriate to elevate the bread and cup together during the Doxology and 'Amen'.

The Lord's Prayer

The Lord's Prayer is first recorded as a devotion before communion in the late fourth century, the phrase 'daily bread' being identified with the bread of the Eucharist, and in early Western rites it is generally placed between the fraction and the communion. Gregory the Great (590–604) is regarded as being responsible for changing its position in the Roman rite so that it came between the eucharistic prayer and the fraction. Originally said by the priest and people together, in the Middle Ages it came to be said by the priest alone, despite its introductory words, *audemus dicere*, 'we are bold to say'.

In 1549 this format was retained, with the congregation saying just the last line, 'But deliver us from evil.' In 1552, with its different structure of the rite, the Lord's Prayer came after the communion, the introduction was omitted, the doxology added, and it was said by all, the congregation repeating each line after the priest. Series 1 permitted its use in either the 1549 position with introduction or the 1552/1662 position without introduction. Series 2 made a significant change, moving the prayer to after the fraction, retaining the introduction, and omitting the doxology. Series 3 kept the position, but restored the doxology and added a simpler introduction. *ASB* Rite A followed the majority practice of modern rites, and reverted to a position immediately after the eucharistic prayer, which is retained in *CW*.

The prayer is not part of the eucharistic prayer but rather a communion devotion. In the *ASB* it was printed after the heading 'The Communion', which grouped together the third and fourth of the four dominical acts, the breaking and the sharing. In *CW* it appears with its own heading, as there is no over-riding heading. It may be said in either its modern language form, or else a traditional form. Different introductions are provided for each. As in the *ASB*, the modern translation differs from the ELLC text at line 9, 'Save us from the time of trial and . . .' The ecumenically agreed version had not met with general acceptance in the Church of England in 1980 (even after a period of use in Series 3 in its ICET form), and the same was true in 2000. Each time, the General Synod eventually agreed to retain the traditional English form, 'Lead us not into temptation but . . .' However, the ELLC text is printed in the main volume of *CW* in the section, 'Prayers for Various Occasions', and Note 19 permits it to be used 'on suitable occasions', and the *BCP* form may also be used instead.

Breaking of the Bread

The breaking of the bread can be seen simply as a means of breaking the bread or wafers into convenient pieces prior to distribution, a sharing-out of the one bread among the many who are one body, in the now well-known phrase from Augustine, commenting on 1 Corinthians 10.17. It can also be seen as an imitation of the third of the dominical acts at the Last Supper, or as a symbolic representation of our Lord's broken body at Calvary.

Various traditions grew up around what originated as a purely practical action. The Roman practice of commixture – putting a piece of consecrated bread into the wine – evolved as a symbolic representation of the restorative effect of resurrection, in which body and blood are reunited. A piece of bread consecrated by the bishop (the *fermentum*) was sent to outlying parishes, where it could be added to the chalice as a symbol of the unity of the Church across space. Such unity across time was represented by the *sancta*, a piece which was reserved until the following Mass. Not surprisingly, Cranmer abandoned all of this, and did not refer to the fraction at all in 1549. He did, however, state that the wafers must be broken at least into two pieces. 1552 stipulated ordinary bread, but of good quality. 1662 retained this but added a fraction during the institution narrative itself. 1928 kept this, but Series 1 allowed for a further fraction between the Lord's Prayer and the communion.

Series 2 marked a turning-point, removing the fraction from the institution narrative and giving it a new section, 'The Breaking of the Bread', immediately after the eucharistic prayer had finished, and providing a text from 1 Corinthians 10.16–17 to accompany it, along with the optional use of the *Agnus Dei*.

Here, at last, the third dominical action was clearly laid out in Anglican liturgy. It appeared not only as a practical action before the distribution, but also as a symbol of the unity of the Church in Christ. Series 3 omitted the irrelevant reference to the cup from the words, while the *ASB* moved the fraction to follow the Lord's Prayer rather than precede it. *CW* retains this arrangement as well as the *ASB* text, but with an alternative form adapted from 1 Corinthians 11.26, and with permission in Note 20 for neither form to be used on days other than Sundays and Principal Holy Days.

Agnus Dei

This anthem, which derives from John 1.29, 36 was first used in the East, probably in Syria, and was introduced into the Roman rite by the Syrian Pope Sergius I (687–701). It was sung at the fraction, a single line repeated as often as was necessary while the bread was broken for all the communicants. As the number of communicants decreased, and with the use of separate hosts, the number of repetitions was standardized at three. And as the anthem was sung in close proximity to the exchange of the Peace, the third response was changed to 'grant us peace'. In the later Middle Ages this anthem, like other sung parts, became the subject of increasingly elaborate settings, and it was sung during the communion of the priest and people. Thus it came to be regarded as a communion anthem, and Cranmer retained it for this purpose in 1549. It was omitted in 1552.

Series 1 re-introduced it as an optional communion anthem; Series 2 re-instated it as an optional fraction anthem; but in Series 3 it was again a communion anthem. In the *ASB* it was printed for optional use at the fraction, but the rubrics allowed its use at the distribution. In *CW* it is again an optional fraction anthem (see Note 20), and as in the *ASB*, two forms are printed, both being ELLC texts. The first is a traditional form, differing from that in the *ASB* in that 'sin' is in the singular rather than the plural. The Latin, *peccata mundi*, is in the plural, an idiom to translate the sense of expanse in the Greek singular. This is not so necessary in English, and ELLC preferred to keep the singular here, as in the *Gloria in Excelsis* and in the invitation to communion.

The second form was the work of Geoffrey Cuming and is a freer version in which the name of Jesus is made the focal point by prefixing each line with the name. Lines 2 and 3 provide free renderings of the Latin *qui tollis peccata mundi*: the verb *tollis* can be interpreted as 'bear' or 'take away', and so the two lines give the dual meaning. The wording of the final petition is altered from that in Series 3 and the *ASB* so as to be identical to the first form.

Giving of Communion

This is the last of the four dominical acts. There has been a variety of different practices for the distribution and reception of communion. The ancient posture, still retained in the East, is standing – a sign that the communicants are God's children, rather than his submissive slaves, and also a reminder of the

Passover tradition of eating in haste and ready to depart. Communicants received in both kinds, receiving the bread in their hands, as Cyril of Jerusalem instructed: 'Make your left hand a throne for the right, since it is to receive a king.' The president communicated first, followed by the other ministers, and then the laity.

In the late Middle Ages in the West the custom spread of kneeling to receive. Both changes in piety and the danger that the elements might be taken away for profane or superstitious use led to other changes in practice. In the East and some parts of the West, intinction, using a spoon, became customary, while in the West from the ninth century wafers were introduced and placed directly into the mouth, and later the chalice was withdrawn from the laity altogether.

In 1548, Cranmer directed communicants to kneel to receive, and the chalice was restored to the laity. 1549 omitted the direction to kneel but added that they should receive the bread into their mouths. 1552, by contrast, required communicants to kneel, and the bread was to be put into their hands. It was specifically denied that by kneeling 'adoration is intended unto any real and essential presence'. The declaration on kneeling was omitted in the 1559 *BCP*, but restored in 1662, though the word 'corporal' replaced 'real and essential', so changing its sense.

From Series 2 onwards, nothing has been said about kneeling, nor about receiving the bread in the hands. Until 1980 the rubrics specified that the priest should receive first, then the other ministers, and then the laity. In the *ASB*, followed by *CW*, the rubric is more general and allows the president and other ministers to communicate after the congregation if desired, which may be more appropriate in the modern cultural context. In any case, following the practice of the Eastern churches, it is desirable that all – including the president – should *receive* communion at the hands of another rather than *take* it for themselves.

Invitation to Communion

The first form of invitation to communion derives from the words of administration of the 1662 *BCP*. The words were first used in this way as an option in 1928; the form was simplified in Series 2; Series 3 revised it, turning the passive verbs into active ones; it was revised again for the *ASB*, and that version is retained in *CW*.

The second form first appeared in the Church of England in the *ASB* in the appendices to Rite A, and was derived with one modification from the form in the modern Roman rite ('Jesus is . . .' rather than 'This is . . .'). The word 'sin' now replaces the *ASB*'s 'sins', as in the *Agnus Dei* (see above), and 'Blessed' has been substituted for 'Happy'. This form has been associated with the Roman rite since the Synod of Aix in 1585. The versicle is derived, like the *Agnus Dei*, from John 1.29, together with a reference to the marriage supper of the Lamb from Revelation 19.9. The response derives from the words of the centurion in Matthew 8.8.

The third form is a revision of the second alternative form in the *ASB*. This is Eastern in origin, appearing as early as the late fourth century. The fourth form, again slightly revised from the *ASB*, is based on 1 Corinthians 5.7–8. Like the opening Trinitarian invocation, the second and third options are deliberately printed in a lighter typeface in response to the desire of the General Synod to give less weight to some options.

Prayer of Humble Access

After the decline in the frequency of communion by the people, private prayers by the priest for worthy reception came into common use. The 1548 Order of Communion, an English insertion into the Latin Mass, provided for congregational use the confession and absolution, the Comfortable Words and then this prayer for worthy reception, followed immediately by the administration. A new composition at the time, it does not seem to have been based on any single source, and similarities can be found with phrases from the Liturgies of St Basil and St James, Daniel 9.18, Mark 7.28, John 6.56, Leviticus 17.11, the Hereford and Westminster Missals, the German Church Orders, Thomas Aquinas, Florus of Lyons and Paschasius Radbert.

The 1549 Book kept this arrangement, but the 1552 revision placed the distribution immediately after the institution narrative, and separated the Prayer of Humble Access from the rest of the penitential material, moving it to a position after the *Sanctus*, which was retained in 1662. This move is said to have been a response to Bishop Stephen Gardiner's contention that the prayer, said kneeling after the consecration, taught the adoration of Christ's flesh in the sacrament.

The 1928 book re-attached the prayer to the end of the penitential material, and this position was retained in the revised services that led to the *ASB* and in that book itself, although its use was now optional. This position was criticized by some on the grounds that no such prayer is necessary at that point, when communicants had just confessed their sins and received absolution. *CW* restores the prayer to its 1548/1549 position, as a prayer for worthy reception immediately before communion.

The original form contained an additional phrase ('in these holy Mysteries') and the order of the clauses was different. In 1552 this extra phrase was removed, and the clauses rearranged to provide a better climax. Gilbert Burnet, Bishop of Salisbury (1689–1714), in his *History of the Reformation* argued that the final clauses had caused grave disquiet because they seemed to suggest that the body of Christ preserved the body of the communicant, and the blood the soul. The 1548 words of administration, which immediately followed the prayer, say the same, and together with the prayer might bring many to an incorrect understanding. In 1549 the words of administration were changed to 'body and soul' for both bread and wine, and the danger diminished. In Series 2 and 3, the words 'that our sinful bodies may be made clean by his body, and our souls washed through his most precious blood' were omitted, as they were in the *ASB* Rite A, and they appeared in brackets as an optional omission in Rite B. Nonetheless, the problem was well understood in the medieval period, when the doctrine of concomitance and reception on one kind had been a leading topic of theologians such as Anselm and Aquinas, and the danger should not be overstated. The words are restored in *CW*.

An alternative version of the prayer is also provided. Written by Professor David Frost, it first appeared in the draft Series 3 service in 1971. It was rejected by the General Synod at that time, but was included in an appendix in the *ASB* Rite A. It is related to George Herbert's poem 'Love', and also alludes to the parable in Matthew 22.1–10 and Luke 14.16–24, to Psalm 24.3–4 and James 4.8, to the Canaanite woman in Matthew 15.27 and Mark 7.28, to the feeding with heavenly manna in Exodus 16.4, and concludes with a glimpse of the heavenly banquet. A prayer such as this will bear constant repetition, and the allusions provide great depth for further reflection.

Words of Distribution

Early forms of these words seem to have been simply, 'The body of Christ' and 'The blood of Christ', to which the communicant replied 'Amen'. Whilst in the East liturgies tended to expand these forms by adding reverential epithets (e.g. the Liturgy of St Mark used: 'The holy body/The precious blood of our Lord God and Saviour Jesus Christ'), the Roman Sacramentaries are silent on the matter. The only evidence in the York and Sarum Missals is the formula used when communicating the sick, which took the form, 'The body of our Lord Jesus Christ keep your body and soul in eternal life'. The 1548 Order used something similar for both bread and wine: 'The body/blood of our Lord Jesus Christ, which was given/shed for thee, preserve thy body/soul unto everlasting life' (see the discussion on the Prayer of Humble Access above). The words 'which was given/shed for thee' were derived from Luther and other German forms. In 1549 the second parts of the two formulae became the same: 'preserve thy body and soul unto everlasting life'.

These words were entirely changed in 1552, the new form being strongly reminiscent of a form by the Reformer John à Lasco: 'Take and eat this, in remembrance that Christ died for thee, and feed on him in thy heart by faith, with thanksgiving' and 'Drink this in remembrance that Christ's blood was shed for thee, and be thankful'. In 1559, the 1549 and 1552 forms were combined, and this was continued in 1662. 1928 introduced a general invitation (see above), and then either the 1549 or 1552 forms for each communicant, or else for each row of communicants. Series 2 reverted to the more primitive form, the minister saying simply 'The Body/Blood of Christ', with the response 'Amen'. The 1559/1662 words were also allowed as an alternative. Series 3 provided the single form 'The Body/Blood of Christ keep you in eternal life', with the response 'Amen'. The *ASB* Rite A provided two main forms, the words found in Series 3 and the simple form from Series 2, while the 1559/1662 form was also permitted as an alternative.

The main text of the *CW* service contains none of the words of distribution, but five different forms appear in the Supplementary Texts. The first is the 1559 form, the second the words found in Series 2, and the third the words from Series 3. The other two are new forms.

Supplementary Consecration

By the end of the first millennium it was accepted that further supplies of the sacrament could be consecrated by contact, unconsecrated wine being added to consecrated wine, and unconsecrated bread being sprinkled with consecrated wine. By the thirteenth century a theology of consecration by formula had been developed: in the West the institution narrative was accepted as the formula, and in the East the invocation of the Holy Spirit upon the bread and wine. This led to greater scruples about additional elements, and the Western Church outlawed the practice, but allowed the repetition of the narrative where there was a defect in the first consecration (such as the priest forgetting to put wine in the chalice). This rule appears in the Sarum use, and is followed in the 1548 Order for situations where insufficient wine had been consecrated.

Using the medieval formula for supplementary consecration in this way was without precedent, and nothing is said about it in the 1549, 1552, and 1559 Prayer Books. In 1573 the Puritan, Robert Johnson, was tried and convicted for adding more wine to the chalice without any words, despite his defence that there was no rubric to prove him wrong. However, Canon 21 of 1604 did require the institution narrative to be said over bread and wine 'newly brought', and this was followed in the Scottish 1637 book and in 1662. It was not considered entirely satisfactory by all, however, and in the proposed 1689 book the repetition of the narrative was preceded by a brief petition. Charles Wheatley in 1710 argued that the whole prayer should be repeated, or at least the section from 'Hear us, O merciful Father'. The Scottish book of 1764 required the whole of the prayer from 'All glory be to thee' through to the *epiclesis*, and this practice was followed in the first and subsequent American books. 1928 required only the relevant part of the institution narrative and an *epiclesis*. Series 1 and Series 2 made no provision.

In 1968 the Liturgical Consultation of the Lambeth Conference and the Doctrine Commission both looked at the matter, and there was general agreement with the Liturgical Commission on the principle that new bread and/or wine should be brought into sacramental action before the exhaustion of the original supplies. This was put into practice in Series 3. The president returns to the holy table, adds more, and uses words which establish that these elements belong to the same context as the original elements. *ASB* Rite A modified the Series 3 words slightly by putting them in the present tense: 'Father, giving thanks over the bread and the cup . . .' *CW* returns to the 1973 form, 'having given thanks', since the *ASB* words might imply that a new giving of thanks was taking place. Despite pleas that the action should be done silently, causing less disruption in a service, none of the *CW* Orders allows this, although the rubric is deliberately silent as to whether public attention should be drawn to the action.

The Ablutions
In the early Church any remaining consecrated elements were kept either on the altar or in the sacristy until the end of the service, and then consumed or used for communion the following day. The early Roman rite speaks of the Pope washing his hands after the communion, and later this was combined with the cleansing of the chalice. In the Sarum rite the ablutions took place before the post communion, and the priest was to consume the remains.

1549 made no mention of the subject; but 1552 allowed the incumbent the use of what remains, making no distinction between consecrated and unconsecrated bread and wine. 1662 states that the incumbent should keep unconsecrated bread and wine for his own use, but that any remaining consecrated elements are not to be removed from the church, but consumed after the service by the priest, assisted if necessary by some of the communicants. The 1928 book controversially permitted some of the consecrated elements to be reserved for the Communion of the Sick. Series 2 directed that 'what is not required for purposes of Communion shall be consumed after all have communicated' by the priest or other ministers; or else it may be consumed after the end of the service. These provisions have remained in each subsequent revision, Series 3, *ASB* and *CW*.

Prayer after Communion
The appearance of a formal conclusion to the service, after the administration of communion, can be dated to the legalization of Christianity in the fourth century and the consequent move to larger, public buildings for worship. While some rites added a fixed post-communion prayer of thanksgiving, the Roman rite, perhaps from the fifth century, had a variable post-communion collect, which was generally a prayer for grace and perseverance, followed at once by the dismissal.

The 1549 book follows this traditional pattern, with a salutation followed by a fixed Prayer of Thanksgiving, but 1552 brought changes to this part of the service. First the priest was to say the Lord's Prayer ('the people repeating him after every petition'), which had previously been placed before communion. Then came one of two prayers, either the Prayer of Oblation, which in 1549 had been part of the eucharistic prayer, or the Prayer of Thanksgiving from 1549; and then the *Gloria in Excelsis* 'shall be said or sung' as an act of praise. This pattern continued in 1662. 1928 re-integrated the Prayer of Oblation into the Prayer of Consecration and restored the Lord's Prayer to its earlier position, and so reduced the post-communion section to the Prayer of Thanksgiving followed by the *Gloria in Excelsis* (which could be omitted on weekdays).

Series 1 and Series 2 each provided a range of options, which varied from a brief 1549-style conclusion to a full 1552-style, including the *Gloria*, together with a short congregational prayer. Series 3 had a short seasonal sentence of Scripture, and then either a new fixed presidential prayer, 'Father of all . . .', or the congregational prayer, revised from Series 2, with the option of adding the *Gloria in Excelsis*. The *ASB* was similar, but allowed other suitable prayers to be added. Various post-communion prayers appeared in subsequent service books, including *LHWE* and *PHG*, and these firmly established the idea of variable post communions. *CW* permits the use of any appropriate scriptural sentence (Note 4), but provides a proper post-communion prayer for every occasion for which a collect is provided (see Chapter 8 on Collects). This post communion or another suitable prayer must be used. This may include one of the two *ASB* invariable post-communion prayers, both of which are now congregational, or one of them may be used after the post communion.

The first of the two was written by the Liturgical Commission for Series 2 as a prayer of dedication and was expanded in Series 3 to include thanksgiving. Its first sentence echoes the opening clause of the 1662 Prayer of Thanksgiving; its second sentence is drawn from the 1662 Prayer of Oblation; and its third sentence refers to the work of the Holy Spirit whose presence is necessary for the communicants to live and work in the world to the praise and glory of God.

The second alternative, written by Professor David Frost, has been described as 'an extended thanksgiving for redemption in Christ, with a prayer for the final victory of his Kingdom'. Like his version of the Prayer of Humble Access, it is full of scriptural echo and verbal ambiguity. It begins with an allusion to the parable of the Prodigal Son: though we were far off, God came in Christ to meet the prodigal human race, opening for us the gate to Spirit-filled achievement in this earthly life. Like the apostles, saints and martyrs we drink his cup. Illumined and set on fire by the Spirit, we must not hide our lights under a bushel, but give light to the world. Finally, in the imagery of the letter to the Hebrews, we pray that we may be anchored in the hope that we have grasped, so that as God's slaves we and the whole world may be truly free. Although Series 3 and the *ASB* printed this as a presidential text, it came to be said congregationally in many places, and this is recognized in *CW*.

Four further alternatives to these prayers are provided in the Supplementary Texts, the first three of which are congregational. The first is taken almost unaltered from the 1975 *Methodist Service Book* (the Revision Committee deliberately altering 'people' to 'peoples'); the second is a new composition, deliberately linking Holy Communion with baptism as the result of a suggestion from Barry Rogerson, the Bishop of Bristol, to the Revision Committee; the third is from the Scottish *Book of Common Order*; and the fourth is an adaptation of the *BCP* Prayer of Thanksgiving.

The Dismissal

Blessing

The first evidence for something like a blessing at the end of the Eucharist comes in the fourth century, when the Sacramentary of Sarapion has a prayer with the laying-on (or stretching out) of hands, the equivalent of the prayer said at the dismissal of the catechumens prior to the liturgy of the sacrament, and a similar arrangement is found in later Eastern and Western rites. In the Leonine Sacramentary a prayer over the people (*super populum*) was a feature of every Mass, but in the Gregorian sacramentary it was restricted to Lent, where it was intended primarily for those undergoing penance at that time, though later used for the whole congregation. This Lenten custom remained in the Roman rite until the revision of Paul VI. Blessings as such, however, began as informal acts of the bishop as he left the church, and only later came to be given from the altar, and by priests as well as bishops.

In the 1548 Order, the communicants are dismissed from the altar with the Peace from Philippians 4.7. In 1549 this became the first half of a blessing at the end of the service, which has remained the standard form in Anglican use. Series 3 made a blessing optional and introduced ten seasonal forms, largely the work of E. C. Whitaker. In the *ASB* these were increased to 21. *CW* provides seven other forms for general use, and a further 13 forms for holy days and seasons.

It can be argued that after receiving communion no further blessing is necessary; on the other hand the blessing said by the president is a long Anglican tradition, and also includes any non-communicants attending the Eucharist.

Dismissals

The first unambiguous evidence of a formal dismissal is also from the fourth century. In Eastern rites the deacon would say to the people 'Depart in peace', and a typical response was 'In the name of Christ'. In Rome the usual form was *Ite, missa est* (literally, 'Go, it is the dismissal'), which cannot be documented before the eighth century but may have been used much earlier. As the Roman rite spread, this dismissal came to be used on festal occasions, and the Gallican ending, 'Let us bless the Lord', on ferial occasions. To each of them the response was *Deo gratias*, 'Thanks be to God'. At Easter, Alleluias were added.

Although some reformers retained the dismissal, Cranmer omitted it. Series 2 restored it as a preferred option immediately before the Blessing, but in Series 3 it follows the optional Blessing, and is itself mandatory. The *ASB* provided two forms, the first being an expansion of the Series 3 form. These remain in *CW*, with the Easter variation with Alleluias explicitly printed. Note 1 directs that the people should stand for the dismissal.

Eucharistic Prayers for use in Order One

Early Christian liturgical prayers in general, including eucharistic prayers, followed their Jewish predecessors in being composed of two main elements.

The first was praise in one form or another for all that God had done for his people, more often by telling the story of those salvific acts than by heaping up laudatory epithets (for a biblical example, see 1 Kings 8.15–21). This was usually followed by petition for God to continue to work in that way among his people now. Sometimes the words indicated that the purpose of the request was not for the benefit of the worshippers but so that God's glory might be known in all the world. The prayer always ended on a note of praise.

In the course of the fourth century several distinctive patterns of Christian eucharistic prayer began to emerge in the various geographical regions of the ancient world, largely influenced by the relative positioning of the *Sanctus* and institution narrative, which were then becoming standard features of all such prayers.

It might be said that, broadly speaking and not very surprisingly, the *BCP* tradition maintained the general shape of the medieval Roman eucharistic prayer then being used throughout Western Christendom. This was even true from 1552 onwards, in spite of the opening dialogue, preface, and *Sanctus* then being detached from the beginning of the prayer; the intercessory element moved to an earlier part of the rite; and what had formerly followed the institution narrative deferred until after the reception of communion. In this Roman pattern, the initial praise was very brief and general in character, with Proper Prefaces inserted at particular seasons to emphasize certain aspects of God's acts, and it ended with the *Sanctus*. What followed was chiefly petitionary, with the request for God to consecrate the bread and wine preceding the narrative of institution and *anamnesis*.

It was this basic shape that Series 2, Series 3, and the *ASB* continued in their eucharistic prayers, although restoring the integrity of the prayer once more by bringing the preface and *Sanctus* back together with an *epiclesis* over the bread and wine, the narrative of institution, *anamnesis*, and the concluding petitions and praise. These prayers also included a fuller Trinitarian thanksgiving in their prefaces than the classic Roman prayer had retained. (The only slight exception to this pattern came in the third eucharistic prayer of the *ASB*. Because this had been influenced by the eucharistic prayer from the ancient *Apostolic Tradition*, its preface had more of a sense of narrative or story-telling than the others.) This same shape can still be seen in the prayers in *CW* that are descended from those in the *ASB* (Prayers A, B and C) as well as in the new Prayer E. As Figure 6.2 shows, in all these prayers the Thanksgiving ends at the *Sanctus* (or *Benedictus*) and the remainder is petitionary, with the narrative of institution being set within that context. The other new compositions, on the other hand, are largely patterned after the classic Eastern 'Antiochene' shape, in which the praise has a more extended narrative character, telling the story of salvation history to a greater or lesser degree, and the *Sanctus* and institution narrative are both incorporated within that part of the prayer. Here petition does not begin until later, giving the prayer a quite different feel. Prayer H forms a partial exception, in that the *Sanctus* is placed as the conclusion of the whole prayer.

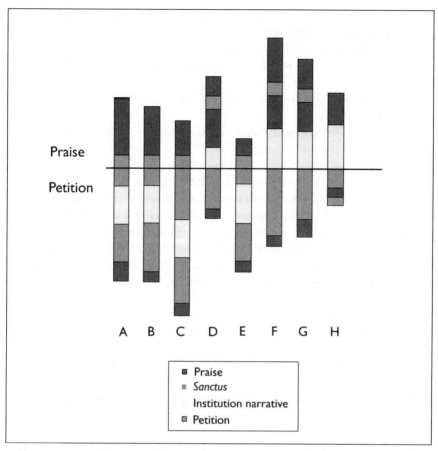

Figure 6.2
Structure of the eucharistic prayers, indicating the relative number of words in each component.

Prayer A
This is a conflation and mild revision of the first and second eucharistic prayers from the *ASB*, which in turn were derived from Series 3 and Series 2 respectively. It largely follows the text of the first *ASB* prayer, but with some phrases from the second. As with the second *ASB* prayer, the standard preface may be omitted if a short Proper Preface is used. Alternatively, the section between the opening dialogue and the *Sanctus* may be replaced with a longer preface from the seasonal provision. The most obvious difference from the earlier versions is that the acclamations are moved to a position following the *anamnesis*, rather than immediately after the institution narrative (see above, p. 126). Other notable features include:

- the option of the use of an extended preface in place of the standard one;

- the option of simple, repeated congregational responses or acclamations, 'To you be glory and praise for ever';
- the credal character of the standard preface;
- the *epiclesis* over the bread and wine placed before the institution narrative;
- the variety of verbs in the *anamnesis*: 'we remember . . . we proclaim . . . we look for . . .';
- and the inclusion of a further acclamation at the end of the Doxology.

Prayer B
This is a revision of the third prayer from the *ASB*. That prayer had been introduced at a late stage in the revision process, and had received less scrutiny than the other prayers. Its vivid imagery and conscious link with the text of the eucharistic prayer in the ancient *Apostolic Tradition* have given it a recognized place in the Church's worship. It closely follows the second eucharistic prayer of the revised Roman rite, itself based on the *Apostolic Tradition*.

The changes from the *ASB* are minor, principally:

- in the second paragraph 'lived on earth' replaces 'seen on earth', to preclude the possibility of a Docetic interpretation that the incarnate Lord was only an apparition;
- a rearrangement of part of the *anamnesis*, 'As we offer you this our sacrifice . . .';
- the omission from before the Doxology of the phrase, 'from whom all good things come', which was not in the *Apostolic Tradition*.

As with Prayer A, the section between the opening dialogue and the *Sanctus* may be replaced with a longer preface from the seasonal provision. Alternatively, a short Proper Preface may be inserted before the introduction to the *Sanctus*.

Prayer C
This is a conservative revision of the fourth prayer from the *ASB*, in turn deriving from the prayer in the 1662 rite, with its strong emphasis on redemption by the one perfect sacrifice of Christ on the cross. This is stressed even more in this revision, which reinstates some of the earlier wording, especially in the paragraph after the *Sanctus* and *Benedictus*, 'who made there by his one oblation of himself once offered a full, perfect and sufficient sacrifice, oblation and satisfaction for the sins of the whole world'.

Other distinguishing features include:

- the presence of the *epiclesis* over the bread and wine before the institution narrative, in common with the other eucharistic prayers in the *ASB*;
- the use of a single verb in the *anamnesis*: 'in remembrance of . . . we offer you through him this our sacrifice of praise and thanksgiving'.

Prayer D

This is a new composition. It tells the story of redemption in more direct and dramatic language, so that the past may come alive in the present. Proper Prefaces, whether short or long, are not used with this prayer, nor are any of the 'standard' acclamations. Its distinguishing features include:

- use of concrete, not abstract, scriptural images, with short sentences;
- repeated use of a congregational response of praise;
- the use of 'heaven' before and after the *Sanctus* as a link word;
- a shorter institution narrative;
- the use of a single verb in the *anamnesis*: 'we celebrate the cross';
- an *epiclesis* towards the end of the prayer: 'send your Spirit on us now' followed by an allusion to the Emmaus story;
- a further acclamation at the end of the Doxology, as in Prayer A.

Prayer E

Like Prayer D, this is a new composition in a simpler narrative style, using vivid and concrete imagery to tell the story of our redemption. Its distinctive features are:

- a very brief preface, which is intended normally to be replaced by an extended preface (with the short preface this is a relatively brief prayer, shorter than any in *ASB* Rite A);
- a single *epiclesis* placed before the institution narrative;
- in addition to the verbs 'remember' and 'proclaim', the use of 'plead with confidence' together with a reference to 'bringing before' God the bread and cup in the *anamnesis*;
- the acclamations placed after the *anamnesis* rather than directly after the institution narrative.

Prayer F

This is much influenced by the eucharistic prayer of St Basil, an Eastern text which in its oldest form probably does go back to the time of Basil the Great (d. 379). It is still used on occasion in the Eastern Orthodox Church, and abbreviated and revised forms can be found in the modern Roman rite (as eucharistic prayer IV) and in the American 1979 *BCP* (as Eucharistic Prayer D, also used by other American denominations), both of which are more direct translations than the form in *CW*. In keeping with this Eastern origin, the prayer does not provide for any Proper Prefaces, short or long, but is always used as it stands. However, the congregational acclamations, which are not the 'standard' ones, may be omitted.

The prayer rehearses the story of salvation, from the covenant relationship with the Father, through the incarnate activity of the Son, to the invocation of the Spirit near the end. Thus the congregation is explicitly caught up into the life of the Trinity. Distinguishing features include:

- the imagery, such as 'you placed us in the garden of your delight', which is reminiscent of both Genesis and Revelation (in the Greek text there is a stronger emphasis on pleasure and enjoyment);
- the acclamations running through the prayer, which catch something of the fervour of the Eastern tradition (Note 18 suggests that these might be led by a minister other than the president and then repeated by the congregation);
- its description of the glory and power of God being revealed as much by the humiliation of the incarnation and the cross as by the splendour of heaven;
- the range of verbs in the *anamnesis*: 'proclaim . . . celebrate . . . rejoice . . . long for . . .';
- the *epiclesis* positioned after the institution narrative;
- and the brief intercessions towards the end of the prayer ('bless the earth, heal the sick, let the oppressed go free and fill your Church with power from on high').

Prayer G

This derives ultimately from an original eucharistic prayer composed by the Roman Catholic Commission on English in the Liturgy in 1984 but never authorized for use. It first appeared close to its present form in the *PW* report of 1989, and subsequently was one of six eucharistic prayers which failed to gain final approval in the General Synod in 1996. It was included here at a late stage of the revision process. It is revised slightly from the 1996 form, principally by the removal of seasonal insertions at three points in the prayer, the slight rewording of the *epiclesis*, and the addition of the petition for fruitful reception from Prayer 2 in the *ASB* ('build us into a living temple to your glory'), which was not included in Prayer A. Notable features include:

- the opening paragraph 'Blessed are you . . .', echoing Jewish prayers and also the response to the offertory prayers in the modern Roman rite and to the version of those prayers in *CW* (item 4 of the Prayers at the Preparation of the Table);
- a vivid use of paradox in such phrases as 'silent music', found first in the works of John of the Cross, and 'we bring before you these gifts of your creation';
- the use of feminine imagery: 'as a mother tenderly gathers her children' reflecting God's gathering of his people, as in Isaiah 66.13 and Matthew 23.37;
- no provision for Proper Prefaces, short or long;

- the *anamnesis*: 'we plead with confidence . . . we remember . . . we rejoice . . .';
- a single *epiclesis*: 'pour out your Holy Spirit . . . may they [these gifts] be for us the body and blood of your dear Son';
- provision for optional intercession for the Church;
- and a further acclamation at the end of the Doxology, as in Prayer A.

Prayer H

This prayer was developed late in the synodical revision process in response to strong requests for more 'interactive' material. Thus, the congregational texts are not solely acclamation or refrain but integral to the 'forward movement' of the prayer. However, the role of the president as the focus of the unity of the congregation is maintained: in each section of the prayer, the first part is spoken by the president, and the second part by the congregation, so that the president initiates the dialogue. This is a brief prayer, and there is much compression and distillation of the elements normally found in a eucharistic prayer. This was considered acceptable in the context of a range of possible prayers, but it would be an impoverishment to use it as the only or main eucharistic prayer. Other distinctive features include:

- phrases and allusions familiar from other prayers; for example, the first dialogue alludes to the parable of the Prodigal Son, an image already used in one of the prayers after communion in the *ASB* and in *CW*;
- no provision for Proper Prefaces, short or long: this prayer has a single, fixed form;
- the 'standard' acclamations are not used;
- a very brief *anamnesis*: 'we proclaim his death and celebrate his rising in glory';
- a single *epiclesis* after the institution narrative, in similar words to the other prayers;
- the conclusion of the prayer with the *Sanctus* and the omission of the *Benedictus qui venit*. Although there is no congregational 'Amen', the *Sanctus* is itself the assembly's affirmation of the thanksgiving expressed in the prayer as a whole. This pattern may have existed in the very early period of the Church's history, although we have no extant examples of it, but there is some precedent for it, originating with Luther and continuing in various rites. Two of the four eucharistic prayers in *PW* had concluded with the *Sanctus*, but this arrangement failed to survive the revision process even before the prayers were rejected in 1996. Prayer H is thus the first time the *Sanctus* has been used this way in the Church of England, but here it forms a fitting crescendo of praise and a reminder of the bliss in the courts of heaven already present in the grace of Christ.

Proper Prefaces

Two sorts of Proper Preface are provided in *CW*. Some prayers allow short insertions, which have been the style customary in the Church of England since 1549; and some allow a longer thematic seasonal preface which replaces all the material between the opening dialogue and the *Sanctus*. These are a new departure for the Church of England. Prayers A and B allow the use of either a short or an extended Proper Preface. Prayer C, which has a short common preface, only allows the insertion of short Proper Prefaces. Prayer E allows only the use of the extended prefaces, and not the short insertions. Prayers D, F, G and H make no provision for Proper Prefaces at all.

The two extended prefaces for Advent are adapted from the modern Roman Catholic rite, and several others from the (as yet unpublished) Roman Catholic Sacramentary in English: for the Sundays before Lent and after Trinity; from Christmas Day until the Eve of the Epiphany; from Ash Wednesday until the Saturday after the Fourth Sunday of Lent; The Annunciation of Our Lord; from the Fifth Sunday of Lent until the Wednesday of Holy Week; Ascension Day; on days between Ascension Day and Pentecost; and for the feast of Christ the King. The extended preface from the Epiphany until the Eve of the Presentation is from a preface by the Reverend Stephen Mitchell; that for the Presentation of Christ in the Temple is a combination of two prefaces in *PHG* (one of which appears in adapted form as the short preface), with additional lines about Simeon and Anna and Anna's prophecy; that for Easter Day until the Eve of the Ascension is a light revision of the preface for the Wednesday of the second week of Easter from Alan Griffiths' *We Give You Thanks and Praise* (1999); that for the Day of Pentecost is slightly adapted from Michael Perham's *Enriching the Christian Year*; those for All Saints' Day and for the period from the day after All Saints' Day until the day before the First Sunday of Advent are adapted from *PW*; and the rest are the work of the Liturgical Commission.

C. ORDER ONE IN TRADITIONAL LANGUAGE

Most of what has been said above also applies to Order One in Traditional Language, with the obvious exception of linguistic matters. However, it should be noted that several of the principal congregational texts, the *Gloria in Excelsis*, Creed and *Agnus Dei* are not the modern language versions rendered back into traditional language, but the older versions already familiar from Rite B in the *ASB*. This means, among other things, that 'sins' and not 'sin' is used in them, that the reference to the incarnation in the Creed remains 'and was incarnate by the Holy Ghost of the Virgin Mary' and that, while both modern and traditional language versions of the Lord's Prayer are included (though their order is reversed), only the traditional form of the *Agnus Dei* and Prayer of Humble Access are printed and not their modern alternatives. The prayers after communion are also different: the first is the *BCP* Prayer of

Thanksgiving and the second is the shorter first prayer from Order One, both already familiar from the *ASB* Rite B.

Nor is the full range of eucharistic prayers provided, but only Prayers A and C. Prayer A is slightly different from that in Order One. The text is that of the *ASB* Rite B first prayer with a few minor changes rather than a direct rendering of the Rite One version. It lacks the extended prefaces and optional acclamations of that version, as well as the acclamation at the end; and it places the acclamation after the institution narrative later in the prayer, after the *anamnesis*, and makes it entirely optional, with just two instead of four alternative forms. One of these is 'Christ has died . . .', familiar since Series 3; the other, 'O Saviour of the world . . .', is new as a eucharistic acclamation in the Church of England although found in the *BCP* Visitation of the Sick. (Any attempt to put the other two acclamations into traditional language will soon demonstrate why they are omitted.) Prayer C is the second prayer from the *ASB* Rite B, with the same slight adjustments as have been made in the version in Order One, but again with only the two optional acclamations provided in Prayer A. Both these prayers omit the directions for the manual acts which were in the *ASB* Rite B.

D. ORDER TWO

Order Two allows for the equivalent of Series 1, the *BCP* rite as commonly used in many places, with various omissions and additions to it (any additions to the *BCP* text are aligned right so that it is easy to see what the 'straight' Prayer Book text is). Most of the above commentary also applies to the various parts of this service. In addition, of course, the *BCP* order itself remains unchanged and authorized for liturgical use, though not printed in *CW*. Several texts, such as the first Lord's Prayer and the Prayer of Preparation, are printed in normal type, since the *BCP* directs that these be said by the priest. However, this rubric is omitted in several places in Order Two, so that they may be said by the congregation where that is the local custom. Texts such as the Nicene Creed and the *Gloria in Excelsis* are printed as they appear in the *BCP*, rather than as they appear in Order One in traditional language.

The Summary of the Law or the *Kyries* may be used in place of the Ten Commandments, except on the first Sundays of Advent and Lent. The Collect for the Sovereign is made optional, and the salutation, 'The Lord be with you/and with thy spirit' may be used before the Collect of the Day. There may be an Old Testament reading in addition to the Epistle and Gospel, and the 1928 responses before and after the Gospel may be used. The Creed can be omitted except on Sundays and Holy Days; brief biddings may precede the 'Prayer for the Whole State of Christ's Church'; and the exhortations are made optional. The *Sursum corda* is now preceded by the Salutation, the *Benedictus* may be added to the *Sanctus*, the *Agnus Dei* may be used before the giving of communion, and the Lord's Prayer is provided with an optional introduction.

The full rubrics of the manual acts are included in the Prayer of Consecration. Supplementary consecration is also provided for, but in the same form as in Order One.

The Notes, however, permit further adaptation of Order Two. Any of the Supplementary Texts that are compatible with it may be used, and the third form of intercession in the Supplementary Texts may replace that in the main text (Note 25). This appeared as the first intercession in the *ASB*'s Rite B, and derives from the 1928/Series 1 version of the *BCP*'s 'Prayer for the Whole State of Christ's Church'. The sermon may precede the Creed, as in Order One (Note 26), and the shape of the eucharistic prayer may also be modified (Note 27) so that it conforms to that of the Interim Rite described earlier in this chapter: the Prayer of Humble Access may be placed before the *Sursum corda* (or Salutation if that is used), so that the *Sanctus* may lead directly into the Prayer of Consecration, with the Prayer of Oblation following on at the end, and then the Lord's Prayer; the Peace may be inserted between the Lord's Prayer and the *Agnus Dei*, and the breaking of the bread may be deferred from the institution narrative until the *Agnus Dei*. Finally, the short Proper Prefaces of Order One may be adapted for use with Order Two (Note 28), and permission is given to omit the *Gloria in Excelsis* on Sundays in Advent and Lent and on all weekdays that are not Principal Holy Days or Festivals (Note 29).

E. ORDER TWO IN CONTEMPORARY LANGUAGE

There are a number of Anglicans who wish to worship in modern language but still retain the shape of the 1662 Prayer Book Eucharist. To meet their needs, this version of Order Two has been included in *CW*. The *ASB* had provided a similar form as a supplement to Rite A, 'The Order Following the Pattern of the *Book of Common Prayer*'. This supplement contained the complete text for the service after the intercessions. *CW* instead provides a complete order of service. In structure, it is almost entirely the same as Order Two. In language, the texts are wherever possible drawn from Order One.

However, slightly more flexibility is permitted here than in Order Two itself. The first Lord's Prayer is explicitly optional, and the permission is also given to abbreviate the Ten Commandments slightly, and to omit some of its responses. The same wide range of options is provided for the intercessions as in Order One, and the seasonal provisions from that Order may also be used at the appropriate points in the rite. There are alternative forms of confession, and the alternative version of the Prayer of Humble Access and of the Prayer of Thanksgiving after communion from Order One are included. On the other hand, unlike Order Two, no provision is made for an Old Testament reading, a short exhortation must be used before the invitation to confession, and the Salutation is not added to the *Sursum corda*, nor is the option given to use the *Agnus Dei* at the end of the Prayer of Consecration or to defer the breaking of the bread until that point (Note 27).

References and Further Reading

Colin Buchanan, *Eucharistic Consecration*, Grove Worship Series 148, Cambridge, 1998.

William R. Crockett, *Eucharist: Symbol of Transformation*, Pueblo, New York, 1989.

Gregory Dix, *The Shape of the Liturgy*, Dacre, London, 1945.

Alan Griffiths, *We Give You Thanks and Praise*, Canterbury Press, Norwich, 1999.

David R. Holeton (ed.), *Revising the Eucharist: Groundwork for the Anglican Communion, Studies in Preparation for the 1995 Dublin Consultation*, Alcuin/GROW Liturgical Study 27, Nottingham, 1994.

David R. Holeton (ed.), *Renewing the Anglican Eucharist: Findings of the Fifth International Anglican Liturgical Consultation, Dublin, Eire, 1995*, Grove Worship Series 135, Nottingham, 1996.

David R. Holeton (ed.), *Our Thanks and Praise: the Eucharist in Anglicanism today. Papers from the Fifth International Anglican Liturgical Consultation*, Anglican Book Centre, Toronto, Canada, 1998.

ICET, *Prayers We Have in Common*, Chapman, London, 1970.

R. C. D. Jasper and G. J. Cuming, *Prayers of the Eucharist: Early and Reformed*, 3rd edn, Pueblo, New York, 1987.

Enrico Mazza, *The Origins of the Eucharistic Prayer*, The Liturgical Press, Collegeville, Minnesota, 1995.

Michael Perham, *Lively Sacrifice*, SPCK, London, 1992.

Michael Perham, *Enriching the Christian Year*, SPCK/Alcuin Club, London, 1993.

Chapter 7

Initiation Services

A. HISTORY

The Old Testament and Jewish Background

Water has occupied a major place in the symbolism and ritual of many religions, for it is naturally rich in associations. It can express cleansing and purification, or refreshment and regeneration. It can be seen as bringing life, since water is necessary for all life; but equally it can be seen as bringing death by drowning, and in some religions water symbolizes the chaos before life began. In ancient Israelite practice water was used to cleanse from impurity (e.g. Leviticus 15.5–13), and the prophets had spoken of God's people being sprinkled with pure water to be made clean in the messianic age (e.g. Ezekiel 36.25). In the first century AD one Jewish group, the community at Qumran, employed regular lustrations as a means of moral and ritual purification. Moreover, the initiation of converts from pagan backgrounds into Judaism came to include a ritual purification by immersion, in addition to the circumcision of the male candidates. This process was preceded by instruction in the Law, and completed by the offering of sacrifice.

The New Testament

There were therefore plenty of precedents for the Christian adoption of baptism as the ritual initiation of new converts into the messianic community. But the immediate precursor and inspiration appears to have been the practice of John the Baptist, who offered a baptism of repentance for the forgiveness of sins. He, in turn, may have been influenced by the tradition of prophetic symbolism, by the Essene lustrations, by Jewish proselyte baptism, or by a combination of all three. The synoptic Gospels all record Jesus' baptism by John, when the Spirit descended upon him after he emerged from the water, and this greatly influenced the theology and ritual of later Christian practice. It is not clear, however, whether Jesus himself instituted the baptism of his disciples, or whether this was something developed by the Church after the resurrection. The synoptic Gospels contain no account of Jesus baptizing anyone, but John 3.22 and 26 do speak of him doing so. In contradiction of this, John 4.2 states that Jesus, unlike his disciples, did not baptize. Most New Testament scholars would doubt that the command in Matthew 28.19 to baptize 'in the name of the Father and of the Son and of the Holy Spirit' is an authentic saying of Jesus, and would consider it to have been put into his mouth by later Christians who were using this doctrinally developed formula in their initiation practice.

On the other hand, what is clear from elsewhere in the New Testament is that from early times it was the normal custom to initiate new converts into the Church through a process which included baptism, performed no doubt in a river, pool, or domestic bath-house. The effects of this conversion experience are described in a variety of ways by different New Testament writers, including the forgiveness of sins, cleansing, illumination, new birth, incorporation into the death and resurrection of Christ, being clothed with Christ, and reception of the Holy Spirit.

What else besides baptism was involved in the process of Christian initiation in the first century is not made very explicit in the New Testament. There may have been a preparatory period of instruction, but the Acts of the Apostles gives the impression that there was little, if any, delay between an individual's decision to become a Christian and the act of baptism itself, and it implies that the rite included a profession of faith in Jesus. Whether any other ceremonies formed a regular part of the ritual has been disputed. Some would see the reference to a post-baptismal imposition of hands in Acts 8.17f and 19.5f, coupled with the reference to 'ablutions' and 'the laying-on of hands' in Hebrews 6.2, as indicating what was the normal procedure in all acts of initiation, even though not always explicitly mentioned. Other scholars would suggest that the two instances in Acts are of exceptional situations and do not necessarily reflect the regular initiation practice of the Church. They would point to the fact that a post-baptismal imposition of hands was by no means a universal feature of initiation rites in the early centuries, a surprising omission if it were of apostolic origin. Similarly, some would believe that behind references in the New Testament to being 'anointed with Holy Spirit' lies the liturgical practice of a literal anointing with oil in the initiation rite (see, for example, 1 John 2.20, 27), whereas others would see such references simply as a vivid metaphor. There is also uncertainty about whether or not children were baptized along with their parents in New Testament times: much depends upon how references to the baptism of 'households' (Acts 16.15, 31–4; 18.8; 1 Corinthians 1.16) are understood.

The Second and Third Centuries
Documents from these centuries suggest that differences in theology and practice existed both within and between different geographical locations. The descriptions of baptism in the *Didache* and by Justin Martyr give no more than an outline of a rite and, together, make reference to fasting before baptism, the assent of the candidate, a triple pouring of water with Trinitarian formula, and a eucharistic celebration.

By the beginning of the third century, Tertullian describes his North African community baptizing children and adults between Easter and Pentecost, although he maintains that 'any hour, any season, is suitable for baptism'. The bishop is the normal minister of initiation, but may delegate this responsibility to presbyters or deacons. A prayer over the water is followed by a renunciation of the devil and imposition of the bishop's hand; a triple profession of faith is accompanied by a triple immersion before the candidate is anointed and signed with the cross; the bishop then lays his hands on the head of the neophyte 'in benediction, inviting and welcoming the Holy Spirit'. There then follows a Eucharist in which the newly baptized make their first communion.

The *Apostolic Tradition*, traditionally attributed to Hippolytus and thought to have originated in Rome in the early third century, describes a broadly similar process, but with a number of variants in the details. However, because the real origin of this text is so uncertain, it is difficult to use it as independent evidence for third-century Roman practice.

In Syria, the *Odes of Solomon*, *Didascalia Apostolorum* and *Acts of Judas Thomas* provide some evidence of the baptismal theologies and practices of this early period. Unfortunately, however, such information lacks any detailed commentary, and it is only with the fourth-century writings of Aphrahat, Ephrem and Narsai that the liturgical picture becomes clearer. Here rites began with a renunciation of evil, made by the candidate facing west (the region of darkness), followed by an act of adherence to Christ, made facing east (the region of light). In response to this, the bishop would anoint the head of the candidate before deacons anointed the whole body. The Syrian tradition interprets these anointings in many ways. Most commonly, it is seen as the necessary preparation for regeneration in the womb of the font. The oil is the means by which the candidate is marked out: marked out as one who belongs to Christ, marked out for protection from evil, and marked out for the washing away of sins. The immersion was accompanied by the indicative formula, 'I baptize you in the name of the Father, and of the Son, and of the Holy Spirit' – words from Matthew 28.19 which may, itself, have originated in Syria. With the possible exception of some Gnostic groups, there is no post-immersion anointing in the Syrian rite in this period, though it is possible that the *Didascalia* witnesses to the bishop laying on hands with the formula, 'You are my Son. This day have I begotten you', after the immersion as a ritual declaration of the status of the newly begotten neophytes.

Later Developments

Christian initiation underwent a number of significant developments in the fourth century. The large numbers of people wishing to be baptized after the conversion of Constantine resulted in a less rigorous scrutiny of the motives and conduct of potential candidates. At the same time, however, it was believed that the remission of sins conferred in baptism could only be conveyed once and, as a result, there arose a desire to delay baptism for as long as possible in order to be more certain of gaining ultimate salvation. Thus people often remained in the status of 'catechumen' ('learner') for many years, admission to which was marked by the sign of the cross and sometimes other ceremonial acts as well. When they did eventually decide to proceed further, their actual period of preparation (instruction, exorcism, and other ceremonies) usually took place during the season of Lent prior to baptism at Easter.

Since it was no longer invariably the case that candidates for baptism had undergone a conversion experience before becoming a catechumen, the liturgy now adopted theatrical elements from pagan mystery religions designed to produce an intense and life-changing impression upon the candidates. Preachers described initiation as 'awe-inspiring' and 'hair-raising', and striking ceremonial, such as clothing the neophyte in a white robe and giving a lighted candle, was used after the immersion. Moreover, the notion of secrecy, once a necessity in face of persecution, was now employed to create dramatic tension, the various ceremonies only being explained to the candidates after baptism. Thus the emphasis shifted from the rite as an expression of a prior experience to the rite as a means of effecting that experience.

Although in both East and West there existed variety of practice in the way Christian initiation was celebrated, this period also witnessed a borrowing of features from one another, which in the end resulted in a greater conformity of structure. Thus, over a period of time, communities in the East adopted a post-immersion anointing, while the use of the indicative formula, 'I baptize you . . .' gradually spread to the Western Church, the threefold profession of faith now preceding immersion rather than accompanying it. Having exported its formula, the East began to use a passive formula, 'N. is baptized in the name . . .', to express that baptism was the action of God rather than the minister.

Later came the transition from mainly adult to almost exclusively infant baptism. Exactly the same fear of failing to obtain salvation which, at first, had caused the tendency to defer baptism led later to a desire to baptize babies soon after birth, in case they should die unbaptized. Thus, during the period in which the Church was involved in missionary expansion, both adults and children underwent initiation together. Eventually, however, as Christendom became established, adult candidates were rare, leaving only the children of Christian parents to be baptized. They were admitted to the Church by a process intended for adults, and treated as adults who were unable to speak. They entered a brief catechumenate in Lent, during which an element of solemn teaching of the Creed continued to be given to them, and sponsors or godparents answered the questions in the rite on their behalf.

The Medieval West

The basic pattern of the Eastern model has remained unchanged to the present day: babies are baptized, chrismated and become full communicants in one rite. In the West, however, later centuries saw further profound changes in the theology and practice of initiation.

With the enormous increase in the size of the Church from the fourth century onwards, in most parts of the world the great distances and number of candidates involved made it impossible for the church in a diocese to gather round their bishop at Easter for a single celebration of initiation. On the whole, this problem was not solved by creating more bishoprics but, rather, in both East and West, by presbyters deputizing for their bishop and conducting the whole of the rite, performing the anointings with oils previously blessed by the bishop.

In Rome and in southern Italy, where dioceses were quite small and communication easy, this practice was not followed. However, when the bishop was not available, the presbyter would conduct the whole rite, but omitting the post-immersion ceremonies which the bishop himself had performed, namely the prayer for the Holy Spirit accompanied by the laying-on of hands, and the anointing of the head. When the bishop was able to visit that church shortly afterwards, he would perform those parts of the rite which had been lacking. Because this delay in completing the rite could be kept very short, it was still possible to feel that the primitive unity of the initiation process and the bishop's part in it had been maintained.

In the course of time, however, the Roman usage was imposed upon the whole of the Western Church, and in different geographical contexts this solution did not work nearly so well. The delay between baptism and what came to be called 'confirmation' grew longer because of the rarity of episcopal visits. Moreover, when there was an episcopal visit, parents were often negligent in bringing their children to a short service that did not appear to add anything to the full communicant status of the baptized. Because of the uncertainty regarding the origin and meaning of 'confirmation', parish priests found it difficult to justify this practice. To encourage parents, various thirteenth-century Councils fixed age limits by which children should have been confirmed. Thus the Council of Durham in 1249 set the age limit at five, and directed that parents who failed in this duty should be denied entry into the church until the omission had been rectified.

Gradually, however, these *maximum* upper limits came to be widely thought of as the normal *minimum* ages for confirmation, and so by the end of the Middle Ages it generally came to be considered inappropriate for the rite to be administered until the child was seven years old. This delay was encouraged by the popular belief which saw confirmation as bestowing an additional gift of grace which strengthened the Christian to face the struggles and battles of life; clearly such a gift was better received not immediately after baptism but was most needed as the child grew up. This doctrine first appeared in a sermon published in the *False Decretals* of 850. The work of Faustus of Riez, a fifth-century bishop, its false attribution to the fourth-century Pope Melchiades led to its wide acceptance in subsequent years, to the extent that it was quoted by leading medieval theologians, including Thomas Aquinas.

The earlier practice, which saw the majority of baptisms at Easter and Pentecost, was prescribed by canon law in the West until the twelfth century. Nevertheless, because of the high risk of infant mortality, the baptism of babies was encouraged as soon after birth as possible. By the thirteenth century the practice of baptizing throughout the year was becoming widespread, and in the fourteenth century baptism within eight days of a child's birth tended to become the rule.

As a result of this, the catechumenate disappeared from the initiatory process, but the ceremonies which accompanied it were telescoped into the introductory rite of the baptism itself. Thus, at the end of the Middle Ages, the infant was admitted as a catechumen with the sign of the cross at the beginning of the service, and then followed in quick succession all the prayers, exorcistic anointings, and other ceremonies (recitation of the Creed, Lord's Prayer and Hail Mary) which in the earlier Roman rite had been spread over a period of six weeks. The whole of this section took place at the church door, the party not moving inside to the font until the baptismal rite proper. The renunciation had been moved from its position within this sequence to be made immediately before the profession of faith.

For a long time children, like adults, were admitted to communion after baptism, even when confirmation became separated from the initiatory rite. In the twelfth century, however, with the growth of the doctrine of 'realism' with regard to Christ's presence in the eucharistic elements, doubts were expressed about giving the bread to infants, since they would not be able to consume it with sufficient reverence, and so communion was given in the form of wine alone, or by allowing very young children to suck the priest's finger after he had dipped it in the chalice. When the chalice was subsequently withdrawn from the communion of the laity, this unintentionally excommunicated children, and led to the general rule that they should wait until they reached 'years of discretion' (which varied between seven and fourteen) before receiving communion, although in a few places infant communion continued until abolished by the Council of Trent in 1552.

Finally, one other change may be noted. Initiation had originally been celebrated in the context of public worship, but for the sake of convenience and so that there would be no disturbance from babies, the Western rites were eventually moved away from the main Sunday assembly, even though they still generally took place within the context of the Eucharist. Similarly, confirmation, being a brief ceremony, was conducted in private, even at the roadside as the bishop was passing.

The Reformation

Apart from the extreme radicals, the leaders of the Reformation did not question the practice of infant baptism, but proceeded to draw up revised and simplified rites. They dispensed with most of the ceremonies traditionally associated with Christian initiation, since they believed that these had either ceased to be understood or had come to be interpreted in a superstitious sense in the popular mind. Luther's baptism rite of 1526 began with the sign of the cross being made on the infant's forehead, two prayers, an exorcism, the reading of Mark 10.13–16 (the account of Jesus laying hands on children and blessing them, the Matthean version of which had become a part of the late medieval baptismal rite), and the laying-on of hands accompanied by the Lord's Prayer. The baptismal party then moved to the font, where the godparents made a triple renunciation and a triple profession of faith in the name of the child. The child was baptized with the now traditional indicative formula and the service ended with the priest putting the white christening robe on the child while saying a prayer of blessing.

With their customary emphasis on the importance of edification, other Reformers tended to replace the symbolic actions with a wealth of didactic and hortatory words. For some, the idea of addressing the infant, and the godparents making replies on his or her behalf presented difficulties, which they resolved by addressing the questions to the godparents themselves about their own faith. Thus, in the church order from Cologne commonly known as Hermann's *Consultation,* the section on baptism, which was the work of the Reformer Martin Bucer, contained a public 'catechism' of the parents and godparents which was to take place on the Saturday evening prior to the baptism. At this the minister was to read a very long statement, setting out what was held to be the true meaning of baptism, before they were asked a long series of questions concerning their own faith and intentions. A further exhortation followed this, and afterwards came an exorcism of the child, the making of the sign of the cross, two prayers (drawn from Luther's rite), the reading of Mark 10.13–16, and an imposition of hands on the child, while the Lord's Prayer and Creed were recited. This service concluded with the singing of certain selected Psalms and a prayer of thanksgiving and petition for the gift of the Holy Spirit. The baptism itself took place at the Eucharist the following morning, and the order of service began with another lengthy exhortation, the reading of Matthew 28.18–19, and a prayer. The children were then baptized and, after a hymn or Psalm, the Eucharist continued.

With regard to confirmation, the Reformers were unanimous in rejecting the notion that it was in any sense a sacrament instituted by Christ, since there was no New Testament warrant for this. Many were happy to retain a rite in which those baptized in infancy might, at an appropriate age and after due instruction, be examined as to their beliefs, make a solemn profession of their faith, and receive a laying-on of hands from the minister accompanied by a blessing or prayer for the strengthening power of the Holy Spirit. Some were even prepared to retain the name 'confirmation', and some believed, mistakenly, that this had been the original function of the rite of confirmation in the early Church. Such services also generally constituted the rite of admission to full communicant status in the Church.

The 1549 BCP

As can be seen from Table 7.1, the first English Prayer Book contained a conservative revision of the Sarum baptismal rite, which, while retaining some of the traditional ceremonies, also made use of Luther's and Hermann's *Consultation*. Like Sarum, the service began at the church door, but was to take place at one of the offices on a Sunday or other holy day, when most people could be present to witness the baptism and also be reminded of their own baptismal commitment, thus reclaiming baptism as a public service. A private service was also produced for use in emergencies.

Table 7.1: Outline of the medieval and Prayer Book baptismal rites.

Sarum	1549	1552
(at church door)	(at church door)	(at the font)
	Exhortation	Exhortation
	Prayer	Prayer
Sign of the cross	Sign of the cross	
Prayers and exorcisms	Prayer	Prayer
	Exorcism	
Gospel (Matt. 19.13–15)	Gospel (Mark 10.13–16)	Gospel (Mark 10.13–16)
	Exhortation	Exhortation
Lord's Prayer	Lord's Prayer	
Hail Mary		
Creed	Creed	
Sign right hand	Prayer	Prayer
Procession to font	Procession to font	
(Blessing of font)	Exhortation	Exhortation
Triple renunciation	Triple renunciation	Renunciation
Anointing		
Triple profession	Triple profession	Profession of faith
Desire for baptism	Desire for baptism	Desire for baptism
	(Prayers over water)	Prayers
Triple immersion	Triple immersion	Immersion
Anointing	Vesting in white robe	Sign of the cross
Vesting in white robe	Anointing	Lord's Prayer
Giving of candle		Prayer of thanksgiving
Charge to godparents	Charge to godparents	Charge to godparents

'Public Baptism' began with an exhortation to pray for the candidates, based on Hermann, followed by a free translation of one of Luther's prayers. There followed the making of the sign of the cross on each child's forehead and breast, with appropriate words (influenced by Hermann), and a further prayer and exorcism, drawn from the medieval rite. The priest then read Mark 10.13–16 (as in Luther's rite) and an exhortation, which drew attention to Christ's goodwill and desire to give the candidates the blessing of eternal life as evidenced by the Gospel reading, and invited the congregation in return to express their thanksgiving for this by saying the Lord's Prayer and their faith by reciting the Creed. A further prayer from Hermann for the candidates closed this part of the service before the party was led into the church and to the font.

The priest then addressed the godparents, making it clear that the promises which followed were made by the children through the godparents, who were their 'sureties'. A triple renunciation and triple profession of faith (using the Apostles' Creed) were followed by a form of blessing of the baptismal water, to be used whenever the water was changed. Each child was baptized with a triple immersion using the traditional formula. The child was then vested in a white robe and anointed on the head. The service ended with a charge to godparents (influenced by Hermann) to ensure that the children were taught 'what a solemn vow, promise, and profession they have made by you', and were to be brought to confirmation after receiving instruction in the Christian faith.

The 1549 service of confirmation was similarly conservative, its major innovation being the inclusion of a Catechism, which the child was expected to learn before being brought to the bishop. After the central prayer for the sevenfold gifts of the Spirit, the bishop made the sign of the cross on the forehead of each candidate, but without oil, having prayed that God would 'confirm and strengthen them with the inward unction of the Holy Ghost' instead of with the 'chrism of salvation'. An explicit laying-on of hands followed this, whereas before, this ancient gesture had become subsumed into the consignation with oil. The rite ended with 'the Peace', a concluding prayer (based on Hermann), and the blessing. The final rubric reaffirmed the English medieval rule that 'there shall none be admitted to the Holy Communion, until such time as he be confirmed'.

The 1552 BCP

Substantial criticism from Martin Bucer resulted in changes to baptism and confirmation in 1552. He claimed that the first part of the service should take place in the church so that all might hear it; that all who came to baptism did not need to have the devil driven out through exorcism; that the blessing of the water, the anointing, and the giving of the white robe were no longer appropriate as they aroused superstitious opinions; that questions should not be addressed to infants but to their godparents, who should be asked to undertake to ensure that in due course the child would renounce Satan and profess belief in God. Apart from the last, these points all had an effect on the 1552 revision.

Thus, the whole service took place at the font. The exorcism and other 'superstitious' ceremonies were removed so that the only ceremonial acts which remained were the baptism itself and the signing with the cross, which was transferred to a post-baptismal position. The Lord's Prayer and Creed were also removed from their pre-baptismal position. The latter was omitted, since it was duplicated in the profession of faith, and the Lord's Prayer appeared after baptism and the signing with the cross and before the prayer of thanksgiving and blessing, thus becoming parallel in structure with Holy Communion, where the Lord's Prayer and thanksgiving followed the reception of the sacrament. The renunciation and profession of faith were run together, so that each was in the form of a single question and answer.

Confirmation also underwent some significant changes. The opening rubrics reveal that 'confirm' was now being used in a rather different sense, not of the bishop 'confirming' the candidate with the Holy Spirit but in the Reformed sense of the candidates being required to 'ratify and confirm' what their godparents promised for them at baptism. Similarly, the prayer for the sevenfold gifts of the Holy Spirit now asked God merely to 'strengthen them with the Holy Ghost the comforter and daily increase in them thy manifold gifts of grace', instead of asking him to 'send down from heaven . . . upon them thy Holy Ghost the comforter with the manifold gifts of grace', a clear movement away from an understanding of the act as a sacramental outpouring to a view of it as prayer for the continuing activity of the Holy Spirit. The signing with the cross and the Peace were also omitted, and a new prayer accompanied the laying-on of hands:

> Defend, O Lord, this child with thy heavenly grace, that he may continue thine for ever, and daily increase in thy holy spirit more and more, until he come unto thy everlasting kingdom.

The 1662 BCP

In the baptism rite, the Puritans had been unhappy with the continued retention of the unscriptural signing with the cross and the baptismal questions being addressed to uncomprehending infants through their godparents. As for confirmation, they would have wished to abolish it altogether. They were, however, unable to win any concessions either during the reign of Elizabeth I or in the seventeenth century. Indeed, the canons of 1603 had inserted a special canon (30) to explain and defend the use of the sign of the cross: it was a primitive feature of baptism, even though it had been abused in the Church of Rome, but it was not to be thought of as part of the substance of the sacrament itself.

In 1662 an order for Adult Baptism appeared in the Prayer Book for the first time. This was a temporary expedient for those not baptized as infants during the Civil War and Commonwealth as well as 'for the natives in our plantations'. In form it was essentially an adaptation of the Service of Infant Baptism, which was still seen as the norm.

Confirmation similarly remained substantially unchanged. The Catechism was removed from the rite and placed earlier in the Prayer Book. It was replaced by a preface drawn from the opening rubrics of the earlier version of the rite and explained confirmation as a ratification and confirmation of baptismal promises, and this was followed by an act of renewal of baptismal promises to be made by the candidates. The Lord's Prayer was inserted after the laying-on of hands, again parallel to the structure of baptism and Holy Communion. A new final collect was added before the blessing, and the rubric requiring confirmation before admission to communion was amended to allow the exception of those 'ready and desirous to be confirmed' – a reflection of conditions under the Commonwealth when many had not been able to be confirmed because of the absence of bishops at that time.

From 1662 to ASB

Very few changes were made to the baptism service in the proposed revision of 1927/8. Parents were allowed to be godparents; deacons were permitted to baptize in the absence of a priest; and 'in the name of this child' was added to all the questions to be answered by the godparents, so as further to clarify their nature. Confirmation underwent a more substantial theological shift: the preface claimed that, following the example of the Apostles in Acts 8, 'a special gift of the Holy Spirit is bestowed through the laying on of hands with prayer'. In addition, the renewal of the baptismal vows was cast in a more extended form than before, and consisted of a renunciation, affirmation of faith, and promise of lifelong obedience.

A series of reports published in 1938, 1944, 1948, 1949 and 1955 pointed to the need to reform baptismal practice, drawing attention both to the desirability of a new rite and the theological questions raised by the practice of indiscriminate infant baptism. They also bore witness to the fierce theological debate regarding the relationship between baptism and confirmation. On one side there were those who, like Gregory Dix, saw confirmation completing initiation by conferring the gift of the Spirit, while on the other side Geoffrey Lampe and others argued that the fullness of Christian initiation was conveyed in baptism itself.

One proposed solution, for which justification and warrant were found in the practice of the early Church, was to try to create a single integrated rite of baptism, confirmation, and Eucharist in which both baptism and confirmation were clearly initiatory. This was the recommendation of the 1948 report, *The Theology of Christian Initiation*, endorsed later in the same year by the bishops of the Lambeth Conference, and was the theological driving force behind the revisions of Series 2, Series 3, and the *ASB*.

Parallel to Anglican discussions, the reforms of the Second Vatican Council restored the adult catechumenate and incorporated this in the Rite of Christian Initiation of Adults, published in 1972. Some Anglicans also began to experiment with a modern catechumenate and became more aware of pastoral issues associated with the baptism of adults. This was, in part, a result of the growing number of adult baptisms, and the increasing popularity of baptism by immersion, not least in ecumenically shared buildings.

Also of great significance were the 1971 Ely Commission report and the Doctrine Commission report of the same year, *Baptism, Thanksgiving and Blessing*. These reports agreed on a number of radical points. First, that baptism should be recognized explicitly as the full and complete rite of initiation. Second, that there should be a new rite of Thanksgiving after Childbirth. Third, that people should be admitted to Holy Communion after baptism, at the priest's discretion. Fourth, that confirmation should become a commitment rite for adults. Fifth, that those baptized as adults should not be presented for confirmation. Some of these points were taken up in the *ASB*, particularly the Thanksgiving rite, but the rest remain unresolved.

The *ASB* saw complete Christian initiation expressed in a rite of baptism, confirmation and Eucharist. This integrated rite for adults was the archetypal model from which other rites were derived. In the rite for children, questions addressed to parents and godparents were answered 'for yourselves and for this child'. This moved away from the Prayer Book understanding of godparents speaking 'in the name of this child', and articulated a different justification of infant baptism, i.e. that children were baptized on the basis of the faith of their parents and godparents.

The renunciation was turned into 'The Decision', a series of three short questions, the first of which asked 'Do you turn to Christ?', thus restoring an equivalent to the act of adherence to Christ first found in the ancient Syrian rites and retained in the Eastern tradition. This was to be followed by the signing with the cross, which gave it a position more akin to its place in the catechumenate. A fuller provision for the blessing of the water was included, and the declaration of faith was again turned into three short questions.

The theology of confirmation became rather vague at a time when the certainties of the Dixian line were waning. That said, although many came to see initiation as complete in baptism, this did not help to provide a distinctive identity for confirmation, which, even if it could not be justified theologically, continued to have a valuable pastoral role in parishes. While numbers of infant baptisms decreased, there were an increasing number of adult candidates for baptism, which again brought into question the necessity of a post-baptismal rite of confirmation.

The *ASB* permitted the use of oil in baptism and confirmation. Coming at a time when the Maundy Thursday Eucharist for the Blessing of Oils was becoming more widespread, this practice became more prevalent, but never achieved the same degree of acceptance as the giving of the baptism candle.

From ASB to CW

Further factors made the situation more complex. There were international Anglican debates about the nature of baptism which stressed that there is only one baptism, not one for adults and another for children. This resulted in a number of Anglican provinces producing a single liturgy with the most minor variations depending on the age of the candidate. At the same time, the tide had gone even further in the direction of seeing Christian initiation as complete in baptism, with some provinces identifying confirmation as a pastoral rite rather than part of the initiatory process. Indeed, the Fourth

International Anglican Liturgical Consultation (IALC) of 1991 described baptism as 'complete sacramental initiation' which 'leads to participation in the eucharist' and confirmation as a pastoral rite of the renewal of faith which is 'in no way to be seen as a completion of baptism or as necessary for admission to communion'.

Debates about the initiation process continued, with reports suggesting a variety of ways forward. One of the big issues to be settled was whether children who had been baptized but not confirmed could receive Holy Communion. If baptism was 'complete sacramental initiation', then why couldn't baptism be the gateway to the Eucharist? However, if communion did come before confirmation, what would happen to confirmation? Some dioceses, notably Southwark and Manchester, began to experiment widely with the practice of communion before confirmation. In some Anglican provinces it had already become the norm and was encouraged by the 1985 Boston Statement of the IALC, *Children and Communion*. A series of reports recommended that this option should be open to parishes. The Knaresborough report, *Communion Before Confirmation?* (1985), proposed a draft regulation pursuant to Canon 15A (1C). This would have allowed parishes to begin to admit children to Holy Communion.

In 1991 Martin Reardon produced *Christian Initiation – A Policy for the Church of England*. He proposed flexibility, outlining four options and suggesting that the Church allow at least one other initiatory pattern. In 1996 the House of Bishops eventually produced the policy document, *Admission to Communion in relation to Baptism and Confirmation*, which opened the doors for parishes to admit children to communion before confirmation. This has obvious consequences for our understanding of the relationship between baptism and confirmation and, not least, for our liturgical rites.

Meanwhile, ecumenical discussions continue to be of importance. *Baptism, Eucharist and Ministry* (World Council of Churches, 1982) raised questions for all denominations. Confirmation in Local Ecumenical Partnerships has led to the development of joint confirmation services and to the Joint Liturgical Group's *Confirmation and Re-affirmation of Baptismal Faith* (1992). The findings of the Toronto IALC (1991), *Walk in Newness of Life*, were wideranging, setting baptism in the context of mission. It put confirmation in a 'pastoral role' and even suggested that, as in the Roman Catholic Church, it might be delegated by the bishop to presbyters.

One of the most influential documents published prior to *CW* was the House of Bishops' report, *On the Way* (1995). A joint enterprise of the Liturgical Commission, the Board of Education and the Board of Mission, this sets initiation in the context of a nation which can no longer be assumed to be Christian, and asks questions about how people come to faith and how the Church might respond to those who are enquiring. It describes stages of initiation and acknowledges the problem of confirmation 'often drawing attention away from the sacrament of baptism', suggesting that this could be addressed by adopting a 'renewed and extended view of confirmation, akin to the Pastoral Offices, in which the bishop's role is the norm'. Apart from its use for those being confirmed, this extended rite would also be used for those who had fallen away from the Church and who wished to move from another denomination to become full members of the Church of England.

The report also wanted to unite evangelism, teaching and sacrament, while recognizing that many have different personal paths. To that end, it encouraged the use of the catechumenate, which some parishes had been using in conjunction with faith development courses like Emmaus.

B. COMMENTARY: BAPTISM

The complete *CW* initiation services were published and authorized in an interim form in 1998, two years before the *CW* main volume appeared. As this latter volume contains only some of the baptismal material, our commentary is based on the full version of the services. However, through its *Miscellaneous Liturgical Proposals* (GS 1342), the General Synod later responded to criticism by allowing greater flexibility than was permitted in the original text. We have noted the significant points from this in the commentary below.

Unlike the *ASB*, a detailed introduction outlines the theological and liturgical principles which underlie the initiation services. It is clear that the new provision no longer favours the integrated archetypal rite of baptism, confirmation and Eucharist but, instead, places baptism as the theological centrepiece around which the rites of confirmation, affirmation of baptismal faith and reception into the communion of the Church of England are clustered. All these relate to baptism and take seriously the pastoral reality that 'a person's spiritual journey does not always fall into one pattern'. While acknowledging the influence of *On the Way*, the rites also claim to have been shaped by a new appreciation of the baptismal practice of the early Church, reflected in the *BCP*, and 'to fresh thinking about the nature of baptism as expressing the identity and call of the Christian community today'.

These initiation services require a different approach, both in terms of theology and liturgical performance, from those of the *ASB*. Bishops, priests and deacons will be better enabled to perform the rites of Christian initiation if they allow themselves to be informed by the material set out in the introduction as well as in the Liturgical Commission's own commentary which concludes the volume.

Notes

The Notes relate not only to baptism within the context of the Eucharist, but also to a non-eucharistic celebration. The two Orders are helpfully outlined at the beginning of this section, with a clear indication of elements which may be used in alternative positions, as well as texts which may be replaced by seasonal options. Both the Notes and the earlier Introduction reiterate the canonical

Table 7.2: Outline of the 1662 *BCP*, *ASB*, and *CW* Baptismal Rites (without Eucharist).

BCP	ASB	CW
		Greeting
Exhortation	Duties of parents	(Introduction)
	and godparents	[(Presentation of candidates)]
		(Prayer of thanksgiving)
		(*Gloria in Excelsis*)
Prayer		Collect
Prayer		
	Ministry of the Word	Readings
Gospel (Mark 10.13–16)		Gospel
Exhortation		Sermon
Prayer	Prayer for candidate	
Exhortation		(Presentation of candidates)
Renunciation	Decision	Decision
	Sign of cross	Sign of cross
	Blessing of water	Prayer over the water
Profession of faith	Profession of faith	Profession of faith
Desire for baptism		
Prayer for candidate		
Blessing of water		
Baptism	Baptism	Baptism
		(Clothing)
Sign of cross	[Sign of cross]	[Sign of cross]
		Prayer for candidate
		(with chrismation)
	(Candle)	[(Candle)]
		Commission
Invitation to prayer	Welcome	Welcome and Peace
	Prayers	(Prayers)
Lord's Prayer	Lord's Prayer	Lord's Prayer
Prayer of thanksgiving		
Charge to godparents		
	Grace	(Blessing)
		(Candle)
		Dismissal

Round brackets indicate optional parts of the service. Square brackets mark alternative positions for the presentation of the candidates, signing with the cross and the giving of the candle.

expectation that baptism should take place at public worship on a Sunday and that this might include not only the usual principal Sunday service, but also 'a significant celebration of Baptism as the main service of the day'. Further notes highlighting the implications of baptizing children at the Parish Eucharist, at a Service of the Word, and at Morning or Evening Prayer, appear separately.

In line with many of the revisions made in *CW*, all the initiation services are modelled on the familiar modern Western eucharistic shape, whether the Eucharist is celebrated or not. Whereas the *ASB* referred to the officiant as either 'bishop' or 'priest', *CW* adopts the term 'president' to encompass the three ministerial orders, while at the same time acknowledging that the bishop is the chief minister of initiation and that, when present, he should preside over the whole service. In all cases, non-presidential sections, such as the signing with the cross, may be delegated to others.

A distinction is also made here between 'godparent' and 'sponsor'. The former refers to those who present children for baptism, whereas the latter describes those who agree to support the journey of any candidates presented for a rite of initiation.

Preparation

Following the pattern of *CW*'s first eucharistic order, a trinitarian greeting (2 Corinthians 13.13) introduces the Preparation and may be followed by informal words of welcome. There are seven appendices printed at the end of the baptismal liturgies, the first of which is a thanksgiving prayer for a child, which may be inserted between the greeting and words of introduction which follow. One Introduction is printed in the main body of the text, but may be replaced by the President's own words or a selection of seasonal forms printed in Appendix 2, or omitted entirely under the provisions of the *Miscellaneous Liturgical Proposals*. The ferial form refers first to baptismal regeneration, quoting John 3.3ff, and moves from the image of new birth to describe baptism as washing by the Holy Spirit, clothing with Christ, dying to sin and living his risen life. The *ASB* rite was often criticized for relying too heavily on the Pauline theology of dying and rising with Christ (Romans 6). *CW* responds to this by embracing a proliferation of biblical images, to which this introductory material bears witness, and which, together with their biblical roots, are listed in the Liturgical Commission's own commentary. The Preparation does not include a penitential rite, but the *Gloria in Excelsis* may be used when appropriate. As in the Eucharist, this section concludes with the collect. The introductory notes make clear that during the 'closed' periods of the Church's Calendar (from Advent to Candlemas and from Lent 1 to Trinity Sunday), the Sunday collect should be used, whereas at other times the collect provided in the main body of the text or in the appendices may be substituted. The ferial collect is that which was used in the *ASB* whenever initiation was celebrated in the context of the Eucharist and expresses the baptismal vocation of the whole assembly.

Liturgy of the Word

This is almost identical in structure to the eucharistic rite and directs that at least one reading should precede the proclamation of the Gospel (reduced to 'may precede' by the *Miscellaneous Liturgical Proposals*). When children are baptized, this is much more substantial than the two-paragraph summary of biblical teaching which appeared in the *ASB*. As with the collect, the Sunday readings are preferred, but those set out in Appendix 5 may be used at celebrations where 'baptism is the predominant element in the service'. A sermon concludes the Liturgy of the Word: this was made mandatory by the *Miscellaneous Liturgical Proposals*.

Presentation of the Candidates

This is an important new feature of the rite, although the act of presentation itself – but not the spoken texts that follow – was subsequently made optional in the *Miscellaneous Liturgical Proposals*. It follows the sermon, but may, if appropriate, be used during the Preparation after the Introduction. Those able to answer for themselves are invited to express their desire for baptism and may, if appropriate, elaborate by testifying to the call of God which has led them to baptism. Where candidates are able to speak for themselves, the whole congregation responds by promising to welcome and uphold them in their new life. Where there are no such candidates, this involvement of the assembly begins the Presentation and is followed by two questions requiring a commitment from parents and godparents to support the candidates by their prayer and example and help them to take their place within the life and worship of the Church. Although the rubrics do not suggest appropriate moments for sitting or standing, the involvement of the congregation at this stage in the rite may be enhanced if they are invited to stand after the sermon, and the candidates (together with parents and godparents) are brought out to face the people.

Decision

Having established the Church's support, the candidates themselves are required to make their decision to reject evil and to turn to Christ. This section is cast in the form of two sets of three questions, and corresponds to the ancient acts of renunciation and adherence to Christ found in the Eastern tradition, and to Peter's exhortation in Acts 2.38, 'Repent and be baptized'. Repentance (*metanoia*) involves more than simply turning away from evil; it involves changing direction and turning towards Christ, so as to be united with him in his life, death and resurrection. In the words of the president, 'To follow Christ means dying to sin and rising to new life in him'. Thus the Decision sets up a new personal relationship with Christ, to whom the candidates now belong.

Where infants are baptized, it is important to be clear who is answering the six questions, since this has been a cause of controversy and disagreement from the time of the Reformation. The theology of the Sarum rite, continued in 1549 and 1552, was for the questions to be addressed directly to uncomprehending children and for the sponsors to answer as the child's mouthpiece. This position was strengthened in 1662 and reiterated in 1928, making it clear that it was the candidate and not the godparents who were bound by the promise. Thirty years later the Liturgical Commission proposed that sponsors were no longer to reply in the *name* of an infant, but on their *behalf*. However, it was not until Series 2 that the situation changed more substantially and parents and sponsors were asked to make the decision for themselves, being at the same time reminded that it was their duty to bring up the infant to fight against evil and to follow Christ. The sponsors were in fact sureties for the infant, and they could only act in this capacity if they themselves were prepared to do these things. In 1980 the position was clarified and parents and godparents were required to answer for themselves and for the children.

CW has rejected this more recent development and, as the second of the Presentation questions makes clear, reminds parents and godparents that they speak for their children. Thus, in the Decision, the president now addresses all the candidates directly 'or through their parents, godparents and sponsors'. The Decision is therefore made by the candidates and not by their supporters.

The language of these six questions is much stronger than the *ASB*'s three (although the latter may still be used where there are 'strong pastoral reasons'). A different verb is used in each question, as the candidates are first asked to reject the devil and all rebellion against God, renounce the deceit and corruption of evil, and repent of the sins that separate them from God and neighbour before turning, submitting and coming to Christ. The strengthening of this part of the liturgy and the reference to the devil has obvious pastoral ramifications for the preparation of candidates, parents, godparents and sponsors.

The suggestion made at the beginning of this section that 'a large candle may be lit' is clearly intended to encourage the use of the Paschal Candle at baptisms, and lighting it at this point (if it is not already lit) establishes a visual link between the Decision and the lighting of the baptismal candles later in the rite.

Signing with the Cross

The consignation was a feature of the pre-immersion ceremonies in the early Church, not only at the renunciation but also at an earlier stage when the candidate was made a catechumen. It was also found in the Roman rite of the seventh century and in the Sarum rite, when infants were brought to the door of the church and, at the very outset, signed with the sign of the cross on the brow. Immediately after the renunciation they were signed again on the breast and between the shoulder-blades, with oil blessed for the purpose. It was a token of the divine help in the struggle to which the candidates were committed. As St Ambrose had aptly commented (*c.* 400), the candidate was 'anointed as Christ's athlete; as about to wrestle in the fight of this world'. The candidates were also signed and anointed with the oil of chrism immediately after baptism. Sarum therefore had three significant signings. 1549 reduced these to two: the first at the beginning, as in Sarum, when the priest also asked the name of the child, and then addressed the child by name; the second after the baptism with the oil of chrism. 1552, however, made radical changes: the first signing was dropped and there was no reference to the child's name until after the baptism itself; the second signing then occurred without oil immediately after baptism. The baptism therefore came to be associated with the signing and the naming, and this continued in 1662 and 1928.

In 1958 the Liturgical Commission attempted to clarify matters by making the signing one of the 'Ceremonies after Baptism', and by indicating that it should not take place until all the candidates had been baptized. This was continued in Series 2. However, in 1980 the order changed and the *ASB* clearly associated the signing with the Decision before baptism. Oil was also permitted and the priest could address the candidate by name at this point in the rite.

Here *CW* strengthens the theology of the *ASB*. The signing with the cross comes as a ritual response to the decision made by the candidates. Since they have repented of their sins and committed themselves to the way of Christ, the Church marks them with his sign as a symbol of his acceptance of their decision, their belonging to him and their new identity as disciples of the crucified one. Parents, godparents and sponsors may also sign the candidates with the cross to express their support and prayer for what has taken place.

Pure olive oil (traditionally the oil of catechumens blessed by the bishop) may be used for the consignation as the minister says to each candidate: 'Christ claims you for his own. Receive the sign of his cross.' The juxtaposition of cross and oil after the Decision symbolizes God's invitation to salvation, the candidates' acceptance of the same once-for-all act of God in Christ, and the Anointed One claiming them as his anointed children by marking them with his sign, the sign from which flows the grace by which the candidates will be strengthened to 'Fight valiantly as a disciple of Christ against sin, the world and the devil, and remain faithful to Christ to the end of your life.' Thus, in this one ritual act, divine initiative, human response and saving grace are all expressed and made present.

It is interesting to note that the congregational prayer, 'Fight valiantly . . .', which from 1549 to 1928 was said by the priest alone, has been altered to remove some of the militaristic language which remained in the *ASB*. The final prayer expresses the belief that the image of God's glory, in which the candidates were created, will be restored to them as a result of their identification with their anointed and crucified Saviour, the Second Adam, who leads them from darkness to light. Depending on circumstances and the number of candidates, it may be appropriate for the congregation to sit for the whole of the Decision.

Prayer over the Water
The ministers, candidates and, where appropriate, the whole congregation gather at the font for the blessing of the water. If the font is in or near the sanctuary, or if the whole service has taken place round the font, then very little movement will be required. If, however, it is necessary to move from the front of the nave to the baptistery at the west end of the church, then a canticle or

Psalms (see Appendix 5) or a litany (such as that in Appendix 6) or a hymn may cover this movement. This very much depends on the liturgical context in which baptism is celebrated. The baptism of several candidates at the Parish Eucharist will require very different treatment from the baptism of one child on a Sunday afternoon outside the Eucharist. Depending on circumstances, it may be possible to involve children, godparents and others in the procession to the font by carrying a candle (which may be the Paschal Candle), symbolizing the light of Christ leading the candidates to baptism, an icon of the baptism of Jesus, relating Christian baptism to the Jordan event, and the baptismal water itself. If a godparent does carry the water, then the dramatic symbolism of this element of the rite may be enhanced if, once all have gathered and in full sight of the congregation, he or she pours it into the font, so that all can see the water in which the candidates will be baptized. Even if the water is not carried, it would still be better for it to be poured into the font at this point in the liturgy than beforehand and out of sight.

Parallel to the eucharistic prayer, the Prayer over the Water is, arguably, the central prayer of the rite and, without doubt, the one which most clearly and concisely expresses the theology of the sacrament. In the seventh-century Roman rite there was a solemn procession to the font, where the bishop blessed the water in a lengthy prayer: he asked God by the Holy Spirit to give fecundity to the water and to purify it; he then recalled God's mighty acts involving water both in the Old Testament and the New, and finally he prayed that through the water the stain of sin might be erased, human nature might be restored to the divine image, and humanity might 'be reborn in a new infancy of true innocence'. The oil of chrism was then poured into the font in the form of a cross. Essentially the Sarum blessing of the water differed little from this, although there were some Gallican modifications. It was now in a eucharistic form, introduced by the *Sursum corda*, while there were added ceremonies – the plunging of a lighted taper into the font, a triple impregnation with oil and chrism, and the breathing of the priest upon the water. Furthermore, now that baptisms were more frequent, the blessing of the water was not required on every occasion: the water simply remained in the font until it was stale, and only when it was renewed was blessing necessary.

In 1549 there were substantial changes. The blessing of the water was still an occasional ceremony, not used at every baptism; but it appeared as an appendix to the Private Baptism of Infants, with the direction that water in the font should be changed at least once a month. Furthermore, the form was much shorter than that of Sarum and owed little to it. Cranmer took it from some Gallican source, the origin of which is obscure. There is one opening prayer, containing a reference to the Jordan event and the request 'Sanctify this fountain of baptism . . . that by the power of thy word, all those that shall be baptized therein may be spiritually regenerated.' This was followed by eight short prayers, which have been found in a similar series of 16 short prayers in the Mozarabic *Benedictio Fontis*. The form ended with a greeting and a collect for those about to be baptized, mainly from Sarum. All the ceremonies accompanying the blessing were removed, save for the sign of the cross at the words 'Sanctify this fountain of baptism.'

Even more radical changes took place in 1552, largely in deference to Bucer's criticisms. The nine prayers were reduced to four, and the first prayer with the crucial phrase 'Sanctify this fountain of baptism' was omitted. All that remained, therefore, was prayer for the candidates, which was said at the font immediately before the actual baptism on every occasion. 1662, however, restored the blessing of the water by inserting the phrase, 'Sanctify this Water to the mystical washing away of sin' in the final collect – an expedient already adopted in the 1637 Scottish book, although in slightly different words. Further improvement then occurred in 1928 by separating the four short Mozarabic prayers from the collect by the heading 'The Blessing of the Water', and introducing the collect with the *Sursum corda* and the eucharistic formula 'It is very meet, right, and our bounden duty, that we should give thanks.'

The Liturgical Commission's 1958 proposals set a new pattern for the blessing of the water, by returning to a long prayer of thanksgiving which set out to expound the meaning of initiation within the context of our Lord's own baptism and redemptive activity before asking God to 'sanctify this water to the mystical washing away of sin'. This prayer immediately preceded the acts of renunciation and belief. Series 2 followed suit, although this time it was placed between the Decision and the Profession of Faith. In Series 3/*ASB* the prayer remained in the same position, and *CW* has retained this, while lengthening what is now called the Prayer over the Water to include many more biblical images, providing seasonal alternatives in Appendix 2 and responsive forms in Appendix 3. Although the latter are intended to provide greater congregational participation in what would, otherwise, be a presidential monologue, they have the disadvantage of requiring the congregation to be provided with a full copy of the text if they are to participate in this way. Moreover, it should not be forgotten that, as in the eucharistic prayer, no matter how much scripted participation the text contains, it is in all contexts a prayer of the whole assembly.

The ferial prayer, based on a text in the Canadian *BAS* (which was itself derived from the 1979 American *BCP*) and also influenced by the equivalent text in the New Zealand Prayer Book, begins by listing significant biblical events associated with water (creation, exodus and the baptism of Jesus), before giving thanks for the baptismal water in which the candidates are buried and rise with Christ and are born again by the Holy Spirit. The final paragraph uses the verb 'to sanctify' in the imperative to petition God to hallow the water that, by the Spirit, the candidates might be cleansed from sin and born again. Picking up the prayer after the Decision, it states that the water of baptism will renew the divine image in the baptized so that, henceforth, they may walk in the light of the risen Christ.

Profession of Faith

In the early Western Church the profession of faith was closely associated with the immersion. In the *Apostolic Tradition*, the candidate was asked three questions as she or he stood in the water: 'Do you believe in God the Father – the Son – the Holy Spirit?' Each time, having answered in the affirmative, the candidate was immersed. The credal interrogations and the answers *were* the baptismal formula and nothing more was said. In medieval terminology, the profession of faith was the 'form' of the sacrament and the water was the 'matter'. Later it was found convenient to put the questions to all the candidates together before immersion; then they were immersed individually and a Syrian form of words, 'I baptize you in the name . . .', was used over each one. This practice reached Rome by the eighth century and since then it has been used continuously in the West. This was the pattern normally used in 1549: since the blessing of the water was not performed on every occasion, the profession of faith was usually closely associated with the baptism. Now, however, the triple interrogation had become the entire Apostles' Creed, divided into three parts. In 1552, when the blessing of the water disappeared altogether, the Creed took the form of a single question, separated from the baptism by what were now the five prayers for the candidates. 1662 retained the pattern, reintroducing the blessing of the water, and in 1928 the break between the act of faith and the baptism was further emphasized by the additions mentioned above.

The Liturgical Commission attempted to return to a more primitive pattern in its 1958 proposals by placing the acts of renunciation and faith after the blessing of the water and immediately before baptism; but the profession of faith now took the form of a single short question on the Trinity based on the words of the Prayer Book Catechism, followed by a promise to 'obey him in whom you have believed'. Series 2 further improved this by placing the Decision before the blessing of the water, and by making the single interrogation concerning faith into three questions – one for each person of the Trinity – and each requiring the reply 'I believe and trust in him.' This form was continued in the *ASB* and supplemented by a congregational affirmation of faith in the Trinity, an innovation borrowed from the 1969 Roman rite.

CW has departed from this in two important respects. First, once again the profession of faith takes the form of the Apostles' Creed (which is a revised version of an ELLC text) but, unlike 1662, this is divided into three questions. Second, whereas in the Prayer Book the act of faith professed the faith of the child and, whereas in the *ASB* parents and godparents answered for themselves and for their children, in *CW* the whole congregation professes 'together with *these candidates* the faith of the Church'. Thus, the candidates make their statement of faith within the corporate context of the gathered Body of Christ of which they will become members through baptism. Where candidates can speak for themselves, they can express their allegiance to this profession of faith by answering a simple question before they are baptized.

Where there are 'strong pastoral reasons', an *ASB*-style profession of faith, provided in Appendix 7, may be used instead of the Apostles' Creed. Here the three questions describe the activity of the three persons of the Trinity in more detail than the *ASB* and, as with the Creed, the answers are made by the whole congregation who also join together in the popular 'This is the faith of the Church' response. Outside the Parish Eucharist, it is likely that, despite the tone of the rubrics, this will remain the preferred option for many.

Baptism

St Paul's comparison of baptism with our Lord's death and resurrection would suggest total submersion – the disappearance of the old person beneath the waters, and the rising of the new. The Johannine imagery of rebirth also suggests that the candidate should break the baptismal waters and emerge from the baptismal womb of new birth. But it is reasonably certain that from the third century onwards the normal practice was neither total submersion nor sprinkling, but the pouring of water all over the candidate (which can still be described as total immersion). In any case, many fonts would preclude total submersion, especially in the case of adults. It was also normal practice to dip or pour water over the candidate three times, symbolizing either the Trinity or our Lord's three days in the tomb. An exception was the Church in Spain, where a single dipping or pouring was preferred, in the interests of preserving the unity of the Godhead against heretical ideas. Sarum directed that the child should be dipped in the water three times, once with face downwards. 1549 prescribed the same method except in cases where a child was weak. 1552 was much less precise, although immersion seems to have been the norm and nothing was said about the number of times the dipping should be done. 1662 prescribed dipping, but rather less enthusiastically: it should only be under-taken if the godparents could certify 'that the child may well endure it'; otherwise water was poured. Dipping or pouring was used for adults, and again the number of times was not mentioned. These have remained the options ever since, including *CW*, which states that:

> A threefold administration of water (whether by dipping or pouring) is a very ancient practice of the Church and is commended as testifying to the faith of the Trinity in which candidates are baptized. Nevertheless, a single administration is also lawful and valid.

It goes on to encourage the minister to use a 'substantial amount of water'. This adds to the dramatic symbolism of the rite and ties in with what has already been said about pouring water into the font. In every case the indicative Western formula is used, prefaced by the candidate's name. The use of the name simply establishes the identity of the candidate at the moment of baptism. Since baptism is not a naming ceremony, the continued use of the Prayer Book formula 'Name this child' would cause confusion and is not in keeping with the theology of the sacrament.

CW permits the newly baptized to be clothed with a white robe. A note refers to clothing as 'a practical necessity where dipping is the mode of baptism'. This is rather coyly put. Increasingly Anglicans of all traditions are seeing dipping or submersion as most appropriate methods of baptism, especially for adult candidates. As a result, some churches are building new baptisteries. Where new churches are being built, fonts in which candidates may be submerged are often being designed as an integral feature. However the water is administered, the image of the candidate being clothed with Christ has its roots in Galatians 3.27 and Colossians 3.10.

After the baptism or clothing, the presidential prayer over the candidates concludes this part of the rite. This marks the second occasion when oil may be used (this time the perfumed oil of chrism). This is a completely new text and, as with the Decision, needs to be understood within the context in which it is set. Presentation of the candidates, Decision, Prayer over the Water and Profession of Faith all lead the way to the font. Baptism follows and new life begins – born again by water and the Spirit, dying and rising with Christ, sins washed away in the water of the font, filled with the Spirit and made a member of the Body of Christ – all of these and whatever else we believe about baptism have their primary focus in the waters of the font. What more is there to say? The baptismal bath marks the beginning of a new life in Christ; and the prayer which follows looks to the future and the continuation of the journey which has brought the candidate to the font, the journey upon which God is asked to pour the riches of his grace that the candidate might daily be renewed by his anointing Spirit. To anoint with chrism during this prayer is not to say that this is the moment at which the Spirit is conferred. Rather, it is to make use of a vivid sign which identifies the candidate as one who has been reborn, one who has become a new creation, one who has been filled with the life of the Spirit and, then looking forward, prays that this new identity in Christ might characterize the candidate's life from that day forward. The Liturgical Commission's own commentary suggests that, to distinguish this anointing from that at the Decision, the chrism may be applied in the shape of a chi-rho, signifying *Christos*, the Anointed One. However, this is not necessarily a helpful symbol; it is over-fussy and will require explanation during the performance of the rite. More importantly, it does not seem to reflect the language of the prayer, which is not sufficiently Christic to warrant such an image. It would be far simpler and much more powerful to reflect Old Testament practice and, using more oil than for a consignation, pour chrism over the crown of the head – thus making a bold and vivid gesture which can be easily seen and smelt.

Commission

Whereas the *ASB* required parents and godparents to give their assent to certain duties explained by the priest at the beginning of the liturgy, *CW* replaces this section with the Presentation of the Candidates, while the Duties of Parents and Godparents have become a post-baptismal Commission. This is no innovation. The Prayer Books of 1549, 1552 and 1662 all contained an exhortation to godparents at the end of the rite. That said, this marks an important shift from the theological stance of the *ASB* and clearly states that divine grace is not dependent upon human initiative, but that the grace of God in baptism invites human response and responsibility.

If the newly baptized are unable to answer for themselves, a minister addresses not only parents and godparents, but also the whole congregation. Thus the corporate dynamic of the Presentation and the Profession of Faith is continued as the assembly hears that the baptized 'need the help and encouragement of the Christian community'. Parents and godparents are then told that they have 'the prime responsibility' for guiding and helping their children in early years.

The Commission ends with an invitation to pray. Two prayers are printed in the main body of the text, one or both of which may be used. The first prays for those who care for the newly baptized and asks a blessing on their homes. The second asks that all Christians may be faithful to their baptismal calling. In the case of candidates old enough to understand, a minister may then explain to the newly baptized that in baptism they have begun a lifelong journey with God, in which, supported by the community of faith, they will grow in love and service.

For adults and older children able to answer for themselves, the Commission instead takes the form of five questions concerning worship, the Christian life and social action, which the newly baptized answer. This is again derived from the American Prayer Book where, interestingly, it is used before baptism as part of the Profession of Faith. In *CW* its position after baptism reflects both the theology of divine initiative and the relationship between baptism and mission. It was made optional in the *Miscellaneous Liturgical Proposals*.

Prayers of Intercession

These Prayers of the People express the privilege of full membership of the Christian assembly, the royal priesthood of the baptized, whose mission in the world is articulated through its prayer. They were made optional in the *Miscellaneous Liturgical Proposals* and may take place here or after the Welcome and Peace, led by the president or others. Brief biddings are provided in the main body of the text, based on a litany from *CCP*, to which particular intentions may be added. Seasonal alternatives are provided in Appendix 2 and 4.

Welcome and Peace

Having expressed their membership of the Christian community in prayer, the people welcome the newly baptized using a response adapted from the *ASB* and based on Ephesians 4.4–6 and 1 Corinthians 12.13 to express a desire for unity: one Lord, one faith, one baptism, one Spirit. Applause is appropriate after the welcome, although this may more effectively be postponed until the people have responded to the president's greeting of Peace. In such cases the introduction to the Peace (Galatians 3.28) or one of the seasonal options (Appendix 2) may perhaps be omitted so that the assembly's welcome spills over into the greeting and applause followed by an informal exchange of peace.

The Liturgy of the Eucharist

If baptism is not celebrated within the context of the Eucharist, the service continues with the Lord's Prayer and the Sending Out. When the Eucharist is celebrated, it seems appropriate that, where age permits, the newly baptized should bring bread and wine to the altar at the offertory. *CW* provides a Proper Preface containing several of the biblical baptismal images already encountered in the rite. The Prayer after Communion may be that appointed for the day or a seasonal prayer from Appendix 2. The ferial text prays for all the baptized and sets baptismal vocation within the context of eschatological hope.

Sending Out

This final section of the liturgy consists of the Blessing, the giving of a lighted candle and the dismissal. Seasonal blessings are printed in Appendix 2, and that which appears in the main text is from the general provision in paragraph 77 of the *ASB* Rite A.

The giving of the lighted candle in the West is a medieval custom, first attested in an eleventh-century missal and included in Sarum with an exhortation to be like the Wise Virgins. The practice was not included in 1549, and it did not appear until the 1958 proposals, where it was included as an optional second post-baptismal ceremony. Series 2 and *ASB* retained it in this position, but *CW* has separated it from the post-baptismal clothing and pneumatic prayer and made it an optional part of the dismissal rite. There are logistical problems in lighting the candles from the Paschal Candle if this is by the font at the west end. One option would be for the candle to be carried to the east end during the administration of communion so that the baptismal candles could be lit from it, and the Paschal Candle lead the final procession. Alternatively, the procession could move to the west end during a hymn after the blessing, and the congregation turn to face west for the giving of the candle and the dismissal. However this is done, there is no formula to accompany the giving of the candle, as in the *ASB*, but once all have received their candles the president proclaims the status of all the baptized: 'God has delivered us from the dominion of darkness and has given us a place with the saints in light' (Colossians 1.13–14). He then exhorts the newly baptized to walk in Christ's light to the end of their lives, before the congregation replies with the *ASB* response.

The theme of light is picked up in the dismissal, to which during Eastertide Alleluias may be added.

C. COMMENTARY: CONFIRMATION

The change of emphasis which now sees baptism as complete initiation has led to baptism with confirmation being a second section of the initiation services. The Synod of July 1991 had called for a service of 'reaffirmation' and a national service of 'reception' into the Church of England. All of these have been put together into 'one printed rite encompassing all the possible acts of commitment', *The Eucharist with Baptism and Confirmation Together with Affirmation of Baptismal Faith and Reception into the Communion of the Church of England.*

Notes

The Notes begin with the assertion that 'the service is presided over by the bishop'. This, of course, is the Anglican norm, but the wider Church has had a variety of approaches, including presbyteral confirmation with episcopally blessed oil and the delegation of confirmation to presbyters. The latter position is authorized in the Churches of North and South India and in the Roman Catholic Church.

In Anglican history the provision for confirmation services has varied. One approach has been to celebrate a service in a cathedral or in major centres, with thousands being confirmed at once. This was common in the eighteenth century. A second approach has been for the episcopal rite to be performed hastily. Perhaps the most famous account of this is Richard Baxter's confirmation in a churchyard in 1630. At 15 years of age, he says that he was ill-prepared and did not understand the service. Sometimes Anglicans have been very negligent of confirmation. Indeed, confirmation has been for some Anglicans almost non-existent, e.g. with non-resident bishops, or because Anglicans were living in colonies overseas. The more contemporary practice of a parish service where bishops travel round the dioceses would seem to be a Victorian development. It has much to do with the development of the railways, a growing pastoral outreach in baptism and confirmation, and the development of suffragan bishops. *CW* recommends discussion between the parish and bishop in the preparation of the service.

The Notes also include guidance for the baptism of children, particularly when the whole family is to be baptized and the parents confirmed. The Notes make clear that the affirmation of baptismal faith is for those who are already baptized and confirmed, but have recently come to new faith. It is not an act of the whole congregation. Testimony is possible in the service and a note on oil clarifies what happens with chrism, since its use is now also permitted at baptism. Someone baptized and confirmed at the same service would not be chrismated twice.

Preparation

The episcopal greeting, 'Peace be with you', is preceded by a set of responses, drawing first from the Byzantine Orthodox tradition and then from Ephesians

4.4–6, emphasizing the theme of unity, in God as Trinity, in the Church, in faith, and in the sacrament.

Liturgy of Initiation

This begins with the question to baptismal candidates: 'Do you wish to be baptized?', while those being confirmed and any affirming their baptismal faith or being received into the Church of England are asked to declare that they have already been baptized. It is clear from these questions that baptism is understood to be the basis of Christian discipleship. After the candidates have responded, the people of God are called upon to welcome and uphold them.

The Decision follows the pattern in the baptism service, as does the signing with the cross. If there are no candidates for baptism, a prayer for strengthening is provided to conclude the Decision. Signing with the cross should be only for baptismal candidates, as should its accompanying apotropaic prayer. It is to be hoped that those responsible for composing local services will carefully follow the rubrics at this point. While the Revision Committee of General Synod thought it was 'not inappropriate' to use a prayer for deliverance with those who have already been baptized, they provided an alternative prayer to avoid this. Apotropaic prayer originates from within the tradition of having renunciations and prayers of protection before baptism. This was acknowledged in the *ASB*. What is needed is a post-baptismal renewal, not a complete starting again.

Those who are about to affirm their faith or be received declare their intentions after the baptism. This position in the rite was deliberately chosen so that these candidates could 'associate themselves with candidates for baptism' or 'make a conscious association of commitment . . . with the baptism they have received' (*First Revision Committee Report*, GS1152Y). This is given ritual expression in the possibility for the candidates to be sprinkled with baptismal water or for them to approach the font and sign themselves. The rules about reception are found in Canon B28, which is itself being revised as a result of Porvoo and other recent ecumenical agreements. This part of the rite concludes with an *ASB* collect, which once again emphasizes the baptismal context of the declarations.

The bishop and candidates move from the font (if the confirmation is not to take place there) to the place of confirmation and the rite continues with the traditional versicles and responses (Psalms 124.8; 113.2) and the *ASB* version of the traditional confirmation prayer. This version quotes directly from Isaiah 11.2 in an attempt to avoid explicitly stating either that it confers the Holy Spirit or that the Spirit began to work in the candidate from baptism. Supporters of the latter position would claim that confirmation is an unfolding and strengthening of that previous pneumatic experience. Much debate on ancient liturgical texts asks questions that our forebears in faith would not have asked and makes distinctions they would not consider. Just as today an Orthodox would not understand why you would ask whether the Spirit was conferred at water baptism or chrismation, so too the ancient writers of liturgical texts would not understand the question. It comes out of a Western interest in the 'moment' of consecration. Rather, they would affirm that whole rite is both pneumatic and baptismal and the one cannot be divided from the other.

The ancient prayer used here can be found in the writings of Ambrose, the Gelasian Sacramentary and later texts, including the Sarum rite. Ambrose talks of the 'spiritual seal . . . for after the font, it remains for the perfecting to take place'. This, he says, is done by the invocation of the priest. The Gelasian Sacramentary states that 'the sevenfold Spirit is given to them by the Bishop'. This makes it an episcopal act in a way that Ambrose did not, and a performative action rather than an invocation. In Sarum it is titled the Confirmation of Children, the minimum age being seven. It is also included in the Sarum Manual, a priest's book, which suggests that it could be delegated to the priest on occasion.

We have already seen that the use of oil in confirmation was abolished at the Reformation. Indeed, it was not until the twentieth century that it again became part of Anglican practice, with the optional use of chrism being permitted, for example, in South Africa in 1954, and ten years later in the West Indies. In 1980 a note in the *ASB* allowed the use of chrism at confirmation, and in *CW* oil may be used both at the confirmation prayer and at the affirmation. The Liturgical Commission's commentary says:

> Chrism has been used in the rites that follow baptism as a sign of the blessings brought by the Holy Spirit . . . The long Christian tradition of prayer and the use of oil points to the appropriateness of such practice . . . Neat attempts to apportion grace to particular parts of the rite fall foul of history as well as theology.

That said, it is safe to put confirmation in a messianic context where the Christ anoints his people with the Holy Spirit. Increasingly this is symbolized by the use of anointing in confirmation.

The Affirmation candidates now have a prayer said over them. This is also found in the JLG rite, *Confirmation and Re-affirmation of Baptismal Faith* (1992). A similar prayer is also to be found in the 1989 New Zealand Prayer Book. The prayer for those being received is a modification of a similar text found in the JLG rite. The words of reception are also similar to those in the 1979 American *BCP* and the Canadian *BAS*.

The section concludes with the congregation praying for all the candidates in the prayer, 'Defend, O Lord . . .' This prayer was introduced into the 1552 service by Cranmer, where it was used as the confirmation prayer. In the seventeenth century Cosin said that 'this seems to be rather a prayer that may be said by any minister, than a confirmation that was reserved only to a bishop'. In the *ASB* the Church of England acted upon this opinion and made it a prayer of the ministers of the Church for the ministers of the Church, that is, by the baptized for the baptized and, in this case, also those who have joined the communion of the Church of England.

The service continues with the post-baptismal questions found in one option of the baptism rite. Then follows the Welcome of the newly baptized and the Peace. The former was made optional by the *Miscellaneous Liturgical Proposals*, chiefly to deal with situations where it seems inappropriate to single out only one or two who have been baptized from a much larger number being confirmed. The words to introduce the Peace are distinctive for this service, based on 2 Corinthians 1.22 and continuing themes of unity, sealing, the Spirit, and what is to come.

The Liturgy of the Eucharist contains the same Proper Preface, Blessing and Sending Out with a candle as the baptismal rite. However, the prayer after communion is different, asking for the gift of the Spirit to be stirred up in all the faithful.

Instructions are then given as to how to order the service if there are no candidates in one or another category or if there is no Eucharist. In the latter case, extra prayers are provided, as in the *ASB*, drawing on a prayer from 1549, an *ASB* prayer for Christian witness, the prayer ascribed to St Francis, the prayer of St Richard of Chichester, and a prayer produced by a revision committee in 1978.

What is Confirmation?

The Initiation Services commentary discusses the necessity of confirmation for those who are baptized as adults. The present policy is that all adults who are baptized should come to the bishop for confirmation. This is not the policy of all Anglican provinces, e.g. Canada, where those baptized as adults are not of necessity confirmed. The commentary draws the 'ready and desirous to be confirmed' rubric from the *BCP* to support admitting baptized adults to communion prior to their confirmation. However, it ducks the question that if adults are chrismated at baptism (as is now an option), why then do they require confirmation? After all, in some Churches, e.g. the Roman Catholic or Orthodox, such chrismation would be seen as confirmation.

CW has also been unable to solve the more general issue of communion before confirmation. At present there exists a variety of practice, with some diocesan bishops permitting communion before confirmation and some not, together with some parishes adopting the practice, while others, even in dioceses where it is authorized, have not. It remains to be seen whether these new liturgies will be able to cope with the pressure which such a lack of uniformity and coherence will place upon them.

Similarly, ecumenical agreements are increasingly making the Anglican insistence on episcopal confirmation look doubtful. Porvoo leaves unresolved issues which will need further clarification, not least whether members of such Churches who wish to be received into the Church of England need to be confirmed.

Behind all this lies a lack of clear theology of the place of confirmation. The Church of England seems to hold on to it as a necessity, but with little theological justification. One hundred and fifty years of debate have still not led to a conclusion, and the debate looks set to continue. How long will it be before the Church of England is bold enough to include confirmation as a 'pastoral rite', as did the Episcopal Church of the USA in 1979?

References and Further Reading

David Holeton (ed.), *Growing into Newness of Life: Christian Initiation in Anglicanism Today*, Anglican Book Centre, Toronto, 1993.

Maxwell E. Johnson, *The Rites of Christian Initiation: Their Evolution and Interpretation*, The Liturgical Press, Collegeville, 1999.

Simon M. Jones, 'Integration or Separation? The Future of Confirmation within the Church of England', *Theology* 98, 1995, pp. 282–9.

Kenneth Stevenson, *The Mystery of Baptism in the Anglican Tradition*, Canterbury Press, Norwich, 1998.

E. C. Whitaker, *The Baptismal Liturgy*, 2nd edn, SPCK, London, 1981.

N. and H. Whitehead, *Baptism Matters*, National Society/CHP, London, 1998.

Edward Yarnold, *The Awe-Inspiring Rites of Initiation*, 2nd edn, T & T Clark, Edinburgh, 1994.

Chapter 8

Collects and Post Communion Prayers

A. INTRODUCTION

History

In the Christian tradition the collect is a distinctively Western form of prayer. However, prayers constructed on the same lines can be found not only in Hebrew religion but also in classical literature, both Latin and Greek. It is therefore probably another case of the Church using a form which had already been found acceptable in other religions. It was established in Rome in the fifth century, in the shape which has been the model for collect-writing ever since, certainly after the papacy of Celestine (d. 432) and probably during the papacy of Leo (440–61).

The earliest sources for collects are the collections called sacramentaries, which contained the canon of the Mass together with the collects, prefaces and other prayers for seasonal use by the priest through the year. Sacramentaries were in use as late as the thirteenth century, when the missal began to replace them. For our purposes, however, it is their early development that is significant. Three texts are recognized as particularly influential. The earliest is the Leonine Sacramentary (probably sixth century), which is not really a sacramentary as such, but a looser collection of material which would form part of subsequent sacramentaries. Later, the Frankish Church was to use the Gelasian Sacramentary, an eighth-century document alleged to have been compiled by Pope Gelasius I (492–96). Another, slightly later collection (late eighth/early ninth century), the Gregorian Sacramentary, was sent to the Franks at the request of Charlemagne by Pope Hadrian I to cover deficiencies in the existing provisions. The book that the Franks received claimed to be 'the Book of Sacraments published by St Gregory the Great', although it contained a number of post-Gregorian elements. These adjustments are to be attributed to several hands. The theory that Alcuin of York updated the material to make it suitable for the needs of its new users is not supported by modern scholarship.

The sacramentaries provided four prayers sharing a similar structure. These were said after the entrance rite, at the offertory, after the communion, and at the conclusion (the blessing). The Roman books do not give particular names to these prayers: the term *oratio*, sometimes qualified to show a prayer's position in the Mass, covers them all. Only the first of the prayers survived into the *BCP* of 1549 to become what we now know as the collect.

Some confusion has long existed over the derivation of the word 'collect' from the term *ad collectam* given to this prayer in the Gregorian Sacramentary. There have been attempts to represent the prayer as a gathering formula when the people gathered in Rome to proceed to a Mass at one of the stational churches. G. G. Willis points out that this is most improbable. Such services were occasional; but the collect is a variable prayer said at every Mass. Others have argued that *collecta* or *collectio* refers to a gathering of the people's prayers into one summarizing prayer said by the celebrant. So, for example, a prayer said by the celebrant on behalf of the people might have concluded a form of the litany. The collect then acts as a conclusion to the introit. This is a far more likely hypothesis, although, as Willis shows, there is no Roman evidence for the use of this word at all. According to Willis,

> the form *collecta* cannot be traced back in Gallican usage earlier than the seventh century; before that time the word used was *collectio*, a word common in Gallican sacramentaries of the seventh and eighth centuries . . . As applied to prayers after psalmody . . . the term *collectio* first appears in the acts of the Council of Agde in 506. Thus in Gallican circles the notion of 'collecting the prayers' appears in the fifth century, the term *collectio* for such a prayer at the beginning of the sixth, and the term *collecta* in the seventh, though it does not at once replace *collectio*. This is the true derivation of the word 'collect' as used of a prayer . . . It is a purely Gallican term, and it has nothing to do with the Roman term *collecta*, or collection of the people before the procession. (1968, p. 107)

Shape and Form

The collect has a distinctive pattern; and whereas Gallican forms could be rather diffuse, Roman collects were marked by brevity and conciseness, containing normally a single petition. They were also prayers noted for their rhythm. Many were written in the fifth and sixth centuries, when classical oratory flowered; and care was taken that they conformed to the rules of the *cursus*. Many people who subsequently attempted to translate collects into the vernacular attempted to follow the same pattern and style. Cranmer, who was probably responsible for most of the translations and new compositions in the 1549 and 1552 Prayer Books, seems to have had an outstanding gift for collect-writing, and especially for translation of Latin collects into rhythmic and memorable English. The 1662 Prayer Book occasionally makes clarifying adjustments that disturb the balance of earlier models. In the main, however, the Anglican collect has retained its sixteenth-century shape even in modern language versions of the present day.

The collect normally has five components:

1. An address to God the Father. Some later collects were addressed to the Son, and usually they originate in places where Arianism was rife.
2. A relative or participial clause referring to some attribute of God, or to one of his saving acts. This is the ground for the petition. It is not present in all collects.
3. The petition itself, normally a single request on behalf of the Church or those present when the prayer is used. It thus takes the first person plural (*us* or *our*).
4. The purpose of the petition. This, again, is not always included.
5. The conclusion is in the form of a mediation. Prayer is offered to God the Father *through* Jesus Christ the Son of God. A trinitarian doxology ('who is alive and reigns with you and the Holy Spirit, one God, now and for ever') properly follows a collect in this form. Prayers addressed directly to the Son take the doxology 'who lives and reigns with God the Father in the unity of the Holy Spirit, ever one God', or something similar.

The BCP

As we have noted, three of the variable prayers of the Roman rite (the secret, post-communion, and concluding prayer) disappeared from the Order for Holy Communion in the 1549 Prayer Book. Only the collect remained for use at the Eucharist and at the daily offices. Archbishop Cranmer's translations of Latin collects, mainly from the Sarum Missal, are justly acclaimed as a literary monument in their own right. In addition, Cranmer (or other hands working with him) produced a number of new collects. Many of these were for saints' days, and sought to avoid the controversial issues of praying for or through the dead. Their quality is uneven.

The function of the collect in the Prayer Book is a more complex topic than it might at first appear. While there are occasions when it could be taken as the conclusion of the introit, and therefore distinct from the Liturgy of the Word, there are many instances where the collect is closely related to at least one of the appointed readings for the day. The First Sunday in Advent and St Mark's Day are only two examples of a larger trend. Certainly, the value of this short form of prayer as a tool of catechism became embedded in the life of the Church. As late as 1874, Thomas Hardy describes the heroine of *Far From the Madding Crowd* hearing a little boy reciting the collect for the week on the way home, as she stands concealed behind some bushes (Chapter 44).

The ASB

Standing on the brink of modern Anglican liturgical revision, the *ASB* significantly reshaped the language, function, and traditional reference points of the collects. Simpler, contemporary language replaced the latinate Cranmerian style, and the relative clause containing an attribute of God gave way (often with unfortunate results) to a statement about God. The adoption of the two-year thematic JLG Lectionary, with a different construction of the Church's year, and attention to other experiments in modern collect-writing (e.g. The Church of the Province of Southern Africa's *Modern Collects* of 1972) had two obvious consequences. The familiar *BCP* collects for particular Sundays often became detached from their place in the year or disappeared altogether, and the collects that were fixed in the new book were thematically related to the Lectionary. This meant, in turn, that the collect became the introduction to the Liturgy of the Word, often flagging up key themes that would be found in the readings.

From ASB to CW

The main difference to be noted in the move from the *ASB* to *CW* is that the Lectionary ceases to be arranged on a thematic plan through the Church's year. *CW* slightly adapts the three-year *Revised Common Lectionary* (*RCL*) to replace the two-year thematic *ASB* Lectionary. This has once more had an effect on the collects. To make the *RCL* workable, the collects had to be attached either to Sunday names or to sets of lections. The choice fell on Sunday names. This does not, of course, deny their relationship to the biblical passages read during worship; and especially in the seasons of Christmas and Easter, clear connections between collects and readings can be seen.

The *sanctorale* is also greatly expanded, and there is provision for a great many individuals previously covered by commons. The *ASB* had four Principal Holy Days, 32 Festivals and Greater Holy Days, and 80 Lesser Festivals and Commemorations, and there were no collects for this last category. *CW* has nine Principal Feasts, 28 Festivals, 101 Lesser Festivals, and 113 Commemorations, and collects are provided for all except the last group. The additions to the collects often reflect matters of particular concern to the Church's life: the foundations of doctrine (e.g. St Athanasius); ecumenism and Christian unity (e.g. Anskar and Cyril and Methodius); and the tradition of spirituality (e.g. Julian of Norwich, William Law, Teresa of Avila and St John of the Cross). They have also provided scope for some very pleasing original additions to the collect repertoire. The collects for Lancelot Andrewes and George Herbert are just two examples.

The compilers of *CW* have declared their intention of staying close to the *BCP* wherever possible. This has had noticeable effects. The relative clause, largely eliminated from the *ASB*, has returned. Sometimes an older phrase has been restored (for example, at the end of the Ash Wednesday collect). There are some unfortunate instances where an archaic phrase has been retained in a way that puts strain on the collect as a whole. A full set of collects in traditional language has also been compiled. This is to accommodate the need for consistency in places where the Eucharist and offices are conducted in traditional language.

Modern resources have played a significant part, too, in the material now available. The collection draws on writers like Frank Colquhoun, David Silk, and Janet Morley, as well as using the Roman Catholic proposed national propers for the vernacular saints Aelred, Columba, Paulinus, Aidan, Willibrord and Hilda. (A national proper is a collection of celebrations and texts used in one country only. In the greater number of cases, this will consist of feasts and commemorations of local saints.) By using this material, the Church of England sensibly draws on appropriate resources of distinctive quality, and declares its commitment to the unity of the whole catholic Church.

The choice of the long ending for the collects ('who is alive and reigns with you, in the unity of the Holy Spirit, one God, now and for ever') has been the cause of complaint from some quarters. *CW* does not make this mandatory, except on Sundays and major holy days.

Post Communion Prayers

Post communion prayers restore something which has been lost from the eucharistic celebration since the 1549 *BCP*. Prayers with this function appear very early in the history of the Church: several early liturgies include a thanksgiving for communion and a prayer, though there does not seem to be evidence that they were variable from season to season. Their structure is similar to that of the collect. The ancient Roman Mass has a post-communion prayer, and variable forms, adapted to Festivals or seasons, were used there from the time of St Gregory. A little later, the ninth-century Gallican rite ends with a thanksgiving after communion, a collect, and a dismissal.

In *CW*, the post communion prayers are drawn from a number of sources, and it is a happy development that some well-loved Prayer Book collects, which are no longer used as collects, remain in the tradition as post communion prayers. The provision for Trinity 17 is a good example.

That the focus of the *CW* post communion prayers is eucharistic is self-evident. They acknowledge feast days and seasons in their intentions, but it is worth emphasizing a consistent feature of the genre as we encounter it here. Again and again, they are eschatological, reminding worshippers that it is through participation in the Eucharist that we are offered a foretaste of the heavenly banquet.

The following notes indicate the sources of the prayers published in *The Christian Year: Calendar, Lectionary and Collects* (1997), where these are known, and comment briefly on any significant points in the text. For the abbreviations used, see above, p. ix. It should be noted that not all the prayers appear in the main volume of *CW*, although they are in the President's edition. Nor has it been possible to include full details of the lives of the saints, and so readers are encouraged to refer to one of the many dictionaries of the saints which are widely available or to *Exciting Holiness*.

B. SEASONS

The First Sunday of Advent

Collect: Probably from the Gelasian Sacramentary, and certainly a modernized form of the version in the 1549 *BCP*. It draws on the Epistle (Romans 8) for the imagery of waking out of sleep, casting away the works of darkness, and putting on the armour of light. In the *CW* Lectionary, Year A sets Romans 8.11–14 for the Principal Service, while Year C sets the passage for the Third Service.

Post communion: From the Gelasian Sacramentary. It is thematically linked to the collect in images of watchfulness and wakefulness.

The Second Sunday of Advent

Collect: The Sarum Missal gives this collect for Advent 1 and the 1549 *BCP* Advent 4. Though not explicitly linked to the day's readings, it sets the Advent theme of expectation in an eschatological frame.

Post communion: From *PHG* and before that included in Silk (unattributed). Takes up and develops more explicitly the themes of the first and second coming that run through Advent to Christmas.

The Third Sunday of Advent

Collect: From the 1662 *BCP*, and obedient to the traditional concentration on John the Baptist on this Sunday. The *CW* Lectionary sets Gospel readings relating to John the Baptist in each of the three years. In the Sarum Rite this was known as *Gaudete* Sunday, from the opening words of its Latin antiphon (Philippians 4.5), and rose-coloured vestments were worn to signify a respite from the deeper penitential mood of the season. The passage from Philippians is set for one of the services in each of the three years of the *CW* Lectionary.

Post communion: From Westcott House, Cambridge, and again focused on the second coming.

The Fourth Sunday of Advent

Collect: From the Scottish *BCP* and included in *PHG*. This collect draws attention to the Lectionary's concentration on Mary on this Sunday.

Post communion: Taken from Frank Colquhoun's *Parish Prayers* via the *ASB*.

Christmas Eve

Collect: From the *ASB*, and adapted from the 1549 *BCP*. No provision was made for Christmas Eve in the 1552 and 1662 Prayer Books. It articulates the relationship between remembering the first coming and looking forward in awe and joy to the second coming.

Post communion: From *BAS*, and reinforcing the special eschatological note of Advent.

Christmas Night

Collect: Taken from the *ASB*, and ultimately translated from the Latin Missal (the Sarum *Missa in Gallicantu* celebrated before sunrise on Christmas Day).
Post communion: From *PHG*, and based on the apocalyptic image of Christ the Morning Star of Revelation 22.16.

Christmas Day

Collect: Newly composed for the 1549 *BCP*, perhaps suggested by a collect in the Gregorian Sacramentary (No. 58). It concentrates on the redemption of human nature by divine nature in the incarnation, and takes up the motif of adoption in the day's Gospel, John 1.1–14.
Post communion: From *BAS*.

The First Sunday of Christmas

Collect: Taken from the *ASB* (Christmas 2, Year 1) and adapted from the 1928 *BCP*. The *CW* Lectionary provides New Testament readings reflecting the theme of incarnation.
Post communion: From the *ASB*. The preamble comes from a prayer in the 1928 *BCP* rite of infant baptism for the home of the newly baptized child.

The Second Sunday of Christmas

Collect: From the Church of Ireland's *Collects and Post-Communion Prayers* (1995). The emphasis on light entering the world through the incarnate Word of God accords with the day's Gospel, John 1.[1–9] 10–18, in all three years of the Lectionary.
Post communion: From the *ASB* Collect of Christmas Day. Adapted in this form from the 1662 *BCP* Collect of Christmas Day in *MC*.

Epiphany

Collect: From the *BCP*, and originally from the Gregorian Sacramentary, which gave it to the Sarum Missal. The day's Gospel (Matthew 2.1–12) gives the Magi's account of the star that led them to Bethlehem.
Post communion: From *PHG*. Closely associated with Isaiah 60.1–3 (though the passage refers to the New Jerusalem rather than to God). This passage is given as the Old Testament reading at the Second Service in all three years in the *CW* Lectionary.

The Baptism of Christ (The First Sunday of Epiphany)

Collect: From the *ASB*, with substantial adaptation to make clear that baptism is rebirth by water and the Spirit, and that by baptism we become God's adopted children. It is based on a collect from CSI.
Post communion: New composition, expressing the typological connection between the baptism of Jesus and our own baptism, and emphasizing the ongoing work of baptism in the Christian life. Implicit in the prayer is a

reference to the Genesis creation narrative, with its account of the creation of water and humanity for the first time. It is this fallen creation that is redeemed through Christ, and sacramentally marked in baptism.

The Second Sunday of Epiphany

Collect: From the *ASB* collect of Epiphany 4, and adapted from *MC*. Based originally on a prayer in CSI. There are resonances of Revelation 21.5, but it is generally consistent with themes of light, incarnation, transformation and rebirth appropriate to this season.

Post communion: From the 1989 New Zealand Prayer Book, reprinted in *PHG*.

The Third Sunday of Epiphany

Collect: From the *ASB*, and adapted from *MC* for the Seventh Sunday before Easter. The *CW* Lectionary sets John 2.1–11, the miracle at the marriage at Cana, as the Gospel at the Principal Service. The other two years focus attention on the wonder of Christ's coming through readings describing the call to the first disciples, and Jesus' identification of himself in the Temple with the prophecy of Isaiah.

Post communion: From *BAS*. Based on the CSI collect of Pentecost 20.

The Fourth Sunday of Epiphany

Collect: From *PHG*, and originally included in Silk (combining a prayer from the Gelasian Sacramentary with the thought of 2 Corinthians 4.6). It sums up the typological progression from reflection on the creation at the beginning of Advent, and the incarnation, manifestation and second coming through to the end of the season of Epiphany, and leads to the Presentation with its natural emphasis on the 'light to lighten the Gentiles'.

Post communion: PHG, p. 239, Prayer D, though in an extensively revised form.

The Presentation of Christ in the Temple

Collect: From the 1549 *BCP*, and originally from the Sarum Missal and the Gregorian Sacramentary.

Post communion: From *PHG*, adapted from the Roman Missal. It continues the trend of the post communion prayers in this season, which explore the call to mission and witness implicit in the keeping of Advent, Christmas and Epiphany, and inseparable from the Eucharist.

The Fifth Sunday before Lent

Collect: From a prayer in the *ASB* for those taking vows, and based on the 1928 *BCP*.

Post communion: From *BAS*. Based on 1 John 1–4.

The Fourth Sunday before Lent

Collect: From the *BCP* (Epiphany 4). The 1662 *BCP* adapts the version of 1549, which in turn is based on the Sarum Missal's collect of Epiphany 5. It shifts the focus away from Epiphany and Candlemas, and towards the Lenten theme of abandonment in danger and temptation.

Post communion: From the *BCP*, which takes it from the Gregorian Sacramentary. This is one of six collects provided in 1549 for occasions when there is no communion after the offertory. In the original form (beginning 'Prevent us O Lord') it appears in the 1662 ordination rite as the prayer just before the blessing.

The Third Sunday before Lent

Collect: From the 1662 *BCP* collect of Easter 4, and used again in 1928. Adapted in this form by the JLG *Daily Office* and *MC*. The opening words in the 1549 and 1552 *BCP* adopt a literal translation of the original in the Gelasian Sacramentary: 'Almighty God, which dost make the minds of all faithful men to be of one will.' The present version points far more sharply to the need for sinful human beings to be recalled to obedience in the joyful service of God.

Post communion: New composition. As the collect meditates on freedom in obedience, so the post communion prayer meditates on eucharistic obedience as a means to approach God 'in faith and love'.

The Second Sunday before Lent

Collect: A new composition in the *ASB*, where it appears for the Ninth Sunday before Christmas. The preamble is based on the CSI collect of the Ninth Sunday before Easter.

Post communion: *PHG*, originally included in Silk (unattributed). The prayer plays on the paradox of the cross as tree of life and tree of death, and perhaps alludes to the medieval tradition that the cross stood on the site of the tree of life in the Garden of Eden.

Sunday Next before Lent

Collect: Adopts the *ASB* collect of Lent 4. This alludes to the collect for the Transfiguration in the 1928 *BCP*. The *CW* Lectionary gives a Transfiguration narrative as the Gospel at the Principal Service in each of the three years, appropriately reminding worshippers that they are strengthened for the challenges of the Christian life (of which Lent is a cameo) by the certain knowledge of the glory of God in Christ.

Post communion: From *BAS*.

Ash Wednesday

Collect: The *ASB* adapts the 1549 *BCP* collect. *CW* restores 'remission and forgiveness' in the last line, where the *ASB* had substituted 'forgiveness and peace'. It brings together two powerful Lenten strands: reflection on our sinful, abject condition, and redemption through the death and resurrection of Christ as a new creation.

Post communion: From the 1549 *BCP* collect of Easter 2.

The First Sunday of Lent

Collect: Largely based on the *BCP*, although the original understanding of abstinence as a way of subduing the spirit into obedience to God is moderated . in the journey through the JLG *Daily Office* and *MC* to the *ASB*.

Post communion: A masterly interweaving of eucharistic themes of living bread with the temptation in the wilderness. It echoes Jesus' rebuke to Satan's challenge to turn stones into bread. This episode appears in the Gospel for the Principal Service in Years A and C. The Marcan passage set for Year B refers generally to the temptation.

The Second Sunday of Lent

Collect: From the *BCP* collect of Easter 3, and ultimately from a prayer in the Leonine Sacramentary. The theme is suited to Lenten (and arguably catechumenal) reflection on the Christian life and the seriousness of allegiance to Christ.

Post communion: Modern language version of the *BCP* collect of the day, based on the Gregorian Sacramentary and found also in the Sarum Missal. It subtly ties the seasonal focus on temptation to the strength imparted by sharing in the Eucharist.

The Third Sunday of Lent

Collect: Adopted by the 1928 *BCP* from the American collect for the Monday in Holy Week. Written by William Reed Huntington, it was published in 1882. The *ASB* uses it for Lent 3.

Post communion: Follows the *BCP* collect of Trinity 18, with the 1662 change from 'avoyde' to 'withstand'. The source is the Gelasian Sacramentary.

The Fourth Sunday of Lent

Collect: Follows the *BCP* collect of Trinity 24. The present text has 'chains', a word more resonant of imprisonment for modern people than the *BCP*'s 'bands'. This collect works with the polarized concepts of sin and forgiveness. Other Lenten collects exploit the tensions of joy and pain, error and truth.

Post communion: From the *ASB*, which adapted it from the American *BCP*. The reference is to Isaiah 50.6.

Mothering Sunday

Collect: By Michael Perham, and published in Michael Perham (ed.), *Enriching the Christian Year* (1993).

Post communion: As above.

The Fifth Sunday of Lent
Collect: The *ASB* adapts this from *MC*. It originates in a Latin collect translated for the 1929 Scottish *BCP*.
Post communion: The *ASB* takes this from the JLG *Daily Office* and *MC*. It is based on a prayer attributed to St Augustine.

Palm Sunday
Collect: From the *BCP*, which takes it from the Sarum Missal. The Latin version appears earlier in the Gregorian Sacramentary.
Post communion: From the Church of Ireland's *Alternative Prayer Book* (1984), based on the collect above.

Maundy Thursday
Collect: From *LHWE*. Based on 1 Corinthians 11.26, which is part of the New Testament reading at the Eucharist. This text reminds us that the day is both the beginning of the Passion, and the inauguration of the Eucharist.
Post communion: Adapted from the 1928 *BCP* and the 1929 Scottish *BCP*. It is based on a medieval Corpus Christi collect, attributed to Thomas Aquinas.

Good Friday
Collect: From the *BCP*. In 1549 it was the collect for Mattins, and it was assumed that the Holy Communion would be celebrated subsequently. It is a translation of the *oratio super populum* in the Roman Mass for the Wednesday in Holy Week. A post communion prayer is inappropriate on this day and on Easter Eve, because the liturgy is not completed until the end of the first Eucharist of Easter.

Easter Eve
Collect: From the 1662 *BCP*, which appears to take it from the Scottish Prayer Book of 1637. The central biblical reference is to Romans 6. This is especially suitable where the Easter liturgy is to incorporate the rites of initiation.

Easter Day
Collect: From the *ASB*. Earlier than this, it appears in *MC* and the American Prayer Book of 1928. The images seem to be distilled from Romans 8.
Post communion: Sums up all the Lenten polarities in the triumphant opposition of dying to sin and rising to new life with Christ. There is close correlation with 1 Corinthians 15.1–31. The death and life imagery lends itself to occasions when baptism is part of the Easter liturgy.

The Second Sunday of Easter
Collect: From the 1549 *BCP*, where it was used at the second celebration of Easter Day, on the Tuesday in Easter Week, and on the First Sunday after

Easter. It is based directly on the Epistle for the second celebration of Easter Day (1 Corinthians 5.6–8).

Post communion: From the *ASB* collect of Pentecost 3, and originating in *MC* for the same day. As on other occasions through the season of Easter, there are allusions to the *BCP* funeral collect, which takes its assurances of resurrection from John 11.25–26 and 1 Thessalonians 4.13–16.

The Third Sunday of Easter

Collect: From the *ASB* provision for Easter 1, composed by the Liturgical Commission. With the Lectionary, it concentrates on the post-resurrection appearances of Jesus. For this Sunday, Years A and B set Luke's account of the Supper at Emmaus as the Gospel reading, while Year C has the draft of fishes from John's Gospel.

Post communion: Alludes powerfully to the Supper at Emmaus, and ties this to the recognition of Christ, through faith, in eucharistic worship. From *BAS*, and written originally for the 1928 American Prayer Book by J. W. Suter, Jr.

The Fourth Sunday of Easter

Collect: A new composition first found in the JLG *Daily Office* and *MC*, and adopted by the *ASB*. It is adapted from the *BCP* funeral collect, and reminds worshippers that, in sharing Christ's resurrection, their concerns are shifted from the transient things of this life to the timeless life of the kingdom.

Post communion: Based on the Church of Ireland's *Alternative Prayer Book* collect of Easter 2. This is traditionally 'Good Shepherd Sunday', and the prayer takes up the theme of the good shepherd in John 10, which provides the day's Gospel.

The Fifth Sunday of Easter

Collect: From the 1549 *BCP*, where it was the first collect of Easter Day. In this later position, it aids in the continuing meditation on the resurrection, and urges that consciousness of grace be translated into action.

Post communion: From the *ASB* collect for the Ninth Sunday before Easter, composed by the Liturgical Commission. Where the *ASB* sequence sets it at the beginning of a cycle leading up to Easter, in *CW* it shares the concerns of the collect that paschal grace be continued and acted upon by the Easter community.

The Sixth Sunday of Easter

Collect: From *LHWE*, it is a revision of a Mozarabic prayer in Bright's *Ancient Collects*. Again, it encourages worshippers to think eschatologically, connecting life lived in the light of the resurrection with the life of the kingdom.

Post communion: Used as a post communion prayer on Lent 3 in *BAS*. While its biblical reference is to Jesus' encounter with the woman of Samaria at the well (John 4.1–42), which is not in the day's Lectionary, there is a more general emphasis on the desire for God that looks for things eternal.

Ascension Day

Collect: From the 1549 *BCP*, which translates the Sarum Missal collect of the day.

Post communion: From MacDonnell, this prayer uses the physical ascension of Jesus as a figure of the raising up of fallen humanity accomplished by his resurrection and ascension, and celebrated at every Eucharist.

The Seventh Sunday of Easter

Collect: From the 1549 *BCP*, based on the Sarum antiphon for the *Magnificat* at Vespers on Ascension Day. In the *BCP*, it corresponds closely to the promise of the Comforter in the day's Gospel (John 15.26–16.4). *CW* concentrates rather on the glorifying of Christ (John 17), a theme that is strongly developed in this collect.

Post communion: From *BAS*. It is an appropriate reminder to Christians, as they wait for Pentecost, that they have a commission to fulfil until Christ comes again.

Day of Pentecost

Collect: From the 1549 Prayer Book, before that in the Sarum Missal, and ultimately the Gregorian Sacramentary (No. 90).

Post communion: From *BAS*. Alludes to the account of the gift of tongues in Acts 2 in asking God's help for Christians in their mission to bear witness to Jesus Christ.

The Weekdays after the Day of Pentecost

Collect: From the 1549 *BCP*, which translates a prayer in the Gelasian Sacramentary (i.60). It reminds worshippers that the gift of the Holy Spirit at Pentecost is continually available as inspiration and guide throughout our lives.

Post communion: From *BAS*, this prayer meditates on the richness of trinitarian belief celebrated in the Eucharist, and reminds Christians that they are nourished to maturity by this sacrament.

Trinity Sunday

Collect: The 1549 *BCP* translates a Latin collect found in the Sarum Missal and the Gregorian Sacramentary (No. 381).

Post communion: The *ASB* uses this as the second collect of Trinity Sunday. It comes from CSI and recapitulates the theme of the collect above.

Day of Thanksgiving for the Institution of the Holy Communion (Corpus Christi)

Collect: The *ASB* adopts this from 1929 Scottish *BCP* collect of Maundy Thursday. This was in turn based on a medieval Corpus Christi collect attributed to Thomas Aquinas.

Post communion: From MacDonnell. The prayer takes up the Johannine eucharistic themes (especially John 6) which underpin the celebration on this day.

The First Sunday after Trinity
Collect: From the 1549 *BCP*, which translates the Sarum collect of the day. The same collect is found in the Gelasian Sacramentary (i.62).
Post communion: From *PHG*. Appropriately, it emphasizes the theological virtues of faith, hope and love which are to be cultivated in the growing time of the Sundays after Trinity.

Second Sunday after Trinity
Collect: The 1549 *BCP* collect for Quinquagesima, with the 1929 Scottish *BCP* use of 'love' instead of 'charity'. In the *ASB*, this is used for Pentecost 7.
Post communion: From a Maundy Thursday post communion prayer in *LHWE*.

The Third Sunday after Trinity
Collect: From the *ASB* provision for Pentecost 4, composed by David Frost for the Church of England Liturgical Commission. It continues the theme of growth, in freely-given service, towards God, and alludes directly to Romans 8.21.
Post communion: From Janet Morley, *All Desires Known* (1992).

The Fourth Sunday after Trinity
Collect: From the 1549 *BCP*, which translates the Sarum collect of Trinity 4. It is used as the collect of Pentecost 14 in the *ASB*. There is an interesting variation, however. Where Sarum has *bona temporalia* (broadly, 'the *good* things of finite, earthly life'), *BCP* does not suggest that temporal things are in any way intrinsically good. *CW* alters 'that we finally lose not the things eternal' to 'that we lose not our hold on things eternal'. This dispenses with the eschatological urgency of the collect.
Post communion: From *BAS*.

The Fifth Sunday after Trinity
Collect: The collect to be said after the two preceding collects at the communion on Good Friday in the 1549 *BCP*, and the second collect of Good Friday in the 1552 and 1662 *BCPs*. The two later Prayer Books did not provide for a celebration of Holy Communion. It is a translation of the third of the Sarum Good Friday solemn prayers, and is also found in the Gelasian Sacramentary. It is used in the *ASB* both on Good Friday and on Pentecost 2. The theme of the vocation of each of the faithful is significant in the larger reflection on growth that continues through the season of Trinity.
Post communion: *BCP* 1549 translates the Sarum collect of the day.

The Sixth Sunday after Trinity
Collect: The 1549 *BCP* translates the Sarum collect of the day, but where Sarum has *ut te in omnibus et super omnibus diligentes* ('loving you in all things and above all things'), 1549 has only 'in all things'. 1552 follows 1549. 1662 changes to 'above all things'. *CW* restores the full Latin original ('in all things and above all things'), which satisfies accuracy, but destroys balance. It is useful to note that, in the Latin, *super* (above) is balanced by *superant* (exceed).
Post communion: From *BAS*.

The Seventh Sunday after Trinity
Collect: 1549 *BCP* paraphrases the Sarum collect of the day to achieve the elegant metaphor of cultivation and growth, progressing from planting to increasing and nourishing. This is well suited to the preoccupations of the Trinity period. In the *ASB* it is used on Pentecost 17.
Post communion: A post communion prayer from *LHWE* (p. 96), in the section of Prayers on the Passion designed for use in Holy Week. The christological metaphor of the true vine accords well with the growth imagery of the collect.

The Eighth Sunday after Trinity
Collect: A new composition for the *BCP* of the Church in Wales, used for Epiphany 6.
Post communion: A post communion prayer for Trinity Sunday from Perham, *Enriching the Christian Year*, and based on the Liturgy of Malabar.

The Ninth Sunday after Trinity
Collect: New composition by David Frost. (Frost denies the customary genealogy, namely that the *ASB* adapts a collect for Pentecost 8 from the JLG *Daily Office*, which in turn follows a post communion prayer for Whitsunday in the 1929 Scottish *BCP*.) There are allusions to Galatians 5.16–22 and Ephesians 5.9.
Post communion: Taken with slight alterations from a post communion in *PW* (p. 100), which has as its intention the Family.

The Tenth Sunday after Trinity
Collect: From the 1549 *BCP*, which translates the collect of the day from the Sarum Missal (also Gelasian Sacramentary, iii.5).
Post communion: By Kenneth Stevenson, Bishop of Portsmouth.

The Eleventh Sunday after Trinity
Collect: From the 1662 *BCP* collect of the day, which develops its 1549 predecessor (a translation from Sarum) by adding phrases that contribute to balanced cadences, but lose some of the urgency of 1549.
Post communion: From MacDonnell.

The Twelfth Sunday after Trinity

Collect: From the *BCP* 1549/1662. The words, 'but through the merits and mediation . . .' were added in 1662. The Prayer Book version is more of a free paraphrase from the Sarum Missal than a translation, and demonstrates the best skills of vernacular writing, with its contrast between hearing and praying, the alliterative pairing of 'desire' and 'deserve', and the play on words with the same root in 'forgiving' and 'giving'. The *ASB* uses this collect for Easter 5.

Post communion: From *BAS*. The technical devices linking wholeness and brokenness make the prayer particularly compatible with the technique of the collect.

The Thirteenth Sunday after Trinity

Collect: A new composition for Pentecost 12 in the *ASB*. It is based on 2 Corinthians 5.19.

Post communion: From Silk (unattributed). The prayer reminds worshippers of their place in the unfolding of salvation history and of the eschatological vision of the Eucharist. Like the wandering Israelites whom God fed until they reached the Promised Land, we are fed by the Eucharist through our earthly pilgrimage until we come to the heavenly banquet.

The Fourteenth Sunday after Trinity

Collect: A new composition for Pentecost 20 in the *ASB*. It takes its inspiration from Hebrews 10.19–23 and John 4.24.

Post communion: From *BAS*.

The Fifteenth Sunday after Trinity

Collect: From Silk, based on a prayer in the Gelasian Sacramentary.

Post communion: The 1549 *BCP* collect of the day, translated from the Sarum Missal.

The Sixteenth Sunday after Trinity

Collect: From the 1549 *BCP* collect of Epiphany 1. It translates a collect from the Gregorian Sacramentary (No. 16), and may be loosely based on the Epistle, Romans 12.1ff.

Post communion: The *ASB* adapts this prayer for Pentecost 16 from the Leonine Sacramentary. It is based directly on Romans 13.10 and Matthew 23.39.

The Seventeenth Sunday after Trinity

Collect: This prayer was composed by David Frost and used for Pentecost 18 in the *ASB*. It is based on Augustine's *Confessions*, Matthew 5.8, and 1 Corinthians 13.12.

Post communion: 1549 *BCP* collect of Trinity 17. It translates the Sarum collect of the day, which derives from the Gregorian Sacramentary (No. 172). The

CW version exchanges the *BCP*'s 'prevent and follow' for 'precede and follow'. This captures part, but not all of the sense of the original.

The Eighteenth Sunday after Trinity

Collect: Composed by David Frost and used in the *ASB* on Pentecost 19. It adopts the image of running the way of God's commandments from the 1549/1662 collect of Trinity 11. Its other references are to Philippians 3.13, Hebrews 12.1, and 1 Corinthians 9.24–25.

Post communion: Based on an ancient prayer, this might be taken as an expression of the notion of *anamnesis*.

The Nineteenth Sunday after Trinity

Collect: From the 1549 *BCP* collect of the day, which translates the Sarum collect (descended from the Gelasian Sacramentary, iii.14) but inverts the sequence of ideas, so that human inadequacy precedes divine mercy.

Post communion: Slightly adapts a post communion prayer from *PW* (p. 96) applicable to the following intentions: the Spirit, Pentecost, Gifts, Healing, Baptism and Confirmation.

The Twentieth Sunday after Trinity

Collect: A new composition, concentrating on the action of the Spirit in the Church and looking forward to the growth towards eternal life which takes place through the Spirit.

Post communion: From Silk (unattributed). It links the familiar image of Christ the Light (especially John 1.1–14) to the inner illumination that comes through the grace of God in the Eucharist.

The Twenty-First Sunday after Trinity

Collect: From the 1549 collect of the day, which translates the Sarum collect.

Post communion: A new composition, based closely on James 1.17.

The Last Sunday after Trinity

Collect: 1549 *BCP* collect of Advent 2, and inspired initially by the day's Epistle, Romans 15.4ff.

Post communion: From *BAS*. The prayer's reflection on the feeding with living bread that we receive in the Eucharist runs parallel to the collect's reflection on the feeding of our minds and hearts with the living word of God.

All Saints' Day

Collect: From 1549 *BCP*, perhaps influenced by a collect in the Leonine Sacramentary.

Post communion: From the Eucharist of All Saints in *PHG* (p. 57). It reminds worshippers that the communion of saints is a bond existing beyond time and space, and that the eucharistic table prefigures the table where all the saints will gather at the end of time.

The Fourth Sunday before Advent

Collect: From the Gothic Missal and included in Silk. This prayer and the post communion prayer continue the All Saints' tide theme of an earthly pilgrimage towards the eschatological joy of heaven.

Post communion: An ancient prayer, included in Silk (unattributed).

The Third Sunday before Advent

Collect: From the *ASB* collect of Pentecost 15. It is based on Howard Galley's translation of the pre-Vatican II Roman Missal collect for Christ the King, introduced by Pius XI in 1925. The JLG *Daily Office* used an adaptation of this for Pentecost 18.

Post communion: ASB from *MC.*

The Second Sunday before Advent

Collect: 1662 *BCP* collect of Epiphany 6, probably composed by John Cosin. There is no collect for that Sunday in the 1549 *BCP*. The JLG *Daily Office* used the prayer for the Eighth Sunday before Christmas. The *ASB* used that for Epiphany 6.

Post communion: From MacDonnell.

Christ the King (The Sunday Next before Advent)

Collect: From the *ASB* collect of Pentecost 21. It originates in *MC*, where it is used for Ascension Day.

Post communion: From the *BCP* collect of Trinity 25, which translates a collect in the Sarum Missal. In the *ASB*, it is used for the Fifth Sunday before Christmas.

Dedication Festival

Collect: A new composition in the *ASB* for the Festival of the Dedication or Consecration of a Church. The notion of the body as a living temple of the Holy Spirit may be found in the First Epistle to the Corinthians. See 1 Corinthians 3.16 and 6.19.

Post communion: From Westcott House, Cambridge. The prayer reminds the Christian community that they are pilgrims, and that the apparent permanency of the buildings that house the Church on earth must always be measured against the eschatological vision of the new Jerusalem.

C. HOLY DAYS

The Naming and Circumcision of Jesus (1 January)

Collect: From *ASB*, which extensively revises the *BCP* collect of the day. The acclamation of the name of Jesus (Philippians 2.9) is retained, but in the second part of the collect, the *BCP* lament over 'worldly and carnal lusts' gives way to the more positive desire to worship and proclaim Jesus Christ as Saviour.

Post communion: A new composition, again based on Philippians 2.9.

Basil the Great and Gregory of Nazianzus (2 January)
Collect: From *PHG*, p. 363. Both of these fourth-century Cappadocian saints contributed richly to the doctrinal teaching of the Church. Basil in particular was active and successful in combating the Arian heresy, which denied the divinity of the incarnate Jesus.
Post communion: See Common 'Of Teachers of the Faith'.

Aelred of Hexham (12 January)
Collect: Roman Catholic proposed national Proper for England. The original text came from the Proper of the Benedictine Congregation, and was considerably adapted by the subcommittee on the National Calendar and Proper. A twelfth-century abbot of the Cistercian house of Rievaulx, Aelred produced a number of spiritual writings. Among these was a treatise *De Spiritali Amicitia* (On Spiritual Friendship).
Post communion: See Common 'Of Members of Religious Communities'.

Hilary (13 January)
Collect: From *CCP*, and adapted from the American *BCP*. Hilary became Bishop of Poitiers *c*. 353, and almost at once found himself involved in the Arian controversy. His treatise *De Trinitate* (On the Trinity) was written to defend the divine nature of the incarnate Jesus.
Post communion: See Common 'Of Teachers of the Faith'.

Antony of Egypt (17 January)
Collect: From *CCP* and written by a member of SSF. Antony was a third-century hermit, who sold his possessions and adopted an ascetic life in the desert. He emerged briefly *c*. 305 to organize his followers into a community, living under a rule.
Post communion: See Common 'Of Members of Religious Communities'.

Wulfstan (19 January)
Collect: Composed by Robert Jeffery, Dean of Worcester 1987–96. Wulfstan was known for refusing riches and combining monastic discipline with the role of Bishop of Worcester (1062–95). He was a peacemaker, a campaigner against the slave trade in Bristol, and an advocate of clerical celibacy. The collect is appropriately based on Micah 6.8.
Post communion: See Common 'Of Bishops'.

Agnes (21 January)
Collect: From *CCP* and written by a member of SSF. Agnes is venerated as a child-martyr who died in Rome in 304 for her faith. But there is no reliable account of her martyrdom. The similarity of her name to the Latin *agnus*

(lamb) is behind the use of a lamb as her emblem, and explains the shepherd imagery of the collect. Perhaps because so little is known of Agnes herself, the collect makes a strangely disjointed move from the specific to the general in its second half, with a four-line petition based on Ephesians 3.18.
Post communion: See Common 'Of Martyrs'.

Francis de Sales (24 January)
Collect: New composition. Francis was a Bishop of Geneva who died in 1622. His ministry was characterized by love, understanding and persistence.
Post communion: See Common 'Of Teachers of the Faith'.

The Conversion of St Paul (25 January)
Collect: From the *ASB*, which adapts the *BCP* collect for the feast. The collect makes much of the use of light – first in its reference to the light of the gospel, and second in its allusion to the blinding light that confronted Paul (then Saul) on the Damascus Road and called him to follow Christ.
Post communion: See Common 'Of Apostles and Evangelists'.

Timothy and Titus (26 January)
Collect: From the *ASB*, which adapts a collect in the Church of the Province of South Africa's *Liturgy 75* (1975). There are epistles to both Timothy and Titus; the Acts of the Apostles mentions Timothy among Paul's followers (Acts 16 and 17); and the Second Epistle to the Corinthians speaks of Paul's love for Titus (2 Corinthians 7).
Post communion: See Common 'Of Missionaries'.

Thomas Aquinas (28 January)
Collect: From *CCP* and written by a member of SSF. Through his enormous body of writings, Thomas, the great thirteenth-century Dominican philosopher and theologian, has largely shaped subsequent Roman Catholic doctrine.
Post communion: See Common 'Of Teachers of the Faith'.

Charles, King and Martyr (30 January)
Collect: From *CCP*, and adapted from Silk, where it appears unattributed. The collect makes the contrast between earthly kingship, and Christ the King of all. While it cannot analyse the complex and even ambiguous nature of Charles's insistence on the divine right of kings, it can make something of the example he set in praying for his persecutors. The Handelian opening line strikes an appropriately patriotic note for an English king. But on the whole, the composition exemplifies many of the difficulties of commemorating political subjects.
Post communion: See Common 'Of Martyrs'.

Anskar, Archbishop of Hamburg, Missionary in Denmark and Sweden, 865 (3 February)

Collect: New composition.
Post communion: See Common 'Of Missionaries'.

Cyril and Methodius, Missionaries to the Slavs, 869 and 885 (14 February)

Collect: New composition, recalling the achievements in vernacular teaching and worship realized by these two missionaries. The collect also pleads for the reunion of the Eastern and Western Churches. Methodius is the patron of ecumenism.
Post communion: See Common 'Of Missionaries'.

Janani Luwum, Archbishop of Uganda, Martyr, 1977 (17 February)

Collect: New composition. The collect takes its imagery of light and darkness from 1 John 1.5–7, and emphasizes the paradox of the martyr's death, which overcomes the darkness and evil of persecution and murder by accepting them for the sake of Jesus Christ.
Post communion: See Common 'Of Martyrs'.

Polycarp, Bishop of Smyrna, Martyr, c. 155 (23 February)

Collect: From *CCP*, and adapted from the American *BCP*. Polycarp defended orthodox belief against the Gnostics, and died in Smyrna refusing to renounce his 86 years of Christianity. The collect thus stresses the Christian obligation to testify to the faith, no matter what the consequences might be.
Post communion: See Common 'Of Martyrs'.

George Herbert, Priest, Poet, 1633 (27 February)

Collect: This new composition is an example of the best kind of evocative and imaginative collect-writing. It weaves allusions to those of Herbert's devotional poems which have become well-loved hymns ('King of glory, king of peace'; 'Teach me my God and King'; and 'Let all the world in every corner sing') into its texture. Finally, it reminds the worshipper both of the title of Herbert's collection of poems – *The Temple* – while also recalling his sense of the Temple or church building as an emblem for the framework of the spiritual life, dedicated in humility to the praise and worship of God.
Post communion: See Common 'Of Pastors'.

David, Bishop of Menevia, Patron of Wales, c. 601 (1 March)

Collect: Taken from *CCP*, which adapts a version in the Church in Wales *BCP*. The earliest written evidence of David's career comes from Ireland, and tells how the people received the Mass from Bishop David and others.
Post communion: See Common 'Of Bishops'.

Chad, Bishop of Lichfield, Missionary, 672 (2 March)

Collect: From *CCP* and written by a member of SSF. The biographical details are drawn from Bede's *Ecclesiastical History*, and remind us that, just as Chad conducted his missionary work among his own people, modern Christians are still called to bear witness to their faith in their particular situations.

Post communion: See Common 'Of Missionaries'.

Perpetua, Felicity and their Companions, Martyrs at Carthage, 203 (7 March)

Collect: From *CCP* and written by a member of SSF. Perpetua had a number of visions, both as she awaited martyrdom, and even in the amphitheatre. One of these showed a ladder leading into a beautiful garden. These visions were a great encouragement to her and to her fellow-martyrs.

Post communion: See Common 'Of Martyrs'.

Edward King, Bishop of Lincoln, 1910 (8 March)

Collect: From *CCP*, which uses a form adapted by Canon Rex Davis from an earlier prayer used at Lincoln Cathedral. The scriptural references come from Ephesians 3.19, which speaks of a rootedness in Christ that opens us to 'the love that passes knowledge', and to 1 Peter 2.25, referring to Christ as 'the shepherd and guardian of your souls'.

Post communion: See Common 'Of Bishops'.

Patrick, Bishop, Missionary, Patron of Ireland, c. 640 (17 March)

Collect: New composition. Patrick's legend recounts that he kindled the new Easter fire in defiance of the Irish Kings – a wonderful image for the inauguration of Christian practice and the need to keep it constantly alive.

Post communion: See Common 'Of Missionaries'.

Joseph of Nazareth (19 March)

Collect: Written by Michael Perham and included in *CCP*, this collect reminds us that Joseph, too, belonged to the line of David, that he has an integral, active and protective role in the Holy Family and in the scheme of the incarnation, and that his obedience, as well as Mary's, was necessary so that Christ could enter the world in human form.

Post communion: New composition. This presents a complex array of references in simple form. First, it recalls Joseph and Mary's anxiety as they searched for the boy Jesus in Jerusalem. When he was found in the Temple, Jesus explained that he was about his Father's business, thus marking the difference between his adoptive father and God the Father. Afterwards, Luke tells us, he grew 'in wisdom and stature, and in favour with God and man' (Luke 2.41–52). Second, it opens up the paradoxical relationship between Joseph's work as a carpenter, and Jesus' work of salvation, accomplished on the wood of the cross.

Cuthbert, Bishop of Lindisfarne, Missionary, 687 (20 March)

Collect: Adapted from Durham Cathedral, which houses Cuthbert's shrine. It develops along the lines of Cuthbert's career, from shepherd of his father's sheep, to life in a monastic community, and finally to episcopal leadership. The move from Cuthbert's shepherding to the call to all Christians to 'bring those who are lost home to [God's] fold' is perhaps rather precarious, resulting in a certain lack of elegance.

Post communion: See Common 'Of Missionaries'.

Thomas Cranmer, Archbishop of Canterbury, Reformation Martyr, 1556 (21 March)

Collect: A new composition, which alludes to the recantations of the last days of Cranmer's life. But the phrasing is too general to express the poignancy of Cranmer's weakness, and in any case, a collect is not the place for political analysis of the actions of its subject. The appellation 'Mediator and Advocate' comes from the Prayer for the Church (later the Prayer for the Church Militant), originally included in the eucharistic prayer of 1549.

Post communion: See Common 'Of Martyrs'.

The Annunciation of Our Lord (25 March)

Collect: From the *BCP*, and new in 1549. It is based on a post-communion prayer in the Gregorian Sacramentary. The collect draws together all the events in the history of salvation: incarnation; crucifixion; resurrection.

Post communion: New composition, and used as a Common for all feasts of the Blessed Virgin Mary. It applies the traditional language of accounts of the incarnation to our own spiritual experience, inviting the Holy Spirit to 'overshadow' us with the power of God, keep us obedient to God's commands, and so enable us to bring to birth the outward signs of holiness.

William Law, Priest, Spiritual Writer, 1761 (10 April)

Collect: From *CCP* and written by a member of SSF. Alludes to Law's own work, *A Serious Call to a Devout and Holy Life*, and encourages us to follow his example in seeking God through perseverance in prayer.

Post communion: See Common 'Of Teachers of the Faith'.

Alphege, Archbishop of Canterbury, Martyr, 1012 (19 April)

Collect: New composition. Alphege defended orthodox Christianity against the invading Danes, who martyred him at Greenwich.

Post communion: See Common 'Of Martyrs'.

Anselm, Abbot of Le Bec, Archbishop of Canterbury, Teacher of the Faith, 1109 (21 April)

Collect: From *CCP* and composed by a member of SSF. The petition is based on words from the opening of Anselm's *Proslogion*.

Post communion: See Common 'Of Teachers of the Faith'.

George, Martyr, Patron of England, c. 304 (23 April)
Collect: Written by Michael Perham and included in *CCP*. The collect has no focus: the same might be said of any Christian martyr. It remains debatable whether a composition based on the very doubtful legend would have provided something sharper.
Post communion: See Common 'Of Martyrs'.

Mark, Evangelist (25 April)
Collect: From the *ASB*, and ultimately from the *BCP*, though with considerable adaptation. The earliest version of the collect was based on the Epistle for the day (Ephesians 4.7–16), and saw grounding in Scripture as a protection against 'blasts of vain doctrine'. Later versions have taken a less combative view.
Post communion: See Common 'Of Apostles and Evangelists'.

Catherine of Siena, Teacher of the Faith, 1380 (29 April)
Collect: From *CCP* and written by a member of SSF, this collect celebrates Catherine's devotion to Christ's Passion.
Post communion: See Common 'Of Teachers of the Faith'.

Philip and James, Apostles (1 May)
Collect: From the *BCP*, a new composition in 1549. It is based on the day's Gospel (John 14) in which Jesus explains to Philip that anyone who has seen him has seen the Father. Earlier in the same passage, he tells Thomas that he is the way, the truth and the life. The collect is therefore an instruction to worshippers to seek Jesus, and through him, the Father.
Post communion: See Common 'Of Apostles and Evangelists'.

Athanasius, Bishop of Alexandria, Teacher of the Faith, 373 (2 May)
Collect: From *CCP*, which adapts the form in the American *BCP*. The collect bears witness to the incarnational faith that Athanasius defended, and alludes to his own work, *De Incarnatione* (On the Incarnation).
Post communion: See Common 'Of Teachers of the Faith'.

English Saints and Martyrs of the Reformation Era (4 May)
Collect: A new composition, this collect is an excellent model of acknowledgement of sin tempered by understanding and compassion. It embraces all who died for their faith under successive waves of persecution by dominant parties, and sustains the vision of unity which is the communion of saints.
Post communion: From *PHG*, p. 57 (prayer after communion for Eucharist of All Saints).

Julian of Norwich, Spiritual Writer, c. 1417 (8 May)
Collect: Written by Michael McLean and included in *CCP*, this collect has its

source in Mother Julian's own experience of the vision of Christ as a series of 'Showings', recorded in *The Revelation of Divine Love.*
Post communion: See Common 'Of Members of Religious Communities'.

Matthias (14 May)

Collect: New in the 1549 *BCP*, the collect takes the case of Matthias (Acts 1.26) as the ground of a general prayer for faithful ministry and protection against false teaching.
Post communion: See Common 'Of Apostles and Evangelists'.

Dunstan, Archbishop of Canterbury, Restorer of Monastic Life, 988 (19 May)

Collect: From *CCP* and composed by a member of SSF. The collect lays special emphasis on Dunstan's important reorganization of the monastic orders in England.
Post communion: See Common 'Of Bishops'.

Alcuin of York, Deacon, Abbot of Tours, 804 (20 May)

Collect: New composition based on one of Alcuin's own prayers in his book on the Psalms, *De Psalmorum Usu Liber.* The end of the prayer refers to the light, strength and mercy of God, and prays for assistance in leading the kind of life that will bring the speaker at last into the presence of God with all his saints.
Post communion: See Common 'Of Members of Religious Communities'.

John and Charles Wesley, Evangelists, Hymn-writers, 1791 and 1788 (24 May)

Collect: From *CCP* and composed by a member of SSF. The collect alludes both to the Wesleys' influential style of preaching, and to their gifts as hymn-ographers.
Post communion: See Common 'Of Pastors'.

The Venerable Bede, 735 (25 May)

Collect: From *CCP*, and adapted from a form used in Durham Cathedral, which houses Bede's tomb. The prayer is a reshaping of the last words of Bede's *Ecclesiastical History*, Book V, Chapter 24.
Post communion: See Common 'Of Members of Religious Communities'.

Augustine of Canterbury, 605 (26 May)

Collect: From *CCP*. The collect underlines the call to mission that is intrinsic to the Christian calling.
Post communion: See Common 'Of Bishops'.

Josephine Butler, Social Reformer, 1906 (30 May)

Collect: From *CCP* and written by a member of SSF. The *CCP* calendar commemorates her on 30 December.

Post communion: New composition. Alternatively, see Common 'Of Any Saint'.

The Visit of the Blessed Virgin Mary to Elizabeth (31 May)
Collect: From the *ASB*, this collect is based on Luke's account (Luke 1.39–56) and weaves into its fabric parts of Mary's song, the *Magnificat*.
Post communion: New composition, which tellingly compares the pregnancies of Mary and Elizabeth to the work of God, received in the Eucharist, within each one of us.

Justin, Martyr at Rome, c. 165 (1 June)
Collect: From *CCP* and written by a member of SSF. The collect plays on the Pauline paradox that to those who perish, the preaching of the cross is folly, but to those who are saved it is the power of God (1 Corinthians 1.18–21).
Post communion: See Common 'Of Martyrs'.

Boniface (Wynfrith) of Crediton, 754 (5 June)
Collect: From *CCP* and written by a member of SSF. The prayer recalls Boniface's martyrdom in Germany, and sets forth his example of faith as a pattern for a living and active faith.
Post communion: See Common 'Of Martyrs'.

Thomas Ken, Bishop of Bath and Wells, Nonjuror, Hymn-writer, 1711 (8 June)
Collect: From *CCP* and written by a member of SSF. The collect develops its theme of faithfulness in all circumstances from Thomas Ken's devotion in times of difficult Church–State relations. Its first line is a direct quotation from the doxology of his well-loved hymn, 'Praise God from whom all blessings flow'.
Post communion: See Common 'Of Bishops'.

Columba, Abbot of Iona, Missionary, 597 (9 June)
Collect: Roman Catholic proposed National Proper for England. The text came originally from the liturgical commission of the Irish Bishops' Conference, and was adjusted with Scotland and England and Wales for joint use. The collect plays on the Latinized version of Columba's Irish name, meaning 'dove' – the symbol of the Holy Spirit – and leads into a celebration of the three theological virtues of faith, hope and love which are manifestations of the Spirit. It is strongly trinitarian in structure and content, a characteristic emphasis in Celtic Christianity.
Post communion: See Common 'Of Missionaries'.

Barnabas (11 June)
Collect: From the *ASB*, the collect uses the meaning of Barnabas's name (Son of

Encouragement) to outline the pattern for Christian behaviour.
Post communion: See Common 'Of Apostles and Evangelists'.

Richard, Bishop of Chichester, 1253 (16 June)
Collect: New composition, elegantly incorporating the last lines of his own prayer: 'Most merciful redeemer, [friend and brother,] may we know you more clearly, love you more dearly, and follow you more nearly, day by day.'
Post communion: See Common 'Of Bishops'.

Alban, First Martyr of Britain, c. 250 (22 June)
Collect: From *CCP*, and adapted from a form used in the Cathedral and Abbey Church of St Alban. The prayer emphasizes Alban's distinctive dual role as martyr and first British martyr.
Post communion: See Common 'Of Martyrs'.

Etheldreda, Abbess of Ely, c. 678 (23 June)
Collect: Modern language version of a collect written by E. C. Ratcliff (1896–1967), Ely Professor of Divinity in Cambridge and Canon of Ely Cathedral (1947–58). This was part of Ely Cathedral's book of saints' day collects, all of which were written or sourced by Ratcliff.
Post communion: See Common 'Of Members of Religious Communities'.

The Birth of John the Baptist (24 June)
Collect: From the *BCP* and new in 1549. The collect uses the narrative of John's call to repentance as a paradigm for all Christian lives.
Post communion: New composition. Taking John as the last of the prophets, the prayer shows the prophetic nature of the Eucharist. As John proclaimed the incarnate Jesus to be the Lamb of God (John 2.29), so each eucharistic celebration reiterates that title, and connects it eschatologically to the wedding feast of the Lamb at the end of time.

Irenaeus, Bishop of Lyons, Teacher of the Faith, c. 200 (28 June)
Collect: From *CCP* and written by a member of SSF. Irenaeus is best known for his writings against heresy. The first great Catholic theologian, his method of opposing false belief was to lay stress on the traditional elements in the Church: the episcopate; the canon of Scripture; and the religious and theological tradition as established at that stage.
Post communion: See Common 'Of Teachers of the Faith'.

Peter and Paul (29 June)
Collect (where both are celebrated): From the *ASB*, and derived from the Leonine Sacramentary. The collect honours Peter and Paul as founders of the Church, and alludes to Jesus' promise that Peter would be the rock on which he would build his Church (Matthew 16.18).

Collect (where Peter is celebrated alone): From the *ASB*, this collect turns on Peter's special status as the first to acknowledge Jesus as the Christ (Matthew 16.16). It follows with the reference used in the collect above.

Post communion: See Common 'Of Apostles and Evangelists'.

Thomas (3 July)

Collect: From the *ASB*, which uses part of the *BCP* collect composed for the 1549 version. Thomas's commemoration moves from 21 December in the *BCP* Calendar. The revised collect departs from the *BCP*'s disciplinary note ('that our faith in thy sight may never be reproved') to the more positive terms of John 20.29, in which Jesus commends those who have believed without physical evidence.

Post communion: See Common 'Of Apostles and Evangelists'.

Benedict of Nursia, Abbot of Monte Cassino, Father of Western Monasticism, c. 550 (11 July)

Collect: From *CCP* and written by a member of SSF. There is an uneasy transition in the middle of the collect, from matter specific to Benedict's hugely influential monastic rule, to the universal Christian calling to follow the law of Christ.

Post communion: See Common 'Of Members of Religious Communities'.

John Keble, Priest, Tractarian, Poet, 1866 (14 July)

Collect: In *CCP* and originally from Keble College, Oxford. Drawing on lines from Keble's own hymns ('Word supreme, before Creation', 'New every morning is the love' and 'There is a book who runs may read'), the collect sets his sacramental vision of God in all creation as a pattern for present-day worshippers.

Post communion: See Common 'Of Pastors'.

Swithun, Bishop of Winchester, c. 862 (15 July)

Collect: Composed by Michael Perham for use in the Diocese of Winchester. From the little that is known about Swithun, the prayer concentrates on his work of bridge-building and fostering the life of the Church.

Post communion: See Common 'Of Bishops'.

Gregory and Macrina, c. 394 and c. 379 (19 July)

Collect: New composition. Gregory supported the Nicene dogma of the Trinity, and also wrote on the Trinity, incarnation and redemption. The concerns of this collect suggest his defence of Christ's two natures in one Person, and his belief that ultimately all (even the souls in hell and the devils) would return to God.

Post communion: See Common 'Of Teachers of the Faith'.

Mary Magdalene (22 July)

Collect: From the *ASB*, this is a heavily revised version of the 1928 *BCP* collect of the day. The present text lays emphasis on the healing of mind and body, and on the relationship between healing from sin and the gift of grace. This perhaps leans most on Luke's fleeting reference to Mary Magdalene as the woman out of whom Jesus cast seven devils (Luke 8.2).

Post communion: New composition. The prayer centres on Mary Magdalene's unique role as apostle to the apostles, and sets this up as an example to all who have shared in the Eucharist. There is always a prophetic obligation attached to the eucharistic recollection of Christ's death, sharing in his mystical body and celebrating his resurrection.

James (25 July)

Collect: Essentially the 1549 *BCP* collect of the day, with some essential modernizations. The prayer reminds us of the importance of responding to the call of Jesus, and also of the cost of such obedience. Underlying it is the request from James and John, the sons of Zebedee, that they might have honoured places in Jesus' kingdom (Mark 10.35–40).

Post communion: See Common 'Of Apostles and Evangelists'.

Anne and Joachim, Parents of the Blessed Virgin Mary (26 July)

Collect: New composition. We know nothing about the parents of Mary, apart from the account in the apocryphal Gospel of James. The prayer cleverly concentrates on Mary's obedience, and imputes it to her good upbringing.

Post communion: New composition, based on the vision of all earthly and heavenly families in Ephesians 3.15 (used also for 29 July, and 9 and 27 August).

Mary, Martha and Lazarus (29 July)

Collect: New composition. The prayer neatly reflects the domestic tensions arising out of Mary's inclination to listen to Jesus while Martha waited on the household, recounted in the Gospels (Luke 10.38–42). It also includes an allusion to the raising of Lazarus (John 11).

Post communion: New composition, based on the vision of all earthly and heavenly families in Ephesians 3.15 (used also for 26 July, and 9 and 27 August).

William Wilberforce, Social Reformer, 1833 (30 July)

Collect: From *CCP* and written by a member of SSF. The prayer turns on an inversion, thus balancing between Christ's atonement (freeing us from 'the slavery of sin') and Wilberforce's work for the emancipation of slaves (from 'the sin of slavery'). There is an undeniable symmetry in one sense, but there is also a risk of making Wilberforce's achievement, immense though it was, commensurate with Christ's for the sake of linguistic effect.

Post communion: New composition. This prayer is insufficiently specific about the fight against slavery to justify its distinctive role. Alternatively, see Common 'Of Any Saint'.

Oswald, King of Northumbria, Martyr, 642 (5 August)

Collect: From *CCP*, which adopts a prayer used at St Oswald's Church in Durham. Oswald raised the Christian symbol of the cross at the Battle of Heavenfield. He also sent for the Scottish bishop, Aidan, to teach his people the faith. His championing of Christianity in the north of England is a vividly militant paradigm of the Christian obligation to bear witness to Christ.
Post communion: See Common 'Of Martyrs'.

The Transfiguration of Our Lord (6 August)

Collect: From the Church of Ireland's *Collects and Post Communion Prayers* (1995). It corresponds closely to a collect found in the Oxford *Diocesan Service Book* (1920) and later in the 1929 Scottish *BCP*. The earlier versions specifically name Moses and Elijah, but use the word 'decease' where we now have 'exodus'. There are grounds for seeing a deliberate parallelism between the transfiguration of Jesus, and Moses' transformative encounter with God on the holy mountain (Exodus 24–35, especially 24.15 and 35.34–35).
Post communion: From *BAS*. The prayer elegantly makes the analogy between the glory of God shining from the face of Jesus and the love of Christ that should shine in the lives of all who belong to the eucharistic community.

Dominic, 1221 (8 August)

Collect: From *CCP* and written by a member of SSF. The collect recalls that Dominic founded the Order of Preachers, and that a love for the Word of God is integral to sacramental life.
Post communion: See Common 'Of Members of Religious Communities'.

Mary Sumner, Founder of the Mothers' Union, 1921 (9 August)

Collect: New composition, reminding us of the Mothers' Union's special commitment to upholding family life.
Post communion: New composition, based on the vision of all earthly and heavenly families in Ephesians 3.15 (used also for 26 and 29 July, and 27 August). Alternatively, see Common 'Of Any Saint'.

Laurence, Deacon at Rome, Martyr, 258 (10 August)

Collect: From *CCP* and written by a member of SSF. Emphasizes the particular characteristics of the diaconate which Laurence exemplified.
Post communion: See Common 'Of Martyrs'.

Clare of Assisi, 1253 (11 August)

Collect: From *CCP* and written by a member of SSF. There is a play on the ety-

mology of Clare's name, which has its roots in the Latin word for 'clear'.
Post communion: See Common 'Of Religious Communities'.

Jeremy Taylor, Bishop of Down and Connor, Teacher of the Faith, 1667 (13 August)
Collect: New composition. The prayer is broadly based on the notion of 'holy living', which Taylor developed in a devotional treatise of that name.
Post communion: See Common 'Of Teachers of the Faith'.

The Blessed Virgin Mary (15 August)
Collect: Adapted for the *ASB* from *MC*. The prayer exploits the apparent antitheses of lowliness and glory, and shows how these are brought together in Mary as mother of Christ. The difficult issue of the assumption is neatly avoided in the petition that we might 'share with her in the glory of [God's] eternal Kingdom'.
Post communion: New composition which serves as a Common for all feasts of the Virgin Mary.

Bernard, Abbot of Clairvaux, Teacher of the Faith, 1153 (20 August)
Collect: From *CCP* and written by a member of SSF. The collect alludes to Bernard's wide-ranging influence in the twelfth-century Church in Europe, and his achievements in building up the Cistercian Order.
Post communion: See Common 'Of Teachers of the Faith'.

Bartholomew (24 August)
Collect: From the *BCP*, and originally from the Sarum Missal. Bartholomew is mentioned in association with the other apostles on several occasions, but no details of his career are known. The collect wisely focuses on the missionary and prophetic relationship between Church, Word and world, using Bartholomew as an instance of preaching.
Post communion: See Common 'Of Apostles and Evangelists'.

Monica, Mother of Augustine of Hippo, 387 (27 August)
Collect: New composition, recalling the fact that Monica prayed resolutely for her son's conversion to Christianity for many years (Augustine, *Confessions*, Book VIII.xii). Monica's example is an encouragement to all who pray for those who stand outside the household of faith.
Post communion: New composition, based on the vision of all earthly and heavenly families in Ephesians 3.15 (used also for 26 and 29 July, and 9 August). Alternatively, see Common 'Of Any Saint'.

Augustine of Hippo, 430 (28 August)
Collect: From the 1989 South African Prayer Book. The prayer is based on Augustine's autobiographical account of his progression from sinful youth to

Christian devotion in the *Confessions*, and alludes particularly to the famous words, 'Lord, you have made us for yourself, and our heart is restless until it rests in you' (*Confessions*, Book I.i).
Post communion: See Common 'Of Teachers of the Faith'.

The Beheading of John the Baptist (29 August)
Collect: CCP expands the collect which first appeared in the 1928 *BCP* and in the 1929 Scottish *BCP* to include the petition that we may win the unfading crown of glory that comes through living the law of Christ (1 Peter 5.4). The prayer draws on Old Testament and New Testament references to John, notably Malachi 3.1 and Mark 1.2, reminding us aptly on this day that his death, as well as his life, prepared the route that Jesus was to follow.
Post communion: New composition, used also for the Birth of John the Baptist (see 24 June).

John Bunyan, Spiritual Writer, 1688 (30 August)
Collect: From *CCP* and written by a member of SSF. The prayer is imaginatively woven out of Bunyan's own literary–spiritual concerns. His allegorical work, *The Pilgrim's Progress*, describes the Christian soul's journey towards the truth that is found in God. Mr Valiant-for-Truth is one of its characters, and Pilgrim, the chief protagonist, sings a song which has become a favourite hymn: 'He who would valiant be, 'gainst all disaster'. To sum up, we are reminded that the Christian life is always a pilgrimage, and that in some sense we are strangers and exiles here until we find our home in God's kingdom.
Post communion: See Common 'Of Teachers of the Faith'.

Aidan, Bishop of Lindisfarne, Missionary, 651 (31 August)
Collect: Roman Catholic proposed National Proper for England, laying stress on those characteristics of Aidan's life which are models for contemporary Christians. The text draws on Bede and Caedmon. The emphases of Catholic Social Teaching are evident in the composition.
Post communion: See Common 'Of Missionaries'.

Gregory the Great, Bishop of Rome, Teacher of the Faith, 604 (3 September)
Collect: From *CCP* and written by a member of SSF. The prayer quotes Gregory's own description of the Pope as 'servant of the servants of God'. His missionary commitment shines through his decision to send Augustine to convert England in 597. He is a paradigm both for Christian leaders and for those in their care.
Post communion: See Common 'Of Teachers of the Faith'.

The Birth of the Blessed Virgin Mary (8 September)
Collect: Published in Silk and composed by the compiler. This prayer, also used

for the feast of the Conception of the Blessed Virgin Mary (8 December), celebrates the incarnation and its paradoxes. God takes human form to restore the divine image in humanity, and human weakness becomes the essential participant in the project of God's redemption.

Post communion: Used for the four feasts of Mary (25 March, 15 August, 8 September and 8 December). See discussion under the Annunciation (25 March).

John Chrysostom, Bishop of Constantinople, Teacher of the Faith, 407 (13 September)

Collect: From *CCP*, and adapted from the American *BCP*. The collect refers to his exceptional gifts as a preacher (his name comes from the Greek and means 'golden-mouthed') and interpreter of Scripture. It also refers to the persecutions he endured when his trenchant utterances caused him to fall foul of the Empress Eudoxia in Constantinople.

Post communion: See Common 'Of Teachers of the Faith'.

Holy Cross Day (14 September)

Collect: From the *ASB*, and adapted from the 1928 *BCP*. The collect points to the paradox of the cross, which is both instrument of torture and the means of life. It reminds us of the Pauline injunction never to boast or 'glory', except in the cross of Christ (Galatians 6.14), turning this to a willing acceptance of suffering for Christ's sake.

Post communion: From *BAS*. This is a slightly uneasy synthesis of scriptural quotation. It brings together 1 Peter 2.24 and 1 Corinthians 11.26 to weld the sacrifice of the cross to the eucharistic and eschatological theme, and repeats the collect's allusion to Galatians 6.14. But the mixture is too dense to be worked out in such a short text.

Cyprian, Bishop of Carthage, Martyr, 258 (15 September)

Collect: New composition. The prayer refers to Cyprian's career from conversion, to episcopal consecration, and finally martyrdom. It alludes also to his great pastoral gifts, and his desire to restore the lapsed, through penance, to the fellowship of the Church.

Post communion: See Common 'Of Martyrs'.

Ninian, Bishop of Galloway, Apostle of the Picts, c. 432 (16 September)

Collect: From the American *BCP*, this collect commemorates Ninian's missionary work in parts of present day Scotland, and uses the occasion to pray for evangelists in our own time.

Post communion: See Common 'Of Missionaries'.

Hildegard, Abbess of Bingen, Visionary, 1179 (17 September)

Collect: New composition. Hildegard experienced visions of God throughout

her life, and famously described herself as 'a feather on the breath of God'. She was also a gifted musician and composer. The collect weaves her life into a prayer for spiritual insight and joy in praising God.
Post communion: See Common 'Of Members of Religious Communities'.

John Coleridge Patteson, First Bishop of Melanesia, and his Companions, Martyrs, 1871 (20 September)
Collect: New composition. Patteson achieved a great deal as a missionary bishop in the islands of Melanesia, learning the local languages, and fostering education. He and his companions were murdered in a revenge killing.
Post communion: See Common 'Of Martyrs'.

Matthew (21 September)
Collect: An extensively modernized version of the *BCP* collect, newly composed in 1549. It is based on the account of Matthew's calling in Matthew 9, and uses him as an example of someone who gave up a life defined by money for the materially insecure life of following Jesus.
Post communion: See Common 'Of Apostles and Evangelists'.

Lancelot Andrewes, Bishop of Winchester, Spiritual Writer, 1626 (25 September)
Collect: New composition, following the pattern of Andrewes' own book of private devotions, the *Preces Privatae*. This is a particularly pleasing instance of innovative collect-writing, and illuminates the prayerful and meditative centre of Andrewes' preaching and pastoral care.
Post communion: See Common 'Of Bishops'.

Vincent de Paul, Founder of the Congregation of the Mission (Lazarists), 1660 (27 September)
Collect: From *CCP*. With his personal experience of life as a slave, Vincent de Paul came well equipped to his work of alleviating the lot of prisoners, the sick and the poor, and preaching the gospel, especially to country people of France. He exemplifies Jesus' picture of the righteous recorded in Matthew 25.34–36.
Post communion: See Common 'Of Members of Religious Communities'.

Michael and All Angels (29 September)
Collect: BCP 1549 translates the Sarum collect of the feast. Drawing on accounts of the orders of creation (e.g. Romans 8.38; Colossians 1.16), the collect helps us towards an understanding of the angels as God's ministers in heaven and our guardians and companions on earth. There is a distinguished biblical tradition, in both the Old and the New Testament, of angelic visits to human beings.
Post communion: The prayer reminds us of our place in the communion of saints, celebrated in the Eucharist through memory, participation and prayer-

ful expectation. It also rejoices in the eschatological aspect of the Eucharist, which crosses temporal boundaries and brings heaven and earth and all the orders of creation together at Christ's banquet.

Francis of Assisi, 1226 (4 October)

Collect: From *CCP*. The prayer is founded on Francis' apparently foolish rejection of the material security of the world, and his pursuit of a childlike simplicity. Its biblical allusions to a God who chooses to reveal himself to children, to the wisdom of this world, and to the pre-eminent importance of acknowledging Christ crucified, come from Matthew 11.25, 1 Corinthians 3.19, and 1 Corinthians 2.2 respectively.
Post communion: See Common 'Of Members of Religious Communities'.

William Tyndale, Translator of the Scriptures, Reformation Martyr, 1536 (6 October)

Collect: CCP uses a collect from the American *BCP*. Tyndale is a poignant example of someone who suffered for the profession of the gospel. Copies of his translation of the New Testament were burned, and he himself went to the stake as a heretic.
Post communion: See Common 'Of Martyrs'.

Paulinus, Bishop of York, Missionary, 644 (10 October)

Collect: Roman Catholic proposed National Proper for England. The text was assembled from fragments and cast in this shape by the sub-committee on the National Calendar and Proper. Paulinus came to England to support the mission of St Augustine in 601. When Edwin, King of Northumbria, married Ethelburga of Kent in 625, Paulinus was consecrated bishop and accompanied her to York. Edwin and his chiefs were converted and baptized. Under Paulinus, a cathedral was begun in York. He ended his life as Bishop of Rochester.
Post communion: See Common 'Of Missionaries'.

Wilfrid of Ripon, Bishop, Missionary, 709 (12 October)

Collect: Diocese of Chichester, from a customary appointed by Bishop George Bell, and published in 1948. Educated at the monastery of Lindisfarne, Wilfrid worked throughout his life to bring Celtic usage into conformity with Roman liturgy, and Celtic monasticism into conformity with the Benedictine rule. Though his episcopal career was in the north of England, he spent some time in Sussex (681–6) where he did important missionary work among the heathen population. The Chichester Diocesan Liturgical Committee has more recently substituted 'perseverance' for the original 'patience', since the historical testimony suggests that Wilfrid's methods were not those of a patient man.
Post communion: See Common 'Of Missionaries'.

Edward the Confessor, King of England, 1066 (13 October)

Collect: New composition. Edward reigned during the troubled years preceding the Norman Conquest. He occupied himself mainly with religious matters, and achieved a reputation for distinctive piety. He was particularly associated with the building of the Abbey of St Peter in Westminster (Westminster Abbey), consecrated in 1065.

Post communion: New composition for royal saints, used also for Alfred the Great (26 October) and Margaret of Scotland (16 November). The prayer contrasts the earthly and heavenly kingdoms, and reminds worshippers that participation in the Eucharist opens them to the inspiration of the Spirit, whose gift is the passion to proclaim the gospel. Alternatively, see Common 'For Any Saint'.

Teresa of Avila, Teacher of the Faith, 1582 (15 October)

Collect: From *CCP*. Teresa was a Spanish Carmelite nun, whose spiritual writings, of which *The Way of Perfection* is one, have had a profound influence in describing the life of prayer and spiritual experience. The collect alludes both to this book, and to her example of a life disciplined by the desire for holiness, culminating in the 'mystic marriage' or 'perfect union of love' with God.

Post communion: See Common 'Of Teachers of the Faith'.

Ignatius, Bishop of Antioch, Martyr, c. 107 (17 October)

Collect: Composed by G. B. Timms and published in Martin Draper, *The Cloud of Witnesses* (1982). The prayer has a powerfully eucharistic focus. It refers to Ignatius's great longing for martyrdom, but shows also that for Christians the way to eternal life is through life itself, sustained by the saving gifts of Christ.

Post communion: See Common 'Of Martyrs'.

Luke (18 October)

Collect: From the *BCP*, and new in 1549. The tradition holds that Luke was a doctor. This provides a metaphor for the gospel as medicine for the soul. But where the *BCP* prayer asks for the healing of our souls, this version asks that the Church may be strengthened to perform a healing role with the widest possible interpretation.

Post communion: See Common 'Of Apostles and Evangelists'.

Henry Martyn, Translator of the Scriptures, Missionary in India and Persia, 1812 (19 October)

Collect: New composition, which takes Martyn's gift of his talents as an inspiration to people of the present day.

Post communion: See Common 'Of Missionaries'.

Alfred the Great, King of the West Saxons, Scholar, 899 (26 October)

Collect: New composition. Alfred's defeat of the Danes did much to maintain Christianity in England, while his attention to the education of his clergy, especially through the translation of important pastoral works, had a great influence on the Church.

Post communion: New composition for royal saints, used also for Edward the Confessor (13 October) and Margaret of Scotland (16 November). See commentary for Edward the Confessor.

Simon and Jude (28 October)

Collect: From the *BCP* and new in 1549, the collect is based on Ephesians 2.19–22.

Post communion: See Common 'Of Apostles and Evangelists'.

James Hannington, Bishop of Eastern Equatorial Africa, Martyr in Uganda, 1885 (29 October)

Collect: From *CCP* and written by a member of SSF. The prayer uses the familiar paradox of defeat turned into victory to recall Hannington's martyrdom. For modern-day worshippers, this paradox is applied to the triumph of faith over evil.

Post communion: See Common 'Of Martyrs'.

The Commemoration of the Faithful Departed (2 November)

Collect: From *PHG*. The prayer improves on both the 1928 and *ASB* collects for this day by incorporating the whole communion of saints, living and departed, in the hope of the resurrection, and the fulfilment of the promises of Christ in the eternal kingdom.

Post communion: From *PHG*, which adopts a prayer in *BAS*. It is a reminder that at every Eucharist we remember and celebrate the death and resurrection of Christ, and look forward to the consummation of the work of salvation in the life of the kingdom.

Richard Hooker, Priest, Anglican Apologist, Teacher of the Faith, 1600 (3 November)

Collect: Composed by Kenneth Stevenson and included in *CCP*. The prayer alludes to Hooker's *Laws* (V, 54, 5; V, 59, 5), especially in its evocative picture of the incarnation as God making 'the human race his inseparable dwelling place'.

Post communion: See Common 'Of Teachers of the Faith'.

Willibrord of York, Bishop, Apostle of Frisia, 739 (7 November)

Collect: Roman Catholic proposed National Proper for England. The text originated in the Missal for German-speaking countries and was translated and lightly adapted by the sub-committee on the National Calendar and Proper. Willibrord was a successful missionary in Frisia (Netherlands), and later in

Denmark, Heligoland, and Thuringia. He is an example to the present-day Church of the importance of witnessing to the gospel.
Post communion: See Common 'Of Missionaries'.

The Saints and Martyrs of England (8 November)

Collect: Composed by Alexander Nairne. The prayer alludes to the vision of heaven in the Book of Revelation, where a multitude adores the Lamb, and no light is needed because he is their lamp (Revelation 19–22). It emphasizes that the example of holiness must begin in earthly life, and proclaims a reconciling intention by *not* distinguishing the often conflicting causes for which men and women died at various periods of the history of England.
Post communion: From *PHG* (p. 57) for the Eucharist of All Saints.

Leo the Great, Bishop of Rome, Teacher of the Faith, 461 (10 November)

Collect: From *CCP* and written by a member of SSF. Leo is distinguished for his early opposition to Pelagianism, his consolidation of the See of Rome and its influence, and the clarity of his doctrinal teaching. He stands as an example of the Church's duty to teach and defend the faith.
Post communion: See Common 'Of Teachers of the Faith'.

Martin of Tours, Bishop of Tours, c. 397 (11 November)

Collect: From *CCP* and written by a member of SSF. Martin served in the Roman army, during which time he gave half his cloak to a beggar at Amiens. Following this, he had a vision of Christ, was baptized, and left the army for the religious life. In Gaul, he made the evangelism of the countryside a special project. These elements of his hagiography become the inspiration for the military imagery of the collect, and for its concern with the poor.
Post communion: See Common 'Of Bishops'.

Charles Simeon, Priest, Evangelical Divine, 1836 (13 November)

Collect: New composition. Simeon was a leader of the Evangelical Revival, and from his position as Vicar of Holy Trinity, Cambridge (1783–1836), took a key role in the Missionary Movement. He was among the founders of the Church Mission Society in 1799 and a supporter of the British and Foreign Bible Society. The collect reflects the evangelical call to repentance and conversion, and the missionary call to preach the gospel.
Post communion: See Common 'Of Pastors'.

Margaret of Scotland, Queen of Scotland, Philanthropist, Reformer of the Church, 1093 (16 November)

Collect: From *CCP*, and adapted from a prayer in the Scottish *BCP*. The present version of the collect adds line four, thus reinforcing the parallel between the earthly and heavenly kingdoms, and interpreting Margaret's insistence upon replacing local Christian practice with a rigorously Roman form as a project for the advancement of the kingdom of heaven. The royal motif is continued in the petition that we, emulating her good works, may obtain the crown of the saints.

Post communion: New composition for royal saints, used also for Alfred the Great (26 October) and Edward the Confessor (13 October). See commentary for Edward the Confessor.

Hugh, Bishop of Lincoln, 1200 (17 November)

Collect: From *CCP*, which uses a prayer composed for Lincoln Cathedral. Hugh was called to England by Henry II as Prior of the first Carthusian house. Later, as Bishop of Lincoln, he continued to be a confidant of the king, but was never afraid to defend the people's cause against the claims of the crown. He retained his monastic identity throughout his life. He is exemplary as a champion of what was right, even in the face of authority, and as someone who pursued a pattern of holiness.

Post communion: See Common 'Of Bishops'.

Elizabeth of Hungary, Princess of Thuringia, Philanthropist, 1231 (18 November)

Collect: From the Roman Missal. Exiled from the Thuringian court upon her husband's death in 1227, Elizabeth renounced the world for a harsh discipline under her spiritual director in Marburg. She had been active in charitable work from her position at court. In Marburg, she devoted all her time to the sick and the poor. Her example of care is one to be followed by modern Christians.

Post communion: New composition. The prayer pivots on the notion of the Eucharist as both a foretaste of the glory that is to come, and an encourage- ment in preparation for that glory. Elizabeth stands as an example of someone who kept the vision before her. Alternatively, see Common for 'Any Saint'.

Hilda, Abbess of Whitby, 680 (19 November)

Collect: Roman Catholic proposed National Proper for England, drawing on Bede and Caedmon. The prayer recalls Hilda's leadership of a community of men and women at Whitby, and alludes to her decisive role in presiding over the Synod of Whitby in 664, which brought the Celtic Church into confor- mity with the Roman Church.

Post communion: See Common 'Of Members of Religious Communities'.

Edmund, King of the East Angles, Martyr, 870 (20 November)

Collect: From *CCP* and written by a member of SSF. Edmund refused to share the ruling of East Anglia with a pagan Danish conqueror as the price of his freedom after being captured in battle. He was martyred at the hands of Danish archers in consequence. His example is one of faith even to death.

Post communion: See Common 'Of Martyrs'.

Clement, Bishop of Rome, Martyr, c. 100 (23 November)

Collect: From the Roman Missal. Probably the third bishop of Rome after St Peter, and author of some very early Christian literature – though not of all that is ascribed to him. According to a later tradition, he was banished to the Crimean mines by the emperor Trajan. Here, he succeeded so well as a missionary that his enemies had him bound to an anchor and thrown into the Black Sea. The collect therefore has a very slender basis in fact, although it lays down the general principles that shine through the lives of the saints.

Post communion: See Common 'Of Martyrs'.

Andrew (30 November)

Collect: This prayer is closest to the *ASB* collect of the feast, which in turn derives loosely from the *BCP* 1662 version (1549 and 1552 are somewhat different). It intensifies the call to mission by turning the *ASB*'s passive grammatical forms into active constructions.

Post communion: See Common 'Of Apostles and Evangelists'.

Nicholas, Bishop of Myra, c. 326 (6 December)

Collect: Composed by G. B. Timms and published in Draper, *Cloud of Witnesses* (1982). Nicholas's legend recounts his generosity to three girls who would have been forced into prostitution had he not provided them with gold for a dowry. He is the inspiration for Santa Claus who brings gifts to children on 6 December. So there is a popular notion of giving attached to Nicholas, which translates readily in the collect to the theme of the treasures of God's grace, both given and received.

Post communion: See Common 'Of Bishops'.

Ambrose, Bishop of Milan, Teacher of the Faith, 397 (7 December)

Collect: Composed by G. B. Timms and published in Draper, *Cloud of Witnesses* (1982). The collect draws on Ambrose's path from lawyer and regional governor to bishop, establishing him as an example of someone who spoke out for the faith, sometimes in defiance of the secular powers of the day.

Post communion: See Common 'Of Bishops'.

The Conception of the Blessed Virgin Mary (8 December)

Collect: Published in Silk and composed by the compiler. This prayer, also used for the feast of the Birth of the Blessed Virgin Mary (8 September), celebrates the incarnation and its paradoxes. God takes human form to restore the divine image in humanity, and human weakness becomes the essential participant in the project of God's redemption.

Post communion: Used for the four feasts of Mary (25 March, 15 August, 8 September and 8 December). See discussion under the Annunciation (25 March).

Lucy, Martyr at Syracuse, 304 (13 December)

Collect: Published in *CCP*, and written by David Silk. Tradition has it that Lucy was deoculated in the process of being tortured for her Christian belief at the time of the Diocletianic persecution. This, together with the meaning of her name ('light'), suggests the collect's governing theme of light, and especially the light of Christ.

Post communion: See Common 'Of Martyrs'.

John of the Cross, Poet, Teacher of the Faith, 1591 (14 December)

Collect: From *CCP* and written by a member of SSF. This sixteenth-century Spanish mystic testified in his writings to the experience of the 'dark night of the soul' – a despairing sense of total separation from God. Always opposing this was his desire for mystical union with Christ.

Post communion: See Common 'Of Teachers of the Faith'.

Stephen, Deacon, First Martyr (26 December)

Collect: Heavily adapted from the 1662 *BCP* collect of the day. Here, the emphasis is changed to give priority to Stephen's example of prayer, going on to ask God's help in loving and forgiving those who persecute us for witnessing to the truth. Where the *BCP* collect stresses Christ glorified, this version stresses Christ crucified pleading for those he redeemed.

Post communion: *PHG* adopts this prayer from the Roman Missal. Its themes of birth and death are very suitable to a feast that falls immediately after the Nativity of Our Lord, and remind us that martyrdom is a birth into the heavenly kingdom.

John (27 December)

Collect: A modern-language version of the 1662 *BCP* collect, which draws from John's Gospel the themes of light (John 1.4–5), truth and direction (John 14.6). *CW* adds emphasis on the incarnation, which is very much in keeping with John's Gospel, especially John 1.14.

Post communion: *PHG* adopts this prayer from the Roman Missal. It is more emphatic than the collect in its reference to John 1.14, and shows that the incarnation – the celebration of Christ as living Word – is as deeply embedded in the Eucharist as the Passion.

The Holy Innocents (28 December)

Collect: This prayer takes its first three lines from the *ASB*, which in turn departs sharply from the *BCP*'s questionable glorification of child martyrdom. Thereafter, it turns to the possibility of confronting evil with the non-violent witness of Christ's suffering and our own innocence, and thus working for peace. While it is a welcome departure from the *BCP*, and perhaps a better alternative than the *ASB*'s rather politicized reference to defending the weak against the tyranny of the strong, there is arguably a lack of focus in the petition. It is an almost impossible feast for which to write a collect.

Post communion: New composition. In the same way that it is difficult to represent the Holy Innocents in a collect, it is difficult to write a post communion prayer. The third line somewhat factitiously inserts the notion of defenceless innocence; and the assertion that the slaughtered children witnessed 'to the purity of [Christ's] sacrifice' is at least debatable.

Thomas Becket, Archbishop of Canterbury, Martyr, 1170 (29 December)

Collect: From *CCP* and written by a member of SSF. The prayer alludes to Thomas Becket's defence of Papal jurisdiction against Henry II's infringements.

Post communion: See Common 'Of Martyrs'.

D. COMMONS OF THE SAINTS

The Blessed Virgin Mary

Collect: Published in Silk and written by the compiler. This prayer is used for the feast of the Birth of the Blessed Virgin Mary (8 September) and the Conception of the Blessed Virgin Mary (8 December). It celebrates the incarnation and its paradoxes. God takes human form to restore the divine image in humanity, and human weakness becomes the essential participant in the project of God's redemption.

Post communion: Used for the four feasts of Mary (25 March, 15 August, 8 September and 8 December). See discussion under the Annunciation (25 March).

Apostles and Evangelists

Collect: Modern language version of the *BCP* collect of St Simon and St Jude (28 October). See discussion there.

Post communion 1: Composed by David Frost for the Church of England Liturgical Commission, and included as the second collect of Pentecost in the *ASB*. The prayer uses the narrative of the descent of the Holy Spirit on the Apostles (Acts 2.1–4) to remind us of our own call to preach the gospel. The imagery of fire associated with the Holy Spirit appropriately suggests the intensity of God's love, and the passion of the evangelical vision that should call people to that love.

Post communion 2: From *BAS*. This prayer beautifully encapsulates the bond uniting the apostles: theirs was a common teaching mission, a eucharistic fellowship, and a shared joy in their faith. It is an example for all Christian communities.

Martyrs

Collect: New in the *ASB*, and based on the Common of Martyrs in the 1928 *BCP*. This version sheds the archaisms of its predecessor and emphasizes Christian witness.

Post communion 1: From the Roman Missal. The prayer focuses on the theology of the cross in the Eucharist, and plays on the double identity of the cross as both tree of death and tree of life, a conceit that has been part of Christian imagery from a very early stage.

Post communion 2: New composition, suitable for commemorations of martyrs who do not have proper collects. It stresses the sacramental element underpinning the sacrificial character of martyrdom, with its implied comparison between the broken bread of the Eucharist, and the broken bodies of the crucified Christ and those who suffer for his sake.

Teachers of the Faith

Collect: From the 1928 *BCP* (for Doctors or Confessors) and used in the *ASB*. The prayer shows the close connection between the teaching work of the Church and its mission.

Post communion: New composition, based on Proverbs 9.2 which praises Wisdom. The prayer takes an eschatological view of the eucharistic table that always points toward the heavenly table.

Bishops and Other Pastors

Collect 1: From the 1989 South African Prayer Book and based on Ephesians 4, which speaks of growing into Christ.

Collect 2 (for a bishop): From the *ASB* and adapted from the 1928 *BCP*. It was hailed at the time as 'the best of the modern collects among the commons'. Appropriately for bishops, the prayer uses the governing metaphor of the shepherd.

Post communion: New composition that links God's shepherding of his people (cf. Psalm 80 and John 10.14) to the shepherding role of bishops and pastors.

Members of Religious Communities

Collect: *ASB* adapts the 1928 *BCP* collect for an abbot or abbess.

Post communion: New composition, which emphasizes the special dedication of the religious life. The prayer shows, however, that all Christians are called to give themselves wholeheartedly to God. Participation in the Eucharist confirms our vocation to union with God.

Missionaries

Collect: From the *ASB*. This prayer reminds us that the point of mission is to communicate the promise of the gospel, and that commemorations of missionaries are also a time to reflect on our own efforts to live according to its directives.

Post communion: Adapted from the post-communion prayer for use where the theme is the family in *PW* (p. 100).

For Any Saint

All the commons for this occasion set the lives of the saints before the Christian community as patterns of the particular calling in which their devotion was exemplary. Apart from the general collect, which the *ASB* adopted from *MC*, all the other prayers are new compositions. The post communions focus on the Eucharist as the celebration in which the community is renewed, inspired with the will to spread the gospel, assured of God's love, and given a foretaste of the life of the kingdom.

E. SPECIAL OCCASIONS

*Collects that are also in 'Prayers for Various Occasions' in the *Common Worship* main volume are marked with an asterisk.

The Guidance of the Holy Spirit

Collect 1*: From the *BCP* Whitsunday collect, which translates the collect of Pentecost from the Sarum Missal. It is slightly adapted from the wording of the collect of Pentecost in the *ASB*, to free it from the specific reference to the Pentecost season.

Collect 2*: Slightly adapted from the *ASB* collect 'For a Synod'.

Post communion: From the 1989 New Zealand Prayer Book.

Rogation Days

Collects 1* and 2*: From the 1989 South African Prayer Book, and similar to the *ASB* prayers for Rogation Days.

Collect 3: New composition.

Post communion: New composition.

Harvest Thanksgiving

Collect: From the 1989 South African Prayer Book. The prayer takes its inspiration from Psalm 65.11, and pursues the implications of the overwhelming generosity of God for our own concern for those in need.

Post communion: New composition. The prayer elegantly develops the metaphor of growth appropriate to harvest in its petition that reverence, generosity and wisdom might grow in God's people.

Mission and Evangelism

Collect: Adapted from the *ASB* collect of Pentecost 12, and based on 2 Corinthians 5.19, the prayer looks to Christ as mediator between God and human beings. The preaching of the gospel of Christ is therefore an imperative. We are called to bear witness to his reconciling love, expressed in the supreme sacrifice of the cross (see John 12.32).

Post communion: From *BAS*.

The Unity of the Church
Collect 1*: From the *ASB*, composed by the Liturgical Commission.
Collect 2*: From the Roman Missal, where it is used as the introduction to the Peace at Mass. Its origins lie in Germany in the eleventh century, and it became part of the Ordinary of the Mass in the 1570 Roman Catholic Missal. The *ASB* adopted it unchanged, except for addressing it to the Father rather than to the Son. The prayer refers to Jesus' words to his disciples at the Last Supper (John 14.27) as a model for the life of the Church that was to grow from them.
Post communion: Composed by William Temple and included in *PHG*, p. 366.

The Peace of the World
Collect*: From the *ASB*, which adapted one of the 1928 *BCP*'s Occasional Prayers. It was originally written by Francis Paget, Bishop of Oxford, 1902–11.
Post communion: New composition based on Ephesians 2.14–16. The prayer uses the eucharistic metaphor of the brokenness that leads to healing and wholeness to put Christ's sacrificial love at the centre of initiatives towards peace.

Social Justice and Responsibility
Collect 1*: From Frank Colquhoun's *Parish Prayers*, although the actual author is unknown, and centred on 1 John 4.18 (perfect love casts out fear), the prayer seeks to guide people to invest their efforts in righteousness, truth and peace.
Collect 2: From the *ASB* Collect for Civic Occasions.
Post communion: Based on the Beatitudes (Matthew 5), this new composition sets the vision of the kingdom as the goal that sharing in the Eucharist strengthens us to pursue.

Ministry (including Ember Days)
Collect (for the ministry of all Christian people): From the *ASB*, which adapted the 1662 *BCP* second collect of Good Friday both for that day and for Pentecost 2. Its emphasis is on the calling of all Christian people to different forms of ministry within the body of the Church.
Collect (for those to be ordained): From the *ASB*.
Collect (for vocations): Adapted from the *ASB* second collect for Ember weeks, which was a new collect based on the 1928 prayer for the Increase of the Sacred Ministry. *CW* widens the understanding of ministry beyond deacons and priests, and prays for all those who offer themselves for the ministry of the Church.
Collect* (for the inauguration of a new ministry): From the *ASB*, this alludes to the *BCP* Good Friday collect on which the collect 'for the ministry of all Christian people' is based.
Post communion 1: New composition, and arguably one that strains too hard to incorporate a very large range of biblical reference in a short prayer. The ascension, the gifts of Pentecost, and Jesus' firm remarks to his disciples about

seeking privileged positions (Matthew 20.28 and Mark 10.45) are all compressed into the eucharistic vision. Of course, they are present in this, but the whole petition suffers from an overload of information.

Post communion 2: From MacDonnell. The prayer employs the flexible metaphor of the harvest to suggest feeding, the work of the Christian life, and the gathering in of souls in the heavenly kingdom. It is worth noting that a single, multivalent image achieves a much more coherent and yet evocative prayer than the densely referenced model above.

In Time of Trouble

Collect: From the 1989 South African Prayer Book, with strong *BCP* resonances, e.g. to the collects for Trinity 4 and for Baptism.

Post communion: Based on Romans 8.18, this prayer is a reminder to communities in distress that the promise of the kingdom is always greater than present suffering.

For the Sovereign

Collect: From the *ASB*, which adopts the prayer for unity in the *BCP* Accession Service. There is a strong allusion to Ephesians 4.1–6.

References and Further Reading

William Bright, *Ancient Collects*, Methuen, London, 1887.

The Christian Year: Calendar, Lectionary and Collects, Church House Publishing, London, 1997.

Collects and Post-Communion Prayers, Church of Ireland, 1995.

Martin Draper, *The Cloud of Witnesses*, Collins, London, 1982.

Martin R. Dudley, *The Collect in Anglican Liturgy*, ACC 72, The Liturgical Press, Collegeville, Minnesota, 1994.

C. MacDonnell, *After Communion*, Mowbray, London, 1985.

Janet Morley, *All Desires Known*, SPCK, London, 1992.

Michael Perham, *Enriching the Christian Year*, SPCK/Alcuin Club, London, 1993.

J. W. Suter, *The English Collects*, Harper, New York and London, 1940.

Br Tristam SSF, *Exciting Holiness: Collects and Readings for the Festivals and Lesser Festivals of the Church of England*, Canterbury Press, Norwich, 1997.

G. G. Willis, *Further Essays in Early Roman Liturgy*, ACC 50, SPCK, London, 1968.

Chapter 9

The Sunday Lectionary

A. HISTORY

Early Lectionaries

The use of Scripture in worship takes us back to the Jewish synagogue, where systematic reading of the Torah first developed. Such continuous reading was itself a principle of the Law (see Deuteronomy 6.7 and Joshua 1.8), and was a regular feature at least of the Sabbath assembly. The sequence of continuous readings was only interrupted on major feast days, when seasonal material interjected. But precise information is not available: there has been some debate as to whether the continuous reading of the Law took three years, or one year, and it seems unlikely that any fixed or common system was in use in the synagogues before the Christian era. It is possible that in some places material from the Prophets (*Haftaroth*) was also read (as in Luke 4.16–30), but it is not clear whether such readings were regularly part of the worship; nor whether or not they were read as a track of continuous readings or as a carefully selected complement to the Torah. They may even have been freely chosen by the leader.

It is often said that the Psalter was part of the synagogue's staple diet. In the Temple the Levites sang designated Psalms each day at morning and evening sacrifices, and there was a calendar for special feasts. It was this pattern that was eventually taken over for synagogue use, but an exact date is difficult to determine.

Inevitably, early Christian practice was based upon this synagogue pattern. Jewish Christians would have had a natural inclination to read both Jewish and Christian Scriptures, and Gentile congregations inherited this tradition. Much early Christian preaching and teaching draws upon the Jewish Bible, and New Testament books may well have had their origins as expository sermons, which often followed the reading of the Law in the synagogue. St Paul's letters were probably intended to be read aloud at this point in the service (see Colossians 4.16; 1 Thessalonians 5.27). The tradition of following Old Testament with Epistle certainly dates from this practice. The telling of 'gospel' stories also arose in this context.

In second-century Rome, reading of the memoirs of the apostles and of prophetic writings at the Eucharist was commonplace, according to Justin

Martyr. However, there is no evidence that any fixed lectionary existed for this purpose. Passages may have been read on succeeding Sundays, according to synagogue custom, but there was no systematic practice of relating readings to one another within any one service. In the third century, there is evidence of non-eucharistic worship and catechetical gatherings on weekdays at which Christian and pre-Christian writings would be read publicly. The use of such readings provided rare access to Scriptures old and new, given the scarcity and cost of written biblical material. Regular, daily instruction for catechumens involved not only daily lections but also daily commentary (sometimes for up to three hours at a time!). Commentaries for the whole Bible exist from the third century onwards, and they were obviously delivered in appropriate order.

By the fifth century, there is more evidence, and it appears that there were some prescribed readings for particular feasts, although the minister might still exercise choice on other occasions. Thus Easter, the primary Christian Festival, lent itself naturally to accounts of the resurrection, and the 50 days following, to the account of the beginnings of the Church as portrayed in the Acts of the Apostles. That different congregations used these same lections from an early date is hardly surprising, given their obvious link with the flavour of the season. Other, more practical reasons led to the adoption of some regular lections, such as the practice (still retained in the *BCP*) of reading accounts of Jesus' exorcisms as Gospel readings in the period of Lent, pointing catechumens towards the exorcisms which would precede their Easter baptism.

From the seventh century we find a complete Sunday eucharistic lectionary, which also included special holy days. By then, it seems, alongside the practice of reading the Bible continuously, the practice of selecting specifically appropriate readings for different occasions had begun to develop more widely. The number of readings varied. At least in Syria there were four, from the Law, the Prophets, the Epistles, and also from the Gospels. Other places used either Law or Prophets, but not both, and in many places there were only two readings. In the Roman tradition it became usual to hear Epistle and Gospel on Sundays, with Old Testament and Gospel on weekdays. On appropriate saints' days the Old Testament lesson might be replaced by a reading describing the life and death of the saint. In the later monastic tradition, this tendency became a fixture, as the writings of non-scriptural Christian authors regularly accompanied biblical lections.

By the fourth century, Psalm-singing had also become part of the eucharistic liturgy, having first been an element in Christian meal fellowship. Psalms were sung after the Old Testament reading, or between Epistle and Gospel, depending on the local tradition and practice. Local variation also determined whether the Psalm was treated as a reading in its own right, or as a response to the reading it followed, in which case it would be determined by that reading. This complementary role eventually became the norm. Later, Psalms were also sung at other points in the service to accompany liturgical actions, but in the course of the Middle Ages these became abbreviated to no more than an antiphon, a single Psalm verse, the 'Glory be . . .', and the antiphon repeated, as the liturgical action itself came to occupy less time than before.

The BCP

Cranmer's Prayer Book of 1549 inherited and retained the Sarum eucharistic lectionary with only slight changes, additions or substitutions of readings. Those from the Old Testament or Apocrypha were changed for New Testament readings in some cases. With the exception of introits, all other Psalms were eliminated, and even the Psalm introits were abolished in 1552.

For Morning and Evening Prayer, however, a completely new arrangement of Psalms and readings was drawn up. A daily Psalm table was devised, based on a division of the Psalter into 60 roughly equal portions, to be used in numerical order morning and evening throughout each month, as is still the practice in some collegiate and cathedral foundations. On only four days of the year (Christmas, Easter, Ascension and Pentecost) was this routine interrupted by selected Psalms (Ash Wednesday and Good Friday were added in 1662). Scripture was read alongside the Psalter, in such a way that most of the Old Testament was completed once a year, and most of the New Testament three times. Whereas the pre-Reformation Calendar had been full of feast-days and diversions from continuous reading, the 1549 Prayer Book allowed very few, thus, for the first time, offering a lectionary that stayed on track for lengthy periods. In 1559 a full set of proper lessons was appointed for all the major festivals of the year, and at the same time proper first lessons for all the Sundays of the year were introduced, so that Sunday congregations might hear important Old Testament passages and not just the chapter reached in the daily sequence.

The 1662 Prayer Book left the Sunday lectionary provisions largely untouched, as did a major revision of the daily lectionary in 1871, although at that time a second set of Old Testament readings was appointed for Sunday evenings, to be used either as an alternative to the existing set or at a third service of the day, at which the minister might choose his own second lessons from the Gospels. It was not until 1922 that appropriate second lessons for Morning and Evening Prayer on Sundays were provided, along with alternative lessons, and lessons for the eves of holy days. These revisions then found their way into the proposed Prayer Book of 1928. They were not met with enthusiasm, however, so in 1947 a new two-year lectionary was created, which itself was criticized. A new revision of 1955 (slightly amended in 1961) altered the pattern, but kept a two-year cycle.

The JLG Proposals

Into this situation entered the Joint Liturgical Group (JLG), who published proposals for a revision of the Calendar and lectionary in 1967. Their influence was felt in many parts of the Anglican Communion and outside it, although not all of their proposals were taken up (such as the desire for a fixed date of Easter). Nine Sundays before both Christmas and Easter, and six afterwards, were suggested, and a lectionary that provided three readings for each Sunday of the year (Old and New Testament and Gospel) was created, although in the knowledge that some churches would prefer to use only two. A two-year cycle was proposed, so as to offer a wider and richer range of biblical readings. The Gospel reading was always to be used, but on the nine Sundays before Christmas the Old Testament lections were deemed to be most important, while during the Pentecost period (which replaced a 'Trinity' season), the New Testament was preferred. In this way, 'controlling' readings were indicated, the other texts having been chosen to assist them thematically. Once readings had been put into sets in this way, then the themes were determined. The 'themes' indicated the thrust of the passages, and did not exercise rigid control. In 1969 another lectionary for use at a second Sunday service was also offered.

The ASB

In the same year the Liturgical Commission published its own report, which accepted most of the JLG proposals, while making a few amendments and adding material for saints' days. It also included rules on how to handle overlappings of holy days. These were eventually authorized for use in conjunction with the Alternative Services then being tested. Finally, in 1976 the Commission brought forward a complete lectionary for the Eucharist on Sundays and holy days and for Morning and Evening Prayer, and at a later stage a daily eucharistic lectionary (mirroring almost exactly the Roman Catholic provision) was added. After debate and some revision, these were incorporated into the *ASB* of 1980.

The Church of England lived with the *ASB* Sunday eucharistic Lectionary for 20 years. For many, its approach wore thin, and there were other reasons for wanting to rethink how the Bible was read week in and out in church. The themes were not felt to be as helpful as they once were, not only because many preachers had used them for many years, but also because a thematic approach itself is not always desirable, nor is it currently in fashion.

In many churches today, a time-honoured practice of reading through a book of the Bible continuously from one Sunday to the next has proved helpful for teaching purposes. Thus a strong model for reading and preaching from an Epistle over a period of six to ten weeks has become popular, especially in large churches that respond to the rhythms of an academic year. There is clearly a desire for, and advantages to such sustained reading, yet the *ASB* Lectionary did not provide it.

Allied to this was a view among some that such a thematic approach to Scripture is 'improper'. One wonders whether the themes, although plainly stated, were played down a little by the compilers of the *ASB* for this reason (they only appear on page 1092). At a time when continuous reading of sorts was finding currency in churches wanting to 'work their way through' certain biblical books, the *ASB* was offering something quite different. No matter how subtle the theme, preachers were used to knowing what it was, and the Lectionary exerted no small pressure to conform. At the same time, the readings appointed in the second set of lections for the day often turned out to be either somewhat remote from some people's understanding of the 'theme' to which they were allied, or they represented a strong interpretation that was hard to ignore.

These themes emerged from a Calendar which was effectively lectionary-driven. The *ASB* Lectionary had a triune feel, focusing on the Creator God until Christmas, then on Jesus Christ up until Ascensiontide, and thereafter, on the Holy Spirit. Trinitarian in structure as it may appear, this was hardly satisfactory, not least because God the Trinity is not revealed in such neatly divisible packages. Any neglect of two persons of the Trinity in the 'season' of the other would be a cause for theological concern. It is far better for the lectionary to reflect the Calendar, rather than determine it.

Another weakness was the brevity of the two-year cycle. Admittedly it was twice as good as the preceding Prayer Book cycle, but it still neglected a great deal of Scripture. The use of themes sometimes led to fairly obscure passages being chosen, inevitably at the expense of other material. In the same way that a two-year cycle is better than a one-year cycle, a three-year cycle would be better still. It is of course hoped that with any cycle, there is a range of familiar texts which resonate annually, allied to a broad base of Scripture throughout the year. Experience has shown that two years is not enough to satisfy both needs.

While the *ASB* was criticized for not including enough Scripture and for marginalizing women, it was also complained that the readings themselves were sometimes too long. The Roman Catholic Lectionary thus gained favour in some places, because of the shorter readings it employed. It was also said that the weighting of Scripture that the JLG came up with was a little idiosyncratic. There was, for example, a particular emphasis on John's Gospel during the Easter season, based around a collection of 'I am' sayings. Also, a little later in the 'Pentecost' period, there was a heavy emphasis placed on a jumbled-up reading of John 15–17 during Year One. Inevitably with a thematic lectionary that covers two years, the selection of texts can seem erratic, and leave gaps. It is not so much the particular weighting of Scripture that the *ASB* has, but the fact that out of necessity it has to weight it in the first place that caused some concern. A series of readings of Jesus' farewell discourse has value of course, but in majoring so strongly in Year One, questions were begged concerning what other lections are lacking. For example, Matthew 21.28–22.14 was omitted, as was the whole first chapter of Mark and the first chapter of 1 Thessalonians. Naturally, opinions vary over what is important, but the problem is that with a weighted lectionary these opinions must be brought into force and imposed upon the Church.

Another idiosyncrasy of the *ASB* Lectionary concerned the various biblical translations printed and recommended. This did indeed lead to a variety of translations being used, chiefly the *New English Bible*, the *Revised Standard Version* and the *Jerusalem Bible*, but it emphasized the discontinuity of the lections, such that often there was neither continuous reading nor a coherent approach as found in a particular translation. This archetypal 'post-modern' approach, as found in the *ASB*, inevitably dates it, and, unfairly, makes it look a bit like a biblical sweet shop, where texts and translations were being 'picked and mixed' according to the flavours of the day.

Since most of the *ASB* daily Eucharist Lectionary was derived from the Roman Catholic Lectionary, while the Sunday lections were not, there was also a problem of overlap or repetition, which could be inappropriate or frustrating. A need to integrate these provisions therefore arose, particularly in contexts where a daily Eucharist was the norm.

The *ASB* Lectionary was hardly ecumenical when created, and never became so. It was never allied with any Roman Catholic lectionary, and its very separate ethos put the Church of England on a very different calendrical and scriptural footing. The advent of the *Revised Common Lectionary* (*RCL*), shared across nations and churches, has mitigated this unfortunate aspect of recent liturgical history, and will, no doubt, facilitate greater unity in an area over which there is hardly any reason to differ.

B. THE *COMMON WORSHIP* LECTIONARY

The RCL

The *RCL* is the precursor of what the Church of England now offers as part of its *CW* provision. After Vatican II, the Roman Catholic Church sought a reading of Scripture in the context of Sunday worship that made possible a nearly continuous reading of the synoptic Gospels in a three-year cycle. From about 1970, and unexpectedly, this lectionary began to be appropriated by some Anglican and Protestant churches, including the United Church of Canada and the United Methodist Church of the USA. Unfortunately, even in North America, various editions of the Roman Catholic table of readings were circulated, and they were not all accurate. This diversity led to calls for standardization, out of which the Consultation on Common Texts (a North American ecumenical body) set up a working group, the North American Committee on Calendar and Lectionary, in 1978. By 1983 the group had finished its work of standardizing and adapting the Roman Catholic Lectionary for wider use, and a nine-year period of testing of this 'Common Lectionary' was begun. After this triple cycle had been run, and after further consultation, in 1992 the Consultation's Lectionary Task Force published the *RCL*.

The first thing to notice about the *RCL* is that it is a three-year cycle, as opposed to the two-year *ASB* Lectionary, providing three readings and a Psalm for each Sunday. Obviously this leads to a greater use of Scripture, and enables more coherent, continuous reading of biblical books. Each of the three years has a distinctive character, which is determined by the particular synoptic Gospel from which the readings are mostly taken. Thus Year A (2002, 2005, etc.) is the year of Matthew, Year B the year of Mark, and Year C the year of Luke. As well as giving a certain unity to weekly reading of Scripture, this approach also immerses the hearers in the world of that writer, giving a fuller flavour of their style, theology, message and agenda. On the other hand, this unifying principle is not adhered to slavishly – where there is not an appropriate reading from a Gospel for a particular feast day, then another Gospel is drawn upon.

It might be felt that St John does not get his due in this scheme of things. But, in fact, almost as much of John is read as of Luke's Gospel, and even though Mark has his own Year B, there is a fair amount of John used that year, as well as in other years. It tends to be the periods of non-continuous reading (such as Advent and Lent) where John's Gospel is interpolated, and where the semi-continuous reading of one Gospel is suspended, whereas in the period after Trinity, for example, the key synoptic Gospel is read almost continuously. There are some interruptions and omissions (e.g. Matthew 9.14–17 is omitted in Proper 5), but there is a sense of continuity that is both stylistic and real.

For the Old Testament readings during Ordinary Time, there are two alternative provisions, either ones chosen to serve as a complement to the other readings of the day (following the typological approach of the Roman Catholic lectionary), or a continuous 'track' of Old Testament readings, which proceeds independently of the Gospel and Epistle. Either of the provisions can be chosen, but alternating between them too often is not encouraged. The idea is that a long-term choice is being offered where the Old Testament is used. Similarly, churches who use only one other lesson in addition to the Gospel are encouraged to choose either New or Old Testament, and stay with it for many weeks at a time, so as to create a sense of continuity. The New Testament Lectionary provides only one reading: there is no alternative track as with the Old Testament readings. It is not in the spirit of the Lectionary to pick and choose between tracks, or between Old and New Testament lessons. Therefore preachers and leaders need to think ahead and plan what is to be read over many months.

The options for the Old Testament resonate in the Psalms set for Sundays. Generally, the choice of Psalm is affected by the Old Testament reading, so where there are two tracks of readings running, there are complementary Psalms for each track.

In general, the readings are slightly shorter than those in the *ASB* Lectionary. Occasionally a particularly long reading occurs, as during Lent in Year A, when lengthier stories from John's Gospel, such as that of the raising of Lazarus, are found. Aside from the Lenten discipline of listening to longer readings, these stories, if read well, can make a deep impression when heard in full on what is, after all, a rare occasion.

The Church of England's Adoption of the RCL

In 1982 a private member's motion to the General Synod proposed the authorization of the Roman Catholic three-year Lectionary. The 1978 Lambeth Conference had recommended the introduction of a common lectionary, so a natural first step was to consider the Roman Catholic one already in use. The Liturgical Commission were duly asked to prepare a report, contrasting and comparing the *ASB* Lectionary with the Roman Catholic one. The Liturgical Commission reported back in 1983. Thus, so soon after the publication of the *ASB*, alternatives were already being sought.

As well as outlining many of the points so far raised in favour of the *RCL* and against the *ASB*, this report also produced extended tables comparing the two, by listing texts contained in one and not the other, and by listing passages common to both. It was revealing to note from this how many passages of Scripture the Church of England would lose, at least at the Sunday Eucharist. Much more would be introduced, of course, but it was instructive to see that using the *RCL* did not simply entail the introduction of more Scripture. However, other churches were already adopting the *RCL*, and so there was a question as to whether the Church of England could afford to be seen not to join in such an ecumenical venture.

The Church of England's Adaptations of the RCL

In constructing the *CW* Lectionary, the Church of England did not adopt the *RCL* unchanged. There was little difficulty concerning the *RCL*'s approach to the church year. The idiosyncratic nine Sundays before Christmas were abandoned, bringing the new Lectionary in line, not only with Roman use, but also with the *BCP*. Similarly there was no difficulty over the approach to Scripture adopted by the *RCL*. Semi-continuous tracks of readings allowed Scripture to be heard without bias towards any particular imposed theme and gave regular worshippers consistency of text and preaching.

In spite of this, there were some issues which the Church of England wanted to address, particularly over the omission of certain parts of Scripture. Thus, the use of the Book of Revelation in the *RCL* was highly selective. Very few passages occurred, namely 1.9–19; 5.11–14; 7.2–end; 21.1–7; 21.10–22.5; 22.12–20. To counter this in the *CW* Lectionary, other passages from the book were added in the Epiphany season in Year B, and also extensively in the Second and Third Service Lectionaries.

Similarly, the *RCL* offered a reading of Genesis 1 at the Easter Vigil service, and nowhere else. The problem therefore was that for anyone who did not attend that service (and some churches do not even offer it), there was only one other adequate reading of any Creation narrative, that being on Trinity Sunday in Year A (Isaiah 40). This is in marked contrast to the previous *ASB* provision, which effectively treated the Ninth Sunday before Christmas as 'Creation Sunday'. To compensate for this, the Church of England has replaced the *RCL* provision for the Second Sunday before Lent with 'creation' texts.

Again, there was an absence of Old Testament readings in the Easter period, because the *RCL* followed the ancient Roman practice of using the Acts of the Apostles as the first reading in that season. The option is therefore given in the *CW* Lectionary to take the Old Testament lessons offered at the Easter Vigil and read them as Old Testament lessons in the Easter season.

There were some notable omissions of particular stories that many would consider to be of intrinsic theological value. The story of the woman caught in adultery (John 7.53–8.11), in spite of its questionable origins, is nevertheless an important text, whose omission is not justified on those grounds. Consequently, it has been offered as an alternative Gospel reading for Ash Wednesday. Other omissions, such as the story of Cain and Abel (Genesis 4.1–16), have been incorporated into the Second and Third Service Lectionaries. Similarly, individual verses from biblical passages which had been omitted in the *RCL* selections in order to shorten them have also generally been restored in the *CW* Lectionary.

In addition, some minor adjustments were made to the early weeks of Ordinary Time in order to continue the Epiphany 'feel' of the period up to 2 February. Nevertheless, the changes that the Church of England has made to the *RCL* are few and far between; and those that have been made have been carefully considered, not least because they distance it from ecumenical brothers and sisters. Overall, the *CW* Lectionary as used by English Anglicans *is* a 'common lectionary', and this is to be applauded and welcomed.

However, a particular problem was encountered with regard to relating readings and collects in Ordinary Time. In the *RCL* these readings are allocated, not to a particular Sunday (and collect) with which Anglicans are familiar, but as numbered 'Propers', relating to specific weeks of the secular calendar. Thus readings are not set for the 'Fifth Sunday after Trinity', as one might expect, but for 'Proper 9 between 3–9 July'. The Liturgical Commission decided to attach the collects to the Sunday titles, rather than to the Propers. Consequently, the collects can bear no relation to the readings, whereas in the *ASB* collects and 'themes' were closely related. While some would argue that there need not be any connection between the two, others regret this decision. Yet, the solution does not lie in attaching particular readings to particular calendar dates, as this would lead to the Church of England following the same lectionary as everyone else, but often on different dates! In the end, Anglicans may have to consider attaching collects to Propers, rather than calendrical dates; or even abandon those dates altogether.

The Second and Third Service Lectionaries
The *RCL* provides only one set of readings for each Sunday. The *CW* version of this is designated as the 'Principal Service Lectionary', and is intended always to be used at the main service of the day, at whatever hour that service is held, and whether it is a Eucharist or not. Thus, even if a monthly pattern in a particular church contains a mixture of both eucharistic and non-eucharistic

services, the reading of Scripture is to be semi-continuous and common in the best sense of the word.

But since most churches have more than one service on a Sunday, Second and Third Service Lectionaries have also been included in *CW*, each of which provides two readings and a Psalm. These Lectionaries also follow a three-year cycle, but in the Third Service the readings in Ordinary Time are the same for all three years. In any given situation, the minister must decide which is the principal service (probably, but not necessarily, the Eucharist if one is cele-brated). Further services must be prioritized, and their designation as 'Second' or 'Third' service adhered to.

In a church where Morning and Evening Prayer are said or sung in addition to a Eucharist, it is likely that the morning service would carry the Third Service provision, and evening worship, the Second Service readings. The 'Second Service' is not the second one to take place, but rather the second most significant of the day. On those days when the Second Service Lectionary does not include a Gospel reading, an additional Gospel passage is provided, since it is recognized that a Second Service may well be a Eucharist. It has not been assumed that the Third Service of the day would be eucharistic, but rather that it would be an office; the readings are shorter than at the other services, and do not always include one from the Gospels.

Alternative Lectionary Provision

In contrast to the JLG proposals of the 1970s, there is no deliberate link between the Epistle and Gospel in the *CW* Principal Service Lectionary. Both are determined independently, and both also proceed semi-continuously. The lectionaries that are intended for use at other morning or evening services reflect the same seasonal emphases as the Principal Service Lectionary, but again in Ordinary Time no attempt is made to relate the readings to one another or to the Psalm. Thus within the *CW* Lectionary provision there are, on any Sunday, at any given service of the three provided for, several 'tracks' of readings proceeding semi-continuously, and thus offering a sense of continu-ity, which helps churches or congregations who wish to spend an extended period of time in preaching and teaching on one particular book of the Bible.

Nevertheless, the provision also exists for a church leader to follow one of the tracks of a lectionary, and while proceeding through it, to alter the other readings to commentate upon the chosen readings, or otherwise complement them, or even to opt out of the lectionary altogether. This kind of potential will undoubtedly appeal in some circles, but is permitted only outside the 'closed' periods from Advent to the Presentation of Christ in the Temple and from Ash Wednesday to Trinity Sunday, so that the Church may move together during the high points of the Christian year. Yet, even in Ordinary Time, the Liturgical Commission intends the provision for opting out to be employed only occasionally rather than frequently. But if recent trends suggesting that more people come to church less often (i.e. not on a Sunday-by-Sunday basis) are confirmed, then the idea of semi-continuous reading through Scripture may well turn out to be counter-cultural. Only time will tell.

References and Further Reading

The Revised Common Lectionary: The Consultation on Common Texts, Canterbury Press, Norwich, 1992.

Horace T. Allen and Joseph Russell, *On Common Ground: The Story of the Revised Common Lectionary*, Canterbury Press, Norwich, 1998.

Howard G. Hageman, 'A Brief Study of the British Lectionary', *Worship* 56, 1982, pp. 356–64.

T. Lloyd, P. Moger, J. Sinclair and M. Vasey, *Introducing the New Lectionary*, Grove Worship Series 141, Cambridge, 1997.

Gerard S. Sloyan, 'Is Church Teaching Neglected When the Lectionary is Preached?', *Worship* 61, 1987, pp. 126–40.

Chapter 10

The Psalter

A. HISTORY

The canonical Psalms have been continuously used in Christian worship, although in different ways and to varying extents. The Psalms were highly valued by the very first Christians, who believed them to have been written by King David under the inspiration of the Holy Spirit, and they understood quite a number of them to be speaking prophetically of the coming of Christ (see, for example, Acts 2.25–28; 4.25–26). Nevertheless, they seem to have used non-scriptural songs and hymns more or less interchangeably with such Psalms in their worship. The primary context for this use was apparently their community meals, where the Psalms were sung responsorially; that is, one person sang the verses and the rest responded with a refrain after each verse, at first usually just 'Alleluia', but later often a verse from the Psalm itself or even from elsewhere.

By the fourth century, their use had spread to other services, and selected Psalms were used both as part of the liturgy of the Word at the Eucharist and also as hymns of praise at the daily offices, as well as on other occasions. At this time the Church was becoming increasingly concerned about orthodoxy, and preferred to use the Psalms in worship rather than other hymns as a way of avoiding heresy.

The theologian Origen in the third century had extended the prophetic/ christological way of interpreting some Psalms to the whole of the Psalter, and this encouraged the desert ascetics and early monastic communities of the fourth century to use all of the Psalms rather than just a selection in their regular worship. Here they did not function as hymns or prayers, but as a source for meditation on Christ: the community sat and listened to a single voice reciting/chanting each Psalm, and this was followed by a period of silence for meditation, often ending with the Lord's Prayer or a collect.

While the selective use of Psalms at the Eucharist and other services contin- ued, through the monastic movement the idea of using the whole Psalter in the daily offices gradually spread to the rest of the Church. Here the Psalms were now viewed as essentially songs of praise to God, and the silent prayer between them became shortened and eventually disappeared altogether, each Psalm usually being concluded instead with the doxology, 'Glory be to the Father . . .'

In addition to the responsorial method of psalmody employed by the early Christians and the solo usage of the early desert monastic communities, other ways of chanting the Psalms also developed. At first antiphonal singing was adopted: the community was divided into two choirs which sang the refrain after each verse alternately, and sometimes two cantors were also used, alternating the verses between them. Later this gave way to what some call antiphonal psalmody but which is more accurately described as alternating psalmody: the two halves of the community themselves sang the verses alternately, and the refrain (or antiphon, as it was called) was only sung at the beginning and end of the Psalm.

At first, most Christians spoke Greek, and used a Greek translation of the Psalms made by the Jews about 200 BC, but later in the West translations were made from the Greek text into Latin. At the Reformation, vernacular versions of the Psalms began to appear as part of the translations of the Bible. In England the first authoritative translation was what is known as the Great Bible of 1540, the work of Miles Coverdale. The Psalter in this was a revision of Coverdale's earlier translation of 1535. Coverdale made his translation from the Latin and from other Reformation versions rather than from the original Hebrew. The 1540 edition of the Great Bible contained a few small corrections to the Psalms, and it was this version of the Psalter that was bound up with the *BCP* from 1549 onwards.

In Reformation churches on the Continent, metrical versions of the Psalms in the vernacular had also made an appearance and were used in worship. These were introduced into England by the Marian exiles returning in the reign of Queen Elizabeth, and were thereafter widely used as hymns, a number of them down to the present day, although their texts never received any form of official sanction.

By the end of the nineteenth century there was a growing awareness that a more accurate translation of the Psalms was needed for Anglican liturgical use. Although a committee of Convocation in 1916 recommended that some small changes be made to the text, their report was criticized for being insufficiently thorough, and the only result of its work incorporated in the proposed 1928 *BCP* was the permission to omit certain bracketed Psalms or portions of Psalms thought to be 'unedifying'. The next official attempt at revision did not appear until 1963, in the shape of *The Revised Psalter*, which was authorized for permissive use, but it never gained wide popularity.

In 1970 the Liturgical Commission invited one of its members, David Frost, to prepare a modern-language Psalter suitable for liturgical use. It soon became clear that a fresh translation from the Hebrew was necessary, and a panel of eight Hebrew scholars, led by the Reverend Andrew Macintosh, was convened to assist Dr Frost. A sample selection of their work appeared in 1973 as *Twenty-Five Psalms from a Modern Liturgical Psalter*, and the complete text as *The Psalms: A New Translation for Worship* in 1977. This became the Psalter of the *ASB*.

B. THE *COMMON WORSHIP* PSALTER

The Making of the CW Psalter

The *CW* Psalter is the only Psalter to have been specifically prepared to complement *CW* services. It differs from any Psalter previously printed in Church of England service books, and yet is closely related to them. It is cast in 'you' form language, is generally inclusive of men and women, attends to the worshipping traditions which have shaped the Church of England, is rhythmic, is reasonably accessible to a wide range of worshippers and falls within the parameters of contemporary Hebrew scholarship.

The Liturgical Commission's review of the Psalter provision to complement the *CW* services was begun in 1994. A number of criteria were identified which the Commission believed should characterize the Psalter to be printed as part of *CW*. It should:

- pay close attention both to the received Hebrew text of the Psalms and to scholarly discussions about their original form;
- pay close attention to the use of the Psalms in the Christian tradition;
- be sympathetic to the liturgical uses of the Psalter within the traditions of the Church;
- have a quality of language which enables the Psalms to be said or sung with ease;
- be memorable and resonate with known Psalter traditions in the Church of England;
- be more generally inclusive of men and women than Psalters currently in use in Church of England services;
- be couched in language accessible to a wide range of worshippers.

The preliminary work of the Liturgical Commission involved an assessment against these criteria of a range of English language Psalters in use in the mid-1990s in English-speaking churches. No existing Psalter in English was deemed to meet the criteria listed above to a sufficient degree, and the Commission decided that work on a new version of the Psalter for use in *CW* would need to be undertaken.

The Psalter of the Episcopal Church of the United States of America was chosen by the Liturgical Commission as its starting point in English. The preference for this Psalter was in part related to its positive reception among some Anglican religious orders during the late 1980s. In addition, it enjoyed copyright-free status, which meant that amendments to the text were relatively easy to make.

In November 1997 the General Synod of the Church of England debated the Commission's preliminary work. A discussion document, *A New Psalter for Liturgical Use in the Church of England* (GS Misc 504), was published to accompany the debate, containing a sample of 50 Psalms drafted by the Commission, together with an explanation of the review process. At the end of the debate, the General Synod asked the Liturgical Commission to prepare a draft of the complete Psalter, and in January 1999 *The Psalter 1998: A Draft Text for Common Worship* (GS Misc 544) was published.

Members of the General Synod, the 800 parishes authorized to test *CW* experimentally, and members of the public, as well as Hebraists, musicians and English language specialists, were invited to comment on the text during the first six months of 1999. Further revisions of the text were made by members of the Liturgical Commission, and consultations held between Commission members and Hebraists, musicians and English language specialists during the period from April to August 1999. A revised text was published in October 1999 as *A Draft Psalter for Common Worship* (GS Misc 582). Substantial revisions of one verse or more had been made to some Psalms (for example, Psalms 3, 56, 144), and revisions of single words, half-verses or punctuation had been made to a wider range of Psalms in the interests of greater faithfulness to the traditional Hebrew text or of rhythm or of clarity of sense.

In November 1999 the General Synod indicated its support for the Psalter contained in GS Misc 582 to be published as part of *CW*. During the early months of 2000 the Liturgical Commission further refined the text in consultation with experts in Hebrew, and the final version was published in the main volume of *CW* in November 2000.

Some Distinguishing Features of the CW Psalter
1. Echoing known Psalter Traditions
At a few points in a limited number of Psalms the *CW* Psalter retains a very familiar translation of a verse or phrase where to do otherwise would render the Psalm very awkward or difficult to use in worship. For example:

> a) 'God has gone up with a merry noise, * the Lord with the sound of the trumpet' (Psalm 47.5).

A literal translation of this verse from the Hebrew would read, 'God is gone up with a festal shout . . .', but here the *CW* Psalter stays with a traditional rendition of this verse (see the Psalter in the 1662 *BCP*), which has long and familiar associations with Ascension Day celebrations, particularly for those who sing. The Hebrew word rendered as 'trumpet' (verse 5b) is *shofar*, literally a ram's horn. The *shofar* is an instrument more familiar to scholars than parishioners, and 'trumpet' has therefore been retained as a familiar substitute.

> b) ' . . . they pierce my hands and my feet' (Psalm 22.16b).

The Hebrew rendered in the *CW* Psalter as 'they pierce' literally means 'like a lion', which makes no sense in the context of the Psalm. The rendition 'they pierce' follows the sense of the Vulgate and possibly the Septuagint. It makes good sense in context, and forms an important element of the traditional Christian understanding of Psalm 22 when used during Holy Week.

2. Variety of English Vocabulary used in Translation

The traditional Hebrew text of the Psalms contains a range of vocabulary that often runs beyond a simple word-for-word rendition into English. To remain faithful to the profound nuances of Hebrew thought implied by such words as *hesedh* (which means 'goodness' or 'kindness' in a strong sense, with a nuance of covenant fidelity) and *emeth* (which has the broad sense of 'truth'), the *CW* Psalter contains a variety of ways of rendering such words in English. For example, *hesedh* has been variously rendered as 'steadfast love', 'loving-kindness' or (following Coverdale) 'mercy', as in the refrain 'for his mercy endures for ever' (Psalm 136). Similarly *emeth* has a basic undertone of 'sureness' or 'reliability', and is sometimes rendered as 'faithfulness', as in Psalm 54.5.

3. Inclusive Language

The language of the *CW* Psalter is generally inclusive of male and female. A variety of approaches has been adopted in order to make the text inclusive:

a) The use of the first person singular or impersonal or plural pronouns have been variously adopted where the Hebrew pronoun is, in literal translation, in the third person masculine singular. For example:
  - 'This is *the one* who did not take God for a refuge' (Psalm 52.7a);
  - 'How long will all of you assail *me* to destroy *me*' (Psalm 62.3);
  - 'Because *they* have set *their* love upon me, therefore will I deliver *them*' (Psalm 91.14).
b) Abstract nouns have sometimes been used to make a text inclusive:
  - 'Put not your trust in princes, nor in any *human power*' (Psalm 146.2);
  - '. . . no delight in *human strength*' (Psalm 148.11b).
c) Generic terms, such as 'mortals', 'human beings' and 'humanity' have occasionally be used where appropriate:
  - '. . . his eyelids try every *mortal being*' (Psalm 11.5b);
  - 'Young *men and women* . . .' (Psalm 148.12).
  In the interests of strong rhythms, vividness of speech and traditional christological interpretations, the *CW* Psalter is on occasion not entirely consistent in its use of inclusive language. Psalm 8 is rendered in two alternative versions whose differences are demonstrated by a comparison of verse 5:
  - 'What is *man*, that you should be mindful of *him*; * the *son of man*, that you should seek *him* out?'
  - 'What are *mortals*, that you should be mindful of *them*; * *mere human beings*, that you should seek *them* out?'
  Other instances where the text is not inclusive generally occur in single

verses, such as Psalm 80.18, where the *CW* Psalter retains the associations of a text with traditional christological interpretations.

4. Layout

In contrast to some English language Psalters, the *CW* Psalter does not contain any bracketed verses within Psalms. The texts of the Psalms have been left to speak for themselves as a whole, without drawing attention to so-called 'difficult' verses. However, some discreet and light paragraphing is included within some Psalms, marked by a double line-space between two verses. This paragraphing is intended to indicate a clear change of mood or voice in the text, and to aid informed recitation or singing of the Psalms.

Chapter 11

Canticles in the Main Volume

Introduction

The term 'canticle' means 'little song'. The canticles are biblical passages, or collections of biblical verses, or hymns full of scriptural allusions. Some sections of Scripture are clearly identified as songs, such as the *Song of Moses* (*and Miriam*) in Exodus 15 or those in Luke's infancy narrative (Luke 1.46–55, 68–79, and 2.29–32). Some have the appearance of songs, for example Philippians 2.6–11 and Colossians 1.15–20. Other passages are acclamations, such those found in Revelation 4, 5, 7 and 15, which have formed the basis of canticles.

There is evidence for the use of both scriptural and other songs in early Christian worship. The form of these is varied and is generally poetic prose or hymns written in imitation of Psalms. Specific evidence for the use of biblical canticles is found as early as the fourth century. A variety of Old and New Testament passages began to be used alongside the canonical Psalms, especially at morning prayer.

Benedict and others introduced further canticles in later years, beginning a long tradition of taking a passage, or a selection of verses from Scripture, and forming a canticle or song. Several of the *CW* canticles come from this monastic tradition. It is the pattern from which the daily office of the Society of St Francis (SSF) has evolved, and is therefore foundational to our understanding of the provenance of the canticles used in *Celebrating Common Prayer* (*CCP*), so many of which have been adopted in *CW*. Since the late 1960s the SSF in Britain has been experimenting and developing a wide range of liturgical material for use in the community, including the use of many old and new canticles. The progress of this development can be discerned from the loose-leaf collection of the early 1970s and the Office Books of 1970, 1972, 1976 and 1981, which were the forerunners of *CCP*.

Non-biblical canticles were also used in place of psalmody. At times such songs were used to express unorthodox theology, and consequently they tended to be treated more cautiously than biblical canticles or Psalms. Those which have survived the test of time are the *Phos hilaron*, *Gloria in Excelsis* and *Te Deum*, all dating back to around the fourth century.

One of the criticisms levelled against Morning and Evening Prayer in the

1662 *BCP* was the lack of variety and flexibility in the canticles provided. With the exception of the *Benedicite*, the only alternatives provided for the *Benedictus, Te Deum, Magnificat* and *Nunc dimittis* were Psalms, for which provision had been made in 1552 because of objections raised to the canticles by some reformers. The proposed Prayer Book of 1928 did little to extend this provision and it was not until the JLG daily office was published in 1968 that different canticles for each weekday at Morning and Evening Prayer were introduced. This provision was first brought into the Church of England in Series 2 (Revised) and extended yet again in the *ASB* to include a wider range of texts. But while two proper canticles were provided for both Morning and Evening Prayer on weekdays, no alternatives to the traditional arrangement were offered for Sundays. *CCP* has an even more diverse selection of canticles and includes Sundays in its provision of canticles for each day.

In the main volume of *CW* an extensive range of canticles is suggested for use at Morning and Evening Prayer on Sundays. The *Benedictus* for use at Morning Prayer and *Magnificat* for use at Evening Prayer are printed in full in the text. The opening canticles and other Old and New Testament canticles, however, are listed in the notes and vary according to the season. *CW* also prints all the *ASB* canticles as well as those in the *BCP*. In the *ASB* these latter were allowed solely where the musical settings dictated their use. In *CW*, however, they have been restored to their rightful place in A Service of the Word.

One feature of ancient practice, preserved in the monastic tradition, is the use of antiphons in the recitation of canticles. The repetition of a phrase or verse sticks more firmly in the mind. The antiphon or refrain also influences the way the canticle is understood, by giving the theme of the canticle, and linking it into the context in which it is said. This context may be seasonal, linked to the Calendar, or related to the life of the Church – either local or universal. The main volume of *CW* has not used many antiphons.

In general *CW* has kept to a couplet layout as the traditional Anglican shape. Scripture passages and Psalms being used as canticles have been adapted to conform to this shape. The canticles have also been revised according to a policy of using inclusive language where possible.

A. OPENING CANTICLES AT MORNING PRAYER

Benedicite – a Song of Creation
This canticle comes from the second and longer part of the 'Song of the Three' (verses 35–65) added to the third chapter of the book of Daniel in the Septuagint, and is now in the Apocrypha. The first part (verses 29–34) also came to be used as a canticle under the title *Benedictus es (Bless the Lord)*. It purports to be the song sung by the three young men in Nebuchadnezzar's fiery furnace. It has been in use at morning prayer in both the Eastern and Western rites since the fourth century, originally on Sundays to commemorate creation on the

first day of the week. Popular in the breviaries of the late Middle Ages, it survived in the 1549 *BCP* as a Lenten alternative to the *Te Deum* in Morning Prayer, and in 1552 and 1662 as a general alternative to that canticle. An important but informal change took place in the *BBC Psalter* in 1948, which omitted the reference to Ananias, Azarias and Misael, altered Israel to 'people of God' and restored the original doxology in place of the *Gloria Patri*. This had the effect of making the canticle more explicitly Christian. These alterations continued in Series 2 (Revised) Morning Prayer and in the *ASB*. In *CW* it appears in double verses as in *CCP*, although the translation of the two versions differs in other respects.

The shorter version is almost identical to the *ASB* version (verses 1–3a, 19–21), except that an additional refrain has been added after 'O people of God, bless the Lord.'

Venite – a Song of Triumph

The earliest accounts of the Roman daily office indicate that the *Venite*, Psalm 95, introduced the first office of the day, except on special occasions, and Benedict appointed Psalms 3 and 95, with an antiphon, to be used before the hymn and Psalms for the day at the office of Vigils. In the Roman and Sarum breviaries it continued in a similar position, and it was the only Psalm to be said with an antiphon in the ancient manner – at the beginning, between verses, and at the end. The 1549 *BCP* retained it as the introduction to the psalmody, but with no alternative, and with no invitatory antiphons. 1552 directed that the Easter Anthems were to be used instead on Easter Day.

A major development in 1928 was the omission of verses 8–11 of the Psalm, in order to provide a specific call to worship. This was a change first used in the American Prayer Book of 1789. The deleted words introduce the concept of the waywardness of humankind, in the history of Israel and in the temptation to harden our hearts to God's voice. Series 1 reinstated them and then Series 2 dropped them again.

Series 2 (Revised), Series 3 and the *ASB* followed JLG proposals to produce a composite version, Psalm 95.1–8a followed by Psalm 96.13, which is another Psalm that calls to worship. This had the effect of maintaining an element of warning about God's judgement, although it does change the dynamic of the Psalm. *CW* has reverted to straight use of Psalm 95, but allowed for its shortening by omitting verses 8–11. The traditional form in the book is as in the *BCP*, but with verses 8–11 bracketed as optional. The *Venite* is an option in the opening section of A Service of the Word, and particularly recommended for Morning Prayer during Advent and Lent, when the awareness of our sin and God's judgement has particular poignancy. The use of the Psalm in the warnings of Hebrews 3 and 4 is also pertinent to the Christian use of these verses.

Jubilate – a Song of Joy

The *Jubilate*, Psalm 100, was the second of the fixed Psalms at Lauds (morning prayer) on Sundays and holy days in the Sarum Breviary, where it appears before the first reading (Old Testament). It was also used at Prime. It was not in the 1549 Prayer Book but was included in 1552 and 1662 after the second reading (New Testament), as an alternative to the *Benedictus*. This alternative was required on days when the latter was the appointed reading. In Series 2 (Revised), and then Series 3 and the *ASB*, it was put back to the earlier position as an alternative to the *Venite*. As another call to worship, this was more appropriate. *CW* recommends its use particularly in festal seasons, and its subtitle, *Song of Joy*, expresses its nature as a short and powerful expression of joy and praise as we come into God's presence.

The Easter Anthems

From the early times in the Christian Church a collection of verses from Pauline Epistles has been used as an Easter acclamation, known as the *Pascha nostrum*. In traditional monastic offices it was used in place of the *Venite* at Mattins on Easter Sunday and in Eastertide. It consisted of just two passages, Romans 6.9–11 and 1 Corinthians 15.20–22. In Sarum use it was sung during a procession before Mass on Easter Day. In the 1549 Prayer Book it is found with the Easter Day collects and readings, with instructions to use it before Mattins. It was used with Alleluias following the two passages and ended with a versicle and response and a collect. In 1552 it was simplified to being only the two main passages and was to be used instead of the *Venite* on Easter Day. 1 Corinthians 5.7–8 was added to the passages in 1662.

The Anthems are substantially unchanged in recent liturgical revision, apart from the substitution of a modern translation of the passages. In the *ASB* they are permitted as an alternative to the *Venite* and *Jubilate* on any day, being mandatory on Easter Day. In *CCP* they are given as the opening canticle at Morning Prayer on Sundays and in Eastertide. In *CW* they are an opening canticle for any occasion, but particularly during the Easter season.

B. OPENING CANTICLES AT EVENING PRAYER

Phos hilaron – a Song of the Light

This early hymn was already described 'ancient' by Basil of Caesarea (died 385) and its use is described in a number of sources from the fourth century onwards. It was sung as a thanksgiving during evening prayer when lamps were brought in, ceremonially lit and then appropriate Psalms were sung. Thanks were given for light and for Christ as the Light. It therefore became a traditional opening canticle at evening prayer in the Eastern tradition. In *CCP* the Blessing of the Light continues this ancient practice. A candle is lit and prayer said, and then the *Phos hilaron* is sung while other candles are lit.

It was used as an opening canticle at Evening Prayer in Series 2 (Revised), as one of three options, the others being Psalm 134 and the Easter Anthems. Having an opening canticle was part of a move by the Liturgical Commission to give Evening Prayer the same structure as Morning Prayer. The *ASB* rendering of the *Phos hilaron* is a hymn version by Robert Bridges, from the Yattendon Hymnal. In *CW* it appears in two versions, 'O joyful light' and 'Hail gladdening light'. The first is a new translation from the original Greek by Brother Colin Wilfred and Brother Christian for the 1972 SSF daily office book. The second is a metrical hymn by John Keble, as in *Hymns Ancient and Modern Revised*.

Verses from Psalm 141

Psalm 141 is a traditional evening Psalm from early times. It is used as part of the Blessing of the Light at Evening Prayer in *CCP*, adopting a translation from the American 1979 *BCP*. This is one of the few places where the main volume of *CW* uses a refrain with a Psalm, as in ancient practice.

Verses from Psalm 104

Psalm 104 was used in many places in the West in ancient times as a regular evening Psalm in place of Psalm 141, which was more common in the East. It has also been used as a morning Psalm. The precise selection of verses has varied. A refrain is used here also.

C. OLD TESTAMENT CANTICLES AT MORNING PRAYER

A Song of the Wilderness

This canticle, taken from Isaiah 35.1, 2b–4a, 4c–6, 10, appears in *PHG* (5:306, verses 1–4 only), *CCP* (10:195), and *PW* (1Q1:150). The first verse includes the imagery of the desert blossoming and bursting into song, suggesting new life, and as such is suitable for use at Morning Prayer, especially in Advent.

A Song of the Messiah

Suggested for use during the Christmas season and based on Isaiah 9.2–3b, 4a, 6–7, this canticle sets an incarnational theme in its first verse: 'The people who walked in darkness have seen a great light.' It is well known as one of the traditional Christmas readings in the Service of Nine Lessons and Carols. It is the second canticle at Morning Prayer in the SSF 1981 daily office, and on Wednesdays/Christmas season in *CCP* (7:193). In *PHG* (2:303) and *PW* (2Q3:152) it is called *A Song of Joy*.

A Song of the New Jerusalem

Based on Isaiah 60.1–3, 11a, 18–19, 14b, this canticle is suggested for use during Epiphany. In medieval use, entitled *Surge, illuminare*, it was an alternative to the *Te Deum* in Advent at Sunday Mattins, and in the Mattins monthly cycle after the Old Testament lesson. The SSF have been using it in Morning Prayer, under the title *A Song of Isaiah*, at Advent since 1970, and on Wednesdays and Epiphanytide from 1976. It appears in substantially the same version in *PHG* (12:311) and *PW* (3Q5:153), and in an identical text to that in *CW* in *CCP* (15:112/198), where it is the alternative second canticle at Morning Prayer on Thursdays/Epiphany season.

A Song of Humility

The canticle for Lent comes from Hosea 6.1–6 and sets a suitable theme of repentance and forgiveness with its opening verse. It also appears in Morning Prayer for Fridays and during Lent in *CCP* (21:137/202), where it is supplemented by an antiphon. It developed in SSF usage from the early 1970s. The same canticle appears in a slightly different translation in *PHG* (26:323) and *PW* (4Q7:155) under the title *A Song of Hosea*.

The Song of Moses and Miriam

This canticle, taken from Exodus 15.1b–3, 6, 10, 13, 17, sets an Easter theme with its opening verse, 'I will sing to the Lord, who has triumphed gloriously.' Exodus 15 has been used as a canticle from the fourth century onwards. In traditional monastic usage a longer version than that in *CW* was used, which included verses 4–5 about Pharaoh's army drowning in the sea. Called *The Song of Moses*, it was used at Morning Prayer as part of the weekly cycle after the Old Testament lesson. It also appeared in a slightly different version in *PW* (6Q10:157). In *CCP* (1:16/189) it is the alternative second canticle for Morning Prayer on Sundays. In verse 4 the *CCP* translation, 'The Lord fights for his people', has been replaced with the stronger biblical imagery of 'The Lord is a warrior.' The title in both *CCP* and *CW* picks up Miriam's role in Exodus 15.20–21, where she echoes Moses' song and leads the women out with timbrels and dancing. This addition reflects a desire for inclusivity.

A Song of Ezekiel

A theme of renewal suitable for use in Pentecost is suggested in this canticle, from Ezekiel 36.24–26, 28b, by the words 'A new heart I will give you and put a new spirit within you' (verse 3). The theme of regeneration is further strengthened by a refrain which accompanies the canticle in *CCP* (Morning Prayer on Monday, 20:43/201). In traditional monastic usage it is part of the Mattins cycle of canticles for Fridays.

A Song of David

This canticle for Ordinary Time comes from 1 Chronicles 29.10b–13, 14b, where it is attributed to David as a prayer. It has the form of a *berakah* (blessing of God), and is therefore similar to the Jewish grace prayers as used at the Passover and other meals. It will be familiar from the Anglican usage of some of the verses in the Eucharist as a song of praise at the Offertory. Its traditional monastic use was as part of the Mattins cycle of canticles for Mondays. The SSF changed its use to Thursdays and Ascensiontide (1972), and it was then included in substantially the same translation in *CCP* (3:190) as an Old Testament canticle for the Transfiguration.

D. NEW TESTAMENT CANTICLES AT EVENING PRAYER

A Song of the Spirit

This canticle, taken from Revelation 22.12–14, 16–17, is suggested for Sundays during Advent. Its suitability for this season is obvious with its opening words, 'Behold, I am coming soon, says the Lord', and the concluding doxology from Revelation 22.20. It has been used for Advent by the SSF since the early 1970s, and appears in *PHG* (40:333, omitting Revelation 22.16) and in Evening Prayer for Tuesdays in *CCP* (58:77/228).

A Song of Redemption

This canticle for the Christmas season is taken from Colossians 1.13–18a, 19–20a. An incarnational focus is provided by verse 3, 'He is the image of the invisible God, the firstborn of all creation', used as a refrain in *CCP* (45:220). Initially the SSF used this canticle at Evening Prayer on Sundays and in Eastertide (1972), but moved it to Evening Prayer on Wednesdays and in the Christmas season in *CCP* (45:100/220). It also appeared in *PHG* (33:328–9).

A Song of Praise – Glory and Honour

This canticle is based on the song of the elders around God's throne in Revelation 4.11; 5.9b–10, with 5.13b used as a doxology. In it we are reminded of the inclusiveness of the theme of Epiphany in the words 'by your blood you ransomed for God, saints from every tribe and language and nation'. It appeared in the appendix to the Irish Prayer Book in 1926, for use in the Alternative Order for Evening Prayer on weekdays. It was included in the JLG daily office for Friday evenings, and in Series 2 (Revised) under the title *Worthy thou art* as an alternative to the *Nunc dimittis*, a position which it retained in the *ASB* with slightly different wording and under the title *Glory and Honour*. The *CW* wording is substantially the same as *CCP* (52:124/224), where it is an alternative canticle for Evening Prayer on Thursdays, and for use when commemorating Apostles and Evangelists. This version evolved from the daily Evening Prayer canticle entitled *Worthy are you* in the SSF daily office of 1970, which was moved for use at Evening Prayer on Holy Days from 1972, and to Thursday use in 1981 as *A Song of Praise*.

A Song of Christ the Servant

The opening words, 'Christ suffered for you, leaving you an example', make this canticle (from 1 Peter 2.21b–25) appropriate for Lent. It has been in SSF usage since 1972, when it was the second canticle at Evening Prayer on Fridays and in Lent, entitled *A Song of the Passion*. It is used again in this position in *CCP* (49:150/222) under its present title, and also appeared in *PW* (5Q9:156).

A Song of Faith

Based on 1 Peter 1.3–5, 18–19, 21, this canticle for use during the Easter season echoes the resurrection hope. It has been in SSF usage since the early 1970s, but the version in *CW* is a fresh translation, using the *Revised Standard Version* of the Bible as a basis. It is therefore different from that in *CCP* (48:30/223), where it is an alternative second canticle for Evening Prayer on Sundays, and to the *Song of Peter* in *PW* (6Q11:157), which is based on the same verses. This canticle is perhaps best known as the anthem by S. S. Wesley, 'Blessed be the God and Father of Our Lord Jesus Christ.'

A Song of God's Children

The words, 'The Spirit himself bears witness that we are children of God', give this canticle, from Romans 8.2, 14, 15b–19, its place as the choice for Pentecost. The version in *CW* differs from that in *CCP* (41:217), being a fresh translation based on the *Revised Standard Version* of the Bible, and restoring the male pronoun to the person of the Spirit.

A Song of the Lamb

This canticle selected for Ordinary Time is based on Revelation 19.1b, 5b, 6b–7, 9b, with 5.13b used as a doxology. Substantially the same version also appears in *CCP* (55:226) and in *PHG* (38:332). The canticle has been in use by the SSF since the early 1970s, being the second canticle at Evening Prayer for Mondays and during Advent. This earlier version did not include verse 5 of the *CW* text. It was also in the World Council of Churches' Lima Liturgy, *One Lord, One Faith, One Baptism* (1983).

E. GOSPEL CANTICLES

These songs from the infancy narrative in the first two chapters of Luke have been used in Christian worship from quite early times, and are set in the context of the gospel message of the bringing of salvation to the world. They are ascribed to the lips of a handful of people who shared in the extraordinary knowledge that the child born as Jesus, in Bethlehem, was bringing the long-awaited salvation in fulfilment of the prophecies and promises of God. They each burst into the Scriptures as shouts of praise, wonder and acclamation of God's goodness. They are full of Old Testament imagery endowed with the New Testament message, and as such make fitting canticles for regular use related to the reading of Scripture.

The *Benedictus* and *Magnificat* bear some similarity to the victory songs of the Maccabaean wars. A War Scroll found among the Dead Sea documents contains a prayer which adapts an older text, giving thanks to God for his intervention. There are significant parallels between this prayer and the two canticles, and a similar dependence on a rich background of Old Testament ideas, and phrases from the Septuagint.

Benedictus (The Song of Zechariah)

This hymn, Luke 1.68–79, expresses confidence in God. There had been expectation and hope that God's mighty hand would bring freedom and redemption for Israel. Now there is the scent of victory in the air and this song of praise recognizes God's hand at work. What has been promised is just about to be realized, and the child John is to be part of it all and to herald it. Zechariah realizes the importance of this moment in history. For Luke, a good priest and a barren, godly woman epitomize the best of religious people in Israel at that time, the truly faithful remnant.

The *Benedictus* has become a foundational hymn in the Church, expressing the salvation (verses 69, 71, 77), redemption (68) and rescue (74) that have come in Christ. The early Benedictine tradition placed it as the climax of morning prayer, and this was the position in which Cranmer used it in 1549. In 1552 Psalm 100 (*Jubilate*) was allowed as an alternative, but the 1662 *BCP* permitted that option only when the Lukan passage containing the *Benedictus* was the assigned reading.

Series 2 reversed the positions of the *Te Deum* and *Benedictus*, using the latter as a logical link between the Old and New Testament readings, as it is anticipatory in character. It remained in this position in *ASB* Morning Prayer, but *CW* reverts to the older tradition and to Cranmer's position, by placing it after the New Testament reading in both modern and traditional Orders for Morning Prayer on Sunday.

The translation used in *CW* is the ELLC text, which removes unnecessary masculine pronouns and aims to follow the Greek original more closely. In the traditional language Morning Prayer, the *BCP* text is used, although printed in couplet layout to assist in its recitation or singing.

Magnificat (The Song of Mary)

Luke 1.46–55 is composed of a tapestry of Old Testament verses and ideas. In it we hear lines from Hannah's Song (1 Samuel 2.1–10, which it closely resembles), from the Psalms (34.1–3; 18.46; 138.6; 71.19; 103.17; 98.1–2; 18.27; 107.9; 98.3), and from both major and minor prophets (Isaiah 61.10; Habakkuk 3.18; Isaiah 40.10; Ezekiel 21.26; Micah 7.20). As well as the similarity with the victory songs of the Maccabaean wars, there are also resonances with songs by the *anawin* (the poor ones), a group with connection to Qumran who lived in complete dependence on God. So whether of Mary's or Luke's composition, it is clearly a product of the times, written and sung by those steeped in the Scriptures and full of the hope of salvation. The song expresses the particular significance of the coming of Christ as the baby born of Mary, bringing about all the fullness of God's promises through the ages. As such it is not only Mary's song but the song of every believer who expresses wonder at this world-transforming gift.

The Church has taken it as foundational to its daily worship, initially as a morning canticle in the Eastern and Gallican Churches, and then as an evening song in the West from at least Benedict onwards. In 1549 Cranmer used it between the two readings of Evening Prayer, although in 1552 provided the alternative of Psalm 98 (*Cantate Domino*). It remained in this position in the *ASB*, but *CW* places it after the New Testament reading, paralleling the position of the *Benedictus* in Morning Prayer.

The text is that of ELLC with minor variations. ELLC avoided masculine pronouns except where they are clearly intended in the original Greek, but *CW* has not followed suit in instances where the substituted words are obtrusive. In the traditional language Evening Prayer, the *BCP* text is used, although printed in couplet layout.

Nunc dimittis (The Song of Simeon)

This Song of Simeon, Luke 2.29–32, is another canticle which rejoices at the fulfilment of the promises of God. In these verses the sense of longing and waiting on God is very strong. It has many resonances with Isaiah's prophecies, especially from Isaiah 40–55, which is often called the Book of Consolation. The expectation of the consolation of Israel was something to which the nation looked forward, and which had been Simeon's hope for many years.

As a song of faithful waiting rewarded, the promise of salvation fulfilled, and the song of a new dawn for all people, it is an appropriate hymn for evening use. We have evidence of its use as early as the end of the fourth century, and Pope Gregory the Great in the sixth century put it into Compline, although its place there was not firmly established until the eighth century. That then became its normal usage in the monastic tradition. It was also used at festivals linked with the incarnation, such as the Feast of the Presentation of Christ in the Temple.

Cranmer made it the second canticle at Evening Prayer in 1549 and there it remained, as a suitable response to the New Testament reading. However, alternatives to it were provided in 1552 (Psalm 67, *Deus misereatur*), in Series 2 (Revised) (*Glory and Honour*), and in the *ASB* (*Glory and Honour* and the *Song of Christ's Glory*).

In the traditional form of Evening Prayer in *CW* it keeps its place after the New Testament reading, with Psalm 67 (*Deus misereatur*) an alternative, and is arranged in couplet layout. However, it is put back into Compline (An Order for Night Prayer) in the modern language provision. Here the ELLC text is used, but there is also a refrain (which may change seasonally and on festivals) at the beginning and end.

F. OTHER CANTICLES

The Song of Christ's Glory

This is based on Philippians 2.6–11, which is thought by scholars to be an early Christian hymn independent of the rest of the letter. Its theme is Christ's rule and the meaning of the incarnation. In its biblical context Paul makes the point that as self-giving is the definition of what it means to be God, so self-giving service is the definition of what it means to be 'in Christ'. It appeared in Christopher Wansey's *New Testament Psalter* in 1963 and was adopted in the 1975 South African liturgy. In the SSF a form of it was used as a responsive reading at mid-day prayer on Fridays in Eastertide in 1970, and it was set in canticle form for use on Thursdays and in Ascensiontide at Evening Prayer in 1972, where it was called *A Song of the Ascension*. In Series 3 and the *ASB* it was used as an alternative to the *Nunc dimittis*. In *CW* it takes the same form as that which became well known in *ASB*.

Great and Wonderful

This canticle is based on Revelation 15.3–4 with a doxology from Revelation 15.13b. It is the song of the martyrs in the presence of God and has links with the *Song of Moses and Miriam* in Exodus 15. It was called *Great and Wonderful* when it was prescribed for use at Morning Prayer in Lent in the SSF daily office book of 1970, but *The Song of Moses and the Lamb* in 1972, where it was the second canticle at Evening Prayer on Wednesdays and during the Epiphany season. It was used as a canticle for Saturday mornings in the JLG daily office and in Series 2 (Revised), where it was also an alternative to the *Te Deum*. In the *ASB* it appeared as an alternative to the *Benedictus* at Morning Prayer.

Bless the Lord

Part of the 'Song of the Three', this canticle is related to the *Benedicite* (see above). It differs from the version used as an alternative to the *Magnificat* in the *ASB*, in that it addresses God directly rather than in the third person. The canticle was prescribed for Tuesday evenings in the JLG daily office, and in Series 2 (Revised) it was adopted as an alternative to the *Nunc dimittis* at Evening Prayer.

Saviour of the World

This canticle, thought to have been written by Dr Henry Allon, a notable Congregational hymn-writer, first appeared in the *Congregational Hymnal* of 1862. It was included in the JLG daily office as the canticle for Friday morning, and in Series 2 (Revised) and the *ASB* as an alternative to the *Te Deum*. It is based on the antiphon 'O Saviour of the world', which appeared in the Visitation of the Sick in the Sarum Manual and in the 1549, 1552 and 1662 Prayer Books. Biblical texts which have been identified as having been used in this canticle include Psalm 80.2, Isaiah 58.6 and 63.9, Acts 21.13, and 1 Peter 1.18–19.

Te Deum Laudamus

This possibly has pagan roots as a hymn addressed to the emperor, which was then adapted by Christian authors as an address to God. A legend claims it was composed as a duet sung by Ambrose and Augustine at Augustine's baptism. Other suggested authors are Niceta of Remesiana (*c.* 392–414, a stronger possibility), Hilary of Poitiers (355), Hilary of Arles (440), or Nicetius of Treves (535), but in truth its origin remains obscure. It is most likely to have evolved and accrued verses along the way. Portions of it may have derived from eucharistic liturgies.

The first complete text appears in the late-seventh-century *Bangor Antiphonary*. In early forms it lacked the final section, from 'Save your people, Lord . . .' onwards, which was originally a separate series of responses drawn from the Psalms. Known as *capitella* (singular, *capitellum*) such responses were often used between a Psalm or canticle and its collect. In the *Te Deum* they eventually became attached to the canticle more permanently, along with those which went with the *Gloria in Excelsis*. The couplet format in *CW* reflects their responsive origin, and this section can be omitted.

Caesarius of Arles in the sixth century allocated this canticle for festive use at morning prayer, and Benedict assigned it to the night office on Sundays. It was incorporated for daily use in Morning Prayer in the 1549 *BCP*, except in Lent when it was to be replaced by the *Benedicite*. In 1552 the Lenten restriction was removed, and the *Benedicite* became an alternative at any time, as it is in 1662. In *CCP* the *Te Deum* is used on feast days and as a concluding song of praise at Morning Prayer on any Sunday, which is also suggested in *CW*.

The modern text in *CW* is the ELLC version, with minor changes in the layout, but not in wording. *CW* keeps the ELLC 'humbly chose the Virgin's womb', rather than the ICET wording, 'did not abhor', seeing it as a more positive and accurate way of expressing Christ's willingness to be born of a woman. The *BCP* text is retained in the traditional version of Morning Prayer, but with modernized punctuation, and it remains in its place after the Old Testament reading.

G. CANTICLES FROM THE BOOK OF COMMON PRAYER

The history of these has already been outlined above, with the exception of two Psalms which have often been used as canticles in the tradition of the Church. *Cantate Domino* (Psalm 98) was included an alternative to the *Magnificat*, and *Deus misereatur* (Psalm 67) an alternative to the *Nunc dimittis* in 1552 and 1662. Neither of them were so used in the *ASB*, and *CW* includes them only as canticles for the traditional form of Evening Prayer in line with 1662 usage. *Deus misereatur* is used as the opening canticle for Morning Prayer on Thursdays in *CCP*.

References and Further Reading

Edward Foley, *Foundations of Christian Music*, Alcuin/GROW Liturgical Study 22–3, Nottingham, 1992.

George Guiver, *Company of Voices*, SPCK, London, 1988.

Robert Taft, *The Liturgy of the Hours in East and West*, 2nd edn, The Liturgical Press, Collegeville, 1993.

Chapter 12

The Design of *Common Worship*

The Design Brief and Selection of the Designers

The design of a book is an important factor in the impression which it creates, so great care was taken in selecting and briefing the designers and approving the design for *CW*. The Liturgical Publishing Group established a Design Sub-Group to undertake these tasks. The members and staff of the Sub-Group were Professor Christopher Frayling, Rector and Vice-Provost of the Royal College of Art and Chairman of the Design Council; Mrs Alison Baverstock, publisher, marketing consultant and author; Canon Jeremy Haselock, Precentor of Norwich Cathedral; The Reverend Dr William Beaver, Director of Communications for the Church of England; Ms Rachel Boulding, Senior Liturgy Editor, Church House Publishing; and Dr Colin Podmore, Secretary of the Liturgical Publishing Group.

The design brief emphasized three principles: *use* (the books would need to be designed for use as well as for appearance), *excellence* (they should give an impression of excellence and quality) and *long-term value* (the design should be one of lasting appeal). The needs of those who are partially sighted or colour blind or have problems with manual dexterity were to be borne in mind at every relevant point, the visual style was to be of understated elegance and quality, and the design was to have a certain timelessness about it – a look which was classic but not old-fashioned. With regard to the typeface and font size, the design brief singled out readability and elegance of appearance as essential; the needs of the partially sighted and the fact that the books would often be used in conditions of poor lighting were also to be remembered. The layout was to be spacious and never cramped but not extravagant, and there had to be sufficient margin so that the text did not disappear into the gutter of the bound book.

Eighteen designers or design groups were approached with the brief, after recommendations from a number of contacts had been discussed. Eight of these expressed interest in the project, and on the basis of their letters and examples of their previous work, three were short-listed and invited to submit a design sample of three double-page spreads of extracts from the Holy Communion services. After interviews conducted in Westminster Abbey's historic Jerusalem Chamber, Professor Derek Birdsall, RDI, and his colleague John Morgan, of Omnific, were selected as the designers for *CW*.

The Typeface

Derek Birdsall's submission said that his approach would be marked by 'comfort, clarity and poetry'. He felt that the typeface for the Church of England's new worship book should be an English one. The obvious candidates were those of Eric Gill, namely Joanna, Perpetua and Gill Sans. Trial pages were prepared in these types and also – for comparison – in Univers and News Gothic. A clear distinction was required between the ministerial text, the rubrics (commonly printed in red italic), and the congregational text (customarily printed in bold). Thus the ideal typeface would have an equally clear distinction between roman, italic and bold. Early research and trial proofs showed Gill Sans to be by far the clearest typeface. It is designed on humanist lines (particularly the rather cursive italic) and also has the clearest distinction between roman, italic and bold; indeed, they are distinct but obviously related typefaces. (There is an additional light version, which in *CW* is used for less-favoured alternative texts and for 'running feet'.) After identifying the most typical longest lines, 9 point was chosen as the text size (the same point size as the *ASB*), with a leading (space between the lines) of three points (in the *ASB* the leading was half a point).

Derek Birdsall recognized that his recommendation of a sanserif typeface might be controversial. However, much of the text needs to be in bold, and almost every serif bold is disappointing. The supposed greater legibility of serif over sans is not important because most of the prayers are lined out and there is therefore not much continuous text. A sanserif might also be perceived as too modern, but Gill Sans had been in use for 70 years and is firmly part of the tradition in its precedents and ancestry. By the time he made his presentation, Derek Birdsall felt very strongly that if the panel would not accept Gill Sans, he would not want to do the job.

The rubrics in *CW* are printed in red – in accordance with tradition and with the meaning of the word rubric. Appropriately enough, given *CW*'s place in the tradition of English liturgical books, 'Sarum red' was eventually chosen by the Design Sub-Group. Because the rubrics are not only in red but also in italic, they are easily distinguishable by those who cannot tell red from black. Derek Birdsall found that italic printed in red looked smaller than the black Roman type; his solution was to enlarge it by one-tenth of a point.

To help people find their place in the book easily, the page numbers are printed in bold type. The position of the Holy Communion services is highlighted by printing the 'running feet' and page numbers for that section in red.

Format and Layout

Potential designers were asked to produce sample pages with a format of 185mm by 124mm. However, Derek Birdsall suggested that a deeper page size of 202 mm would be ideal, so as to accommodate the Nicene Creed (one of the longest texts) comfortably on a single page. 202mm by 125mm has the added advantage that it is a 'Golden rectangle' (i.e. its sides are in a proportion of 1 to 1.618). This is the same shape as (but slightly larger than) the format used for the majority of Penguin books.

In his submission, Derek Birdsall commented that 'the best layouts appear to have designed themselves'. A fundamental principle of the design for *CW* is the avoidance of page-breaks (even from a left-hand to a right-hand page) in the middle of prayers. Wherever possible, each prayer is complete on a single page, and rather than 'pouring the text in' (as has been done since printing first began – when paper was scarce), if the space at the foot of the page is insufficient for the next prayer, it is simply left blank and the next prayer begins at the top of the next page. This not only avoids the rustle of pages turning during a prayer; it also produces a spacious effect which contributes to clarity and gives a relaxed and comfortable appearance.

A notable feature of the design is the fact that headings such as 'Gloria in Excelsis' or 'The Collect' are ranged right and printed in bold 11 point. The grid is designed with show-through in mind, as the right-ranged headings fall on the left margin of the previous or following page. The ranged-right heading style means that someone following the service through from beginning to end is not disturbed by frequent intrusive headings. By contrast, someone leafing through to find a particular element can do so quickly by scanning down the right-hand side of the page; here the headings are prominent. Thus, the liturgy is provided with clear signposts for those trying to find their way around it – a further element in the overall clarity of the design. Derek Birdsall points out that if all the headings had been on the left, the text would have read as one long stream. Ranging the headings right, he argues, makes them a distinct 'label' above the 'cloud' of each prayer: 'You can read and understand the structure of the page with your eye corners.'

Major sections within a service (such as the Liturgy of the Word) are distinguished with a larger heading (16 point) in red italic and flagged with a traditional paragraph sign (¶). This symbol also marks sections within some of the notes, and appears in outline services and service structures and (appropriately indented) as a substitute for the modern 'bullet point'. Although the paragraph symbol is now most commonly encountered as a 'hard return' on the computer screen, its use in *CW* is particularly appropriate since it originally appeared in church books.

Within the book as a whole, solid red pages are used to separate major sections. At Derek Birdsall's suggestion, the word '*All*', printed in red italic, has been inserted in the margin against congregational texts to make it even clearer to those unfamiliar with the service that these are said by everyone.

The repeated red '*All*' in the margin, the red paragraph symbols and the red pages all have a function, but these flourishes also add colour and exuberance; the pages of the *ASB* look very drab and solemn by comparison. The purple endpapers add further to the sense of joy in the book.

Paper and Binding

For discussion of issues concerning the covers and materials, the Design Sub-Group was augmented as necessary by the Marketing and Production Managers of Church House Publishing (Mr Matthew Tickle and Mrs Katharine Allenby).

The standard and presentation editions and the desk edition are all printed on an ivory-coloured Bible-quality paper from France, which is acid-free and guaranteed to last for 150 years. It is made from elemental chlorine-free wood pulp derived from sustainable forests. The ivory colour enhances the opacity of the paper and so reduces the show-through from one page to the next. Ivory paper blends the red and black gracefully and gives the pages a warmer appearance. It is easier on the eye than the bright white papers often used today and is therefore more pleasurable to read. A 55 gsm stock was chosen in order to minimize the thickness of the book and its weight while being robust enough to withstand reasonable wear. The President's edition is printed on a heavier paper (100 gsm) from Holland, with similar archival qualities, which will enable the user to turn the pages of this large-format book more easily.

The books are bound in a heavy-duty plastic-coated bookbinding material which will be reasonably resistant to scuffing and marking. There are also more expensive presentation editions in bonded leather and in genuine calfskin. All of the books have a sewn binding style to enable them to open as flat as possible – when the book is opened towards the beginning or the end as well as in the middle.

The Liturgical Publishing Group was keen that a cross should appear on the cover of the books. Noticing that the title *Common Worship: Services and Prayers for the Church of England* consisted of two lines, and that 'Common' was nearly the same length as 'Worship', Derek Birdsall suggested that the words of the title should themselves be formed into the cross. After thorough discussion, it was decided to make the cover of the standard edition of the main volume black, with the cross in gold. The gold cross would shine against the black background, and the inside of the book, with its ivory and red pages and much red type, would similarly be even more striking inside a black cover. A black cover would give the book a stylish, contemporary appearance of understated elegance, although it was recognized that for some black would also have resonance with the older tradition of black covers for prayer books. For these reasons respectively, the cover was perhaps more likely to appeal to the young and the old than to the middle-aged (or to the *avant-garde* and the traditional rather than to the middle-of-the-road), but the Design Sub-Group decided to be bold in its choice. Red, the other main *CW* colour, was chosen for both of the ministerial editions – the desk edition and President's edition.

Ribbon markers are an important feature of the *CW* volumes, making it easier to refer to different places in the book. The standard edition of the main volume has two in the *CW* colours (red and black), the desk edition four in the main liturgical colours (green, purple, gold, and red), and the President's edition six (the four liturgical colours plus blue and black).

Derek Birdsall's design for *CW*, as approved by the Liturgical Publishing Group's Design Sub-Group, is aware of and resonant with the tradition, yet innovative and inventive. It is stylish and elegant, yet warm and exuberant. It is marked by careful attention to detail and by technical expertise. It is clear in its structure, and user-friendly. In all of this, it reflects the best of the liturgy which comprises *CW*.

(This chapter, written by Dr Colin Podmore, is based in part on notes supplied by Derek Birdsall and Katharine Allenby and on Quentin Newark's article, 'God is in the Details', *Design Week*, 7 April 2000, pp. 20–2.)

Index